*The Gospels
As You've Never Read Them Before!*

The Gospel Of Jesus Christ

by

Dr. Patrick Pierce

Copyright © 2005 Dr. Patrick Pierce
Second Edition 2018

The Gospel of Jesus Christ
Second Edition
By Dr. Patrick Pierce

Printed in the United States of America

Distributed by DOV Publishing
643 N. 98th St., #144
Omaha, NE 68114

A division of Disciples of Victory

Library of Congress Control Number:

ISBN: 978-0-578-18929-1

All rights reserved solely by the author. The author guarantees all contents are original and do not infringe upon the legal rights of any other person or work. Reproduction or translation of any part of this work beyond that permitted by Section 107 or 108 of the 1975 United States Copyright Act without the permission of the copyright owner is unlawful. Requests for permission or further information should be addressed to the author at 643 N. 98 St., #144, Omaha, NE 68114. The views expressed in this book is not necessarily those of the publisher.

Printed in the United States of America

Preface

Dear Reader:

You are holding in your hands one of the most important new volumes ever published concerning the life of Jesus. Dr. Pierce's unique approach uses a totally new avenue for understanding what influence Jesus had on the people of his day. The step-by-step techniques used by the author help every reader to comprehend how His life touches billions of Christians around the world at the present time.

The easy-to-read format of the book allows every reader, whatever age, or level of Christian maturity, to gain a new understanding of how the gospels of Matthew, Mark, Luke, and John correlate with the teachings of Jesus and how His messages should serve as a guide and compass for every person.

The volume has been constructed to be utilized as a sourcebook for persons in a study course at a church, university, or seminary setting. It will also find wide acceptance as a valuable addition to one's personal library as a reference guide. The author's untiring efforts to translate Biblical data from the Greek to a new, readable version are truly remarkable.

It has been my distinct pleasure to offer assistance and suggestions to Dr. Pierce in the preparation of the book. I can predict a wide appeal for this new and exciting offering among all persons, believers and non-believers alike.

Donald C. Cushenbery, Ed.D.
(Regents Professor Emeritus, University of Nebraska at Omaha and a widely known author and speaker specializing in the application of Biblical principles and how they relate to everyday living.)

Acknowledgements

It takes a community to complete a task of this scope and size. Over the past twenty-five years I have had the pleasure of working with many people who have made this possible.

Carolyn, my best friend and wife, has read and corrected this manuscript until she can quote it by heart. Unfortunately, Carolyn died in 2010 after 46 years of wonderful marriage.

Margaret and Ray Donahue, Carolyn's parents, were an encouragement to a young man who thought he knew more than he really did, and encouraged him anyway.

Don Cushenbery, Ed.D. has been an enormous help in direction and kind correction. A man of great experience and ability that I have been blessed to know.

Dr. Curt Dodd, Senior Pastor on Westside Church, for his encouragement and direction.

Rev. Rodney Caulkins, Episcopal priest, Vicar of St. Luke's Church, Simeon, in Albemarie County, Virginia for his most helpful suggestions and comments.

Mike Stuart for his knowledgeable insight and suggestions.

Joyce, my God sent wife. Joyce lost her husband, Wayne, to cancer after 50 years of marriage. We have been blessed to find each other. She has been invaluable in helping renew my spirit, life and purpose.

Pictures Acknowledgement

All of the pictures in the book including the cover are the art of Jean Keaton. Jean is an exceptional artist and captures the "Friendly" spirit of Jesus in her drawings.

Jean's first drawing of Jesus was after seeing in the news of the abduction and killing of a small boy in England. Jean prayed for the family and received a heavenly commission to draw the baby boy being held up by Jesus, welcoming the boy into the presence of Jesus.

Jean's drawings are available for purchase at www.jeankeatonart.com. Go to her website and see the selection of drawings that she has available.

http://www.jeankeatonart.com/

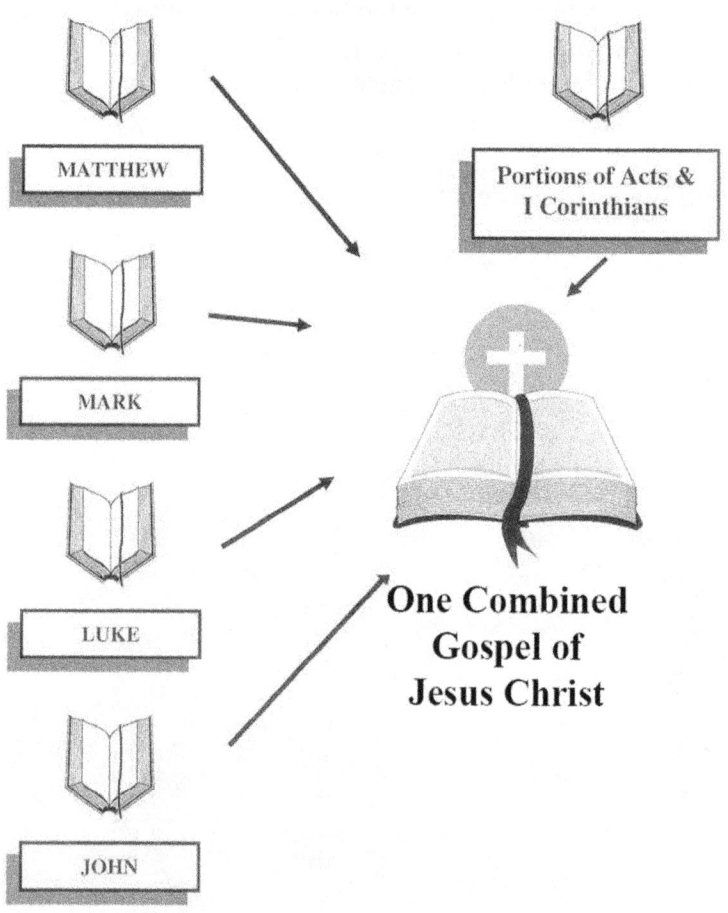

The Gospel Of Jesus Christ

Introduction

The Gospel of Jesus Christ is the four New Testament Gospels presented in a way that makes the gospels of Jesus come alive.

The Gospel of Jesus Christ starts with Almighty God creating the earth before the beginning of time. It continues with God coming to earth as Jesus Christ and covers all the teachings and events of Jesus' life. The Gospel ends with Jesus rising into Heaven and then the ultimate empowerment by the Spirit of God in each believer.

The Gospel of Jesus Christ is presented in the order it happened. Each section shows where and when the event or teaching took place. The Bible's Gospel verses are shown at the beginning of each section. The date that an event happened is also put at the top of each section. There are some sections that the exact day and hour are known. Then there are other sections where the year and season is all that is known.

In combining the four Biblical Gospel accounts into The Gospel of Jesus Christ there is never a conflict among the four Gospels. Each of the Gospel books makes additions to each account that helps us understand what Jesus said, did and meant.

Two Problems

There are two problems in reading the separate Gospels and finding the same account in each of the four Gospels.

The first problem is each Gospel book tells about only selected events and teachings. None of them gives us the entire story of Jesus' life and teachings. This makes it difficult to read about Jesus' entire life because we have to skip from one of the Gospels to the next in order to put Jesus' complete life together.

The second problem is that the four Gospel writers tell their stories in different orders of Christ's life. The accounts don't conflict but have been written in a different order. This can make it confusing to study the entire life of Christ.

In The Gospel of Jesus Christ, Jesus' entire life is presented in the order that is believed to be true. There is also a full listing of Christ's life in which you can find any part of Christ's life and turn to it. Then you can read the entire account as told by all four Gospel writers. You can find all of the events in Jesus' life in the Contents Section.

Chapters and Verses

The Gospel of Jesus Christ is divided into chapters and verses. This makes referring to the scriptures for discussions and teaching easy.

You can refer to a passage as found in:
The Gospel of Jesus 6:35-40
This covers the verses found in:
Matthew 8:14-17
Mark 1:29-34
Luke 4:38-41.

Version:

The Gospel of Jesus Christ is a new version. The author did not use a specific translation of the Bible, but relied on the Greek interlinear, Greek lexicon and Concordances for research. This version was completed by the author in over 25 years of study. A more comprehensive explanation is included at the back of this version as "Explanatory Notes." The version was completed to achieve these goals:

    Easy to read in current American English

    Elimination of male and female when

        "people" in general are referenced

    Combine the Gospel accounts into one Gospel narrative

    Accurate translation from the Greek to

        modern American English

Time Line:

There are several timelines for Jesus' life that have been established. Of course, no one really knows the correct order of the events in Jesus' life or the exact dates. The author used the timeline that provides for Jesus cleansing the Temple twice, once when he started his ministry and second at the end of his ministry. In the author's research, this seems the most reliable timeline.

The date of Jesus' birth is the next unknown date. There are several dates that have been developed. The date that the author used is October, 7 BC.

The Gospel by Matthew

Matthew was an Apostle of Jesus for the last two years of Jesus' ministry. Matthew was an educated person who seemed to take notes and kept track of everything just as he had done in his job as a tax collector. When he followed Jesus, he took his method of recording with him and kept track of what happened and what Jesus said for later reference.

Matthew was a Jew and wrote his Gospel book to his fellow Jews because he wanted to prove to his Jewish friends that Jesus was the promised Messiah of the Old Testament. He took his notes and showed how Jesus fulfilled the Old Testament prophecies.

Matthew combined his notes about Jesus together by teachings, miracles, and parables to write his Gospel story. He didn't try to arrange Jesus' life in the order it happened because he arranged most of Jesus' teachings together and Jesus' miracles together.

Matthew often wrote a factual description of Jesus' actions or a quote of Jesus' words. This is shown by <u>Matthew's account of Jesus leaving Judea and going to Galilee:</u>

Matthew 4:12 (KJV)

Now when Jesus had heard that John was cast into prison, He departed into Galilee.
(Matthew tells just the facts)

The Gospel by Mark

Even though Mark is the second book in the New Testament, Mark wrote the earliest book about Jesus that is included in the Bible. Mark had at least two other accounts of Jesus' life to work from, but these other accounts were not saved.

Mark was a close personal companion to Peter for many years. Because he had been with Peter, many people asked him to write what Peter had told him about Jesus, and this resulted in the Gospel of Mark.

Mark did not cover the birth of Christ, but started out with the beginning of Jesus' public ministry. He wrote a short, almost outline account of Jesus' ministry, probably from notes he had taken from Peter. Since Mark's book was the earliest Gospel to be written, most of the verses in Mark also appear in either Matthew or Luke or both.

There are a few parts of Mark that are inconsistent with other parts of Mark and the other three Gospels. After researching these areas, it was found that the earliest manuscripts did not contain these problem verses. Perhaps these problem verses were added later by some transcribers, and since these parts do not appear to be Mark's earliest manuscripts, they are not included in <u>The Gospel of Jesus Christ</u>.

Mark gives us more information on Jesus' life and events. <u>Let's look at what Mark wrote about the same event that Matthew told about Jesus leaving Judea</u>. Mark is still brief but does add some more information:

Mark 1:14 (KJV)

Now after that John was put in prison, Jesus came into Galilee, preaching the gospel of the Kingdom of God.
(Mark gives us a little more information)

The Gospel by Luke

Luke was an educated and respected doctor and he wanted to make a complete study of all that had been written and said about Jesus to put into one accurate account. Luke explains his careful and complete process of writing his account to Mr. Theophilus in his first four verses of Luke chapter one.

Luke tells about many of the events the other Gospel authors missed. Luke gives us the only description of Jesus' birth as well as many other stories.

Without Luke we would not have any of these stories:

- ✝ Zacharias and Elizabeth
- ✝ John the Baptist's birth
- ✝ God's message to Mary
- ✝ Mary's visit to Elizabeth
- ✝ Jesus' birth
- ✝ Shepherds and angels
- ✝ Jesus as a boy in the temple

We are very glad Luke gave us all of these important stories in Jesus' life. He filled in the parts that Matthew and Mark had omitted.

Luke tells us the same story of Jesus, but gives us more of the background and information.

<u>Luke's account of the same trip made by Jesus from Judea to Galilee tells us the reason for the trip</u>. We also learn, for the first time, why John was put into prison.

Luke 3:29-20 (KJV)

But Herod the tetrarch, being reproved by him [John] for Herodias his brother Philip's wife, and for all the evils which Herod had done, added yet this above all, that he shut John in prison.

(Luke gives us the best explanation)

The Gospel by John

John was the last to write his book about Jesus and was about ninety years old when the book was written. The book was the combined effort of many of John's followers, with John doing the final reviewing and editing.

John's Gospel does not attempt to tell the same story as the other Gospels. John assumed the reader would already know about the life of Jesus from the other Gospel stories.

John's book gives us the teachings of Jesus as well as the private explanations that Jesus told John about those teachings. <u>John tells what Jesus meant and why Jesus was doing what he did</u>.

John was one of the closest Apostles to Jesus and probably spent a lot of one-on-one time with Jesus. After Jesus had done or said something and was relaxing in the evening, John would come to Jesus and ask him about the events and teachings of the day.

When John's book is combined with the other Gospel books the entire gospel is presented. Matthew, Mark and Luke tell what happened, and John tells us why or what was the meaning.

When John tells about the same event we have followed in the other Gospel books, <u>he tells more about the reasons for the trip</u>. Since John was the last of the books written, he also is able to fill in some of the gaps left by the other accounts.

<u>Here is what John says about Jesus leaving Judea to go to Galilee</u>:

John 4:1-4 (KJV)

When therefore the Lord knew how the Pharisees had heard that Jesus made and baptized more disciples than John, (though Jesus Himself baptized not, but His disciples) He left Judea, and departed again into Galilee. And He needed to go through Samaria.

*After this verse follows the story of Jesus and the Samaritan woman at the well in John
4:5-42. In verse 43 John adds this:*

Now after two days He (Jesus) departed then, and went into Galilee.

The Combined Account in The Gospel of Jesus Christ

We can see that to get the whole gospel story of what Jesus did, <u>we must read the account from all four of the Bible's Gospels.</u>

It would be helpful to see all Jesus said and did from all four of the Gospels at one time, and this is exactly what <u>The Gospel of Jesus Christ</u> does.

<u>The Gospel of Jesus Christ</u> gives the combined account of Jesus' life in one story.

<u>The Gospel of Jesus Christ</u> is an easy to read and understand version that is exactly accurate to the original Greek.

On the next page is an example of all four Gospels combined together to give the entire story of Jesus leaving Judea to go to Galilee:

<u>The Gospel of Jesus Christ is the Bible, and it doesn't change the Biblical meaning, words or presentation.</u> <u>The Gospel of Jesus Christ</u> combines the four Bible Gospel books and puts them together in the order they happened which makes the life and teachings of Jesus come alive.

The Gospel of Jesus Christ
Combined Story

JESUS LEAVES JUDEA
MATTHEW 4:12; MARK 1:14; LUKE 3:19-20; JOHN 4:1-4

DATE: Summer, AD 27
PLACE: Judea

But, when Herod the tetrarch was rebuked by John concerning the matter of Herodias, his brother Philip's wife, and concerning all the other wicked things he had done, he added this also to everything else and he locked up John in prison.

When Jesus learned that the Pharisees had heard that He was making and baptizing more disciples than John. (Although it wasn't Jesus Himself who was in the habit of baptizing but His disciples). And Jesus heard that John had been delivered into the hands of the authorities and put in prison, He quit in Judea and went away to Galilee.

THE SAMARITAN WOMAN
JOHN 4:5-42

DATE: Summer, AD27
PLACE: Sychar in Samaria

Now He had to pass through Samaria,...

This is followed by the story of the Samaritan woman at the well found in John's Gospel.

Isn't it interesting to know how all the events with John, Herod, and the Disciples fit together? Now we can see why Jesus left the area because He was probably concerned that Herod would come after Him and His Disciples and imprison them also.

      We can also see the dates and the places the events happened. It's also interesting that on their walk back up to Galilee they met the Samaritan woman at the well. Each Gospel adds more information about the event in Jesus life. <u>Now we can read the entire story only when all of the accounts are combined together to give us the complete story of The Gospel of Jesus Christ.</u>

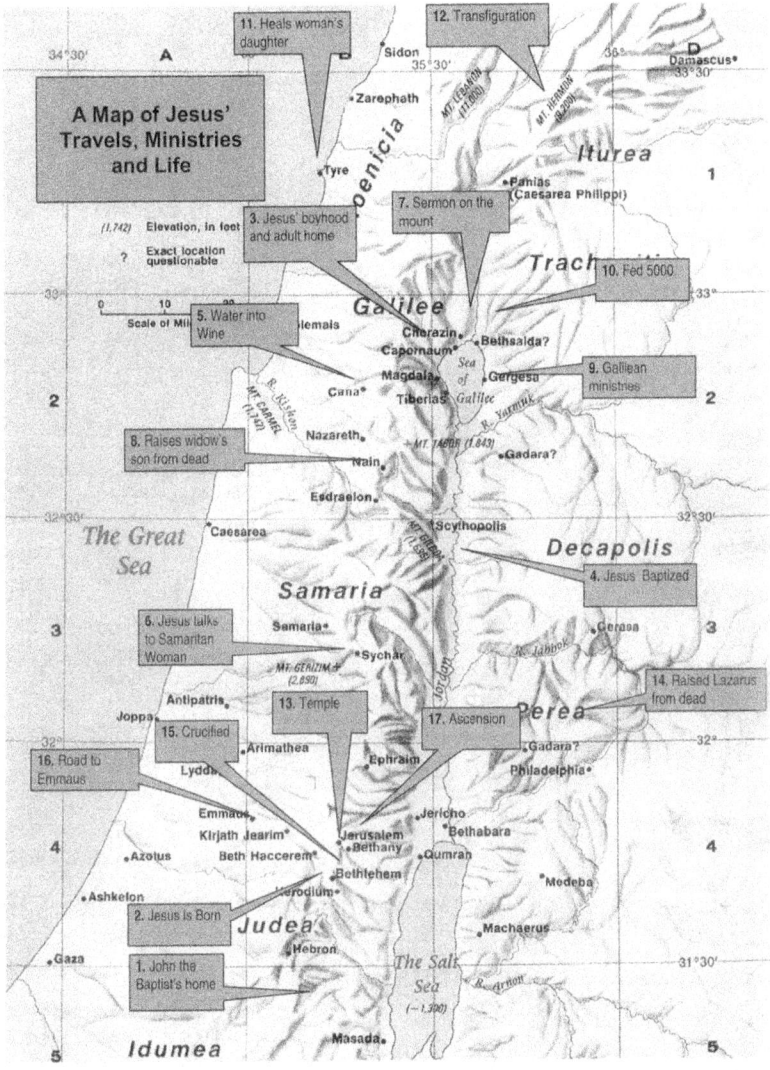

CONTENTS

CHAPTER 1 – THE FAMILY OF JESUS

Before the Beginning   3
The Beginning – Heaven

Joseph and Mary's Genealogies   5

CHAPTER 2 – GOD'S MESSAGE OF JESUS

An Angel Comes to Zacharias   9
September, 8 BC – Jerusalem

God's Message to Mary   11
March, 7 BC – Nazareth

Mary Visits Elizabeth   12
March, 7 BC – Hill Country of Judea

Mary's Song of Praise   13
March, 7 BC – Hill Country of Judea

The Birth of John the Baptist   14
June, 7 BC – Hill Country of Judea

Zacharias' Joy and Prophesy   15
June, 7 BC – Hill Country of Judea

God's Message to Joseph   16
June, 7 BC – Nazareth

CHAPTER 3 – THE BIRTH OF JESUS

October, 7 BC – Nazareth & Bethlehem   19

The Shepherds and the Angels   19
   7 BC – Bethlehem

Jesus in Named and Presented in the Temple   21
   Simeon's Joy
   Anna

The Wise Men   23
   December, 6 BC and later – Bethlehem

Escape to Egypt   24
   6 BC to 2BC – Bethlehem to Egypt

Return from Egypt   25
   2 BC – Egypt to Nazareth

The Boy Jesus in the Temple   26
   *April AD 5 – Nazareth and
      Temple in Jerusalem*

Jesus Growing Up   27
   AD 5 to 25 – Nazareth

CHAPTER 4 – JOHN'S MINISTRY

AD 25 – Wilderness of Judea by the Jordan River
   John's Ministry   29
   John Baptizes – Jordan River
   John Preaches Repentance
   John Declares Christ is at Hand

John Baptizes Jesus   31
   January, 27 – Jordan River

The Temptation of Christ   32
   February, 27 – Judean Wilderness
     Hunger Temptation
     Display Power Temptation
     Gain Power Temptation

The Witness of John   34
    February, 27 – Bethany across Jordan
       John Explains His Ministry
       Jesus Begins His Public Ministry

CHAPTER 5 – JESUS' FIRST PUBLIC ACTS

Jesus Makes His First Disciples   37
    Spring, 27 – At Bethany across the Jordan

Philip and Nathanael   38
    Next Day – Galilee

Jesus' First Public Miracle – Water into Wine   39
    Sprint, 27 – Cana in Galilee

Jesus Cleanses the Temple   40
    April 9, 27 – Jerusalem

Jesus Talks to Nicodemus   41
    April, 27 (Passover) – At Jerusalem

John's Second Testimony   43
    Summer, 27 – Judea and Aenon

CHAPTER 6 – TRIP THROUGH SAMARIA   45

Jesus Leaves Judea   45
    Summer, 27 – Judea

The Samaritan Woman   45
    Summer, 27 – Samaria
       Spiritual Food

Return to Galilee   49
    Summer, 27 – Galilee

Jesus' Teachings 49
   Summer, 27 – Galilee

Jesus Heals the Official's Son 49
   Autumn, 27 – Cana

Jesus' Home in Capernaum 50
   Autumn, 27 – Capernaum

Jesus Calls Four 51
   Autumn, 27 – Capernaum
      Peter and Andrew
      James and John
      Catching Fish Miracle

Jesus Drives Out a Devil 52
   Autumn, 27 – Capernaum

Healing Peter's Mother-in-Law 53
   Autumn, 27 – Capernaum

CHAPTER 7 – PREACHING IN GALILEE

   Fall to Winter, 27 Galilee 55

Jesus Heals a Leper 56
   Early, 28 – Galilee

Jesus Heals a Paralytic 56
   AD 28 – Capernaum
      Emmanuel's Authority

The Call of Matthew 58
   AD 28 – Capernaum

Jesus Heals a Lame Man on the Sabbath 58
   April, 28 – Jerusalem

The Authority of Emmanuel *Jerusalem*	60
Witness to Jesus *Jerusalem*	61
Plucking Grain on the Sabbath *May, 28 – Road from Jerusalem to Galilee*	62
Healing Man With a Withered Hand *Early Summer, 28 – Galilee, Capernaum*	63
Healing Multitudes *Early Summer, 28 – Sea of Galilee*	64
Jesus Chooses Twelve Apostles *Summer, 28 – Near Capernaum* Names of the Twelve Apostles	65

CHAPTER 8 – THE SERMON ON THE MOUNT

Summer, 28 – Near Capernaum Introductory Statements	67
Beatitudes (Promises to Jesus' Followers)	67
Influence and Duties of Jesus' Followers	69
Jesus' Teachings and the Old Testament The Law Killing Giving Debts Adultery Temptation Divorce Oaths Retaliation Love Enemies	70

Giving	73
Prayer	74
The Lord's Prayer	74
Fasting	75
Possessions 　Spiritual Treasures 　Spiritual Insight 　Two Masters 　Worry	75
Judging 　Giving 　Choosing Teachers 　Dealing with Your Own Problems First 　World's Treatment of Heavenly Truths	76
Prayer	77
The Golden Rule	79
False Prophets 　Good Fruit	79
Build on a Rock	80

CHAPTER 9 – GALILEAN JOURNEYS　　81

Healing Centurion's Servant 　*Summer, 28 – Capernaum*	81
Jesus Raises Widow's Son 　*Summer, 28 – Nain in Galilee*	82
Messengers From John 　*Summer, 28 – Galilee* 　　Jesus Praises John 　　Jesus and John Rejected	83

        Penalty of Rejection
        Revelation of Truth
        Rest for the Weary

Jesus' Feet Anointed   86
Fall, 28 – Galilee

Journeys Around Galilee   87
Fall, 28 – Galilee

Blasphemous Accusations   88
Fall, 28 – Galilee
        Accusations and Answers
        Blasphemy
        Good and Bad Fruit

The Demand for a Miracle   90
Same day – Galilee
        Need for God's Spirit of Light

Jesus' Mother and Brothers   92
Same day – Galilee
        Spiritual Kinship

CHAPTER 10 – START OF PARABLES   93

Dining with Scribes & Pharisees   93

Inward State and Legalism   93
Fall, 28 – Galilee
        Hypocrisy Condemned
        Lawyers Condemned

Hypocrisy and Anxiety   95

Parable of Rich Man's Possessions   95
Fall, 28 – Galilee
        Hypocrisy
        Greed

      Worldly Possessions
      Trust God
      Watchfulness
      Division

Repentance Required   99

Parable of the Barren Fig Tree   99
   Full, 28 – Galilee
      Repent or Perish
      Penalty for Fruitlessness

CHAPTER 11 – FIRST GROUP OF PARABLES

   Fall, 28 – Sea of Galilee   101
      Introduction
The Sower   101
   Fall, 28 – Sea of Galilee
      The Sower
      Purpose of Parables
      Sower Explained
      Pay Attention to What You Hear

The Seed Growing by Itself   104

The Weeds   105
      The Weeds
      The Weeds Explained

Mustard Seed and Leaven   106
      The Mustard Seed
      Leaven

Treasure, Pearl and the Net   107
      Treasure
      Pearl
      The Net

CHAPTER 12 – HEALINGS & MIRACLES

Teaching on Sacrifice   109

Jesus Calms the Sea   110
Same day – Sea of Galilee
- Calms Sea

Evil Spirits Ordered Out   111
Fall, 28 – Gerges, now called Khersa

Matthew's Feast   113
Late, 28 – Capernaum
- Eating with Sinners
- Fasting
- The Patch
- Wine Skins

Jairus' Daughter Healed   114
Same day – Capernaum
- Jairus Asks Jesus to Heal Daughter
- Woman Touches Jesus' Garment
- Jesus Raises Daughter

Healing Blind Men   118
Fall, 28 – Capernaum
- Two Blind Men Healed
- Mute Healed

CHAPTER 13 – REJECTION AND JOHN BEHEADED

Jesus is Rejected in Nazareth   119
January 29 – Nazareth
- Rejected in Home Town
- Attempt to Kill Jesus

Jesus Sends the Twelve Apostles   121
January, 29 – Galilee
- Workers Needed

  Apostles Instructed
  Apostles Warned
  Fear God
  God Loves Sparrows
  Confess Emmanuel
  Conflict Over Jesus

Herod Beheads John the Baptist   126
 March, 29 – Jerusalem

Apostles Return   127
 April, 29 – Bethsaida

Feeding Five Thousand   128
 Spring, 29 – Bethsaida

Jesus Walks on Water   131
 Spring, 29 – Galilee

CHAPTER 14 – THE BREAD OF LIFE

 Spring, 29 – Sea of Galilee   133
  Jews Challenge Jesus
  Jews Question Eating Flesh
  Offended Disciples Leave
  Peter Affirms Belief

Jesus Disregards Tradition   138
 Spring, 29 – Capernaum
  Uncleanlinness

Healing a Woman's Daughter   140
 After Passover, 29 – Near Tyre

The Deaf Stammerer Healed   142
 Summer, 29 – Sea of Galilee
  Man Healed
  Many Healed
  Four Thousand Fed

Pharisee's Test	**144**
Summer, 29 – Magadan	
Pharisee's Test	
Warning about Leaders	
Blind Man Healed	

CHAPTER 15 – PASSION FORETOLD

Peter's Confession	**147**
Summer, 29 – Caesarea Phillippi	
Passion Foretold	**148**
Summer, 29 – Caesarea Phillippi	
Suffering Foretold	
Burden of Discipleship	
The Transfiguration	**149**
Summer, 29 – Mount Hermon	
Healing Demonic Boy	**151**
Summer, 29 – Caesarea Phillippi	
Death Foretold Again	**153**
Summer, 29 – Galilee	
Jesus Pays Temple Tax	**153**
Late Summer, 29 – Capernaum	

CHAPTER 16 – GOD'S FAMILY

Autumn, 29 – Capernaum	**155**
Stumbling Blocks to Children	
Lost Sheep	
World's Stumbling Blocks	
Works in Jerusalem	

Sin and Forgiveness in God's Family   157
   Autumn, 29 – Capernaum
      Disputes in God's Family
      Disciple's Authority
      Peter Asks About Forgiveness
      Parable of Servant's Debt

Jesus Advised to Go to Judea   159
   September, 29 – Capernaum

The Journey to Jerusalem   160
   October, 29 – Through Samaria

CHAPTER 17 – JESUS TEACHES IN THE TEMPLE

   October, 29 – Jerusalem   161
      Temple Teaching
      People Talk about Jesus
      Guards Sent to Arrest Jesus
      Spiritual Drink
      People Divided
      Nicodemus Advised

The Adulteress   165
   October, 29 – Jerusalem

Jesus Argues with the Jews   166
   October, 29 – Jerusalem
      Light of the World
      Unbelief
      Spiritual Freedom
      Abraham's Children
      Eternal Existence

CHAPTER 18 – JESUS TEACHES

Jesus Heals a Blind Man — 171
October, 29 – Jerusalem
- Pharisees Questions Miracle
- Jesus Reveals He is Emmanuel

The Good Shepherd — 175
October, 29 – Jerusalem
- The Sheep
- The Gate to the Fold
- The Good Shepard
- People Divided

The Mission of the Seventy — 177
October, 29 – Judea
- Seventy Sent
- Seventy Return
- God's Revelations

The Parable of the Good Samaritan — 179
November, 29 – Judea

Jesus Visits Martha and Mary — 181
November, 29 – Bethany

CHAPTER 19 – HOW TO PRAY — 183

November, 29 – Judea
- Persistence
- Pray with Belief
- Gift of God
- Healing on Sabbath
- Mustard Seed and Leaven

The Feast of Dedication — 186
January, 30 – Jerusalem
- Jesus and Almighty God are One
- Attempt to Stone Jesus
- Almighty God in Jesus

The Narrow Door   187
January, 30 – Perea to Jerusalem
    Jesus Warned
    Lament Over Jerusalem

Dining with a Pharisee   189
January, 30 – Perea
    Place of Honor
    Unselfishness
    The Great Banquet

The Cost of Discipleship   191
January, 30 – Perea
    Salt

CHAPTER 20 – SECOND GROUP OF PARABLES

January, 30 – Perea   193
    Parable of the Lost Sheep

Parable of the Lost Coin   193
January, 30 – Perea

Parable of the Lost Son   194
January, 30 – Perea

Parable of the Shrewd Steward   196
January, 30 – Perea
    Honesty
    Serve One Master
    Things Detestable in God's Sight
    The Law
    Divorce

Parable of Lazarus and the Rich Man   198
January, 30 – Perea

CHAPTER 21 – RAISING LAZARUS

Jesus' Teachings — 201
January, 30 – Perea
- Stumbling Blocks
- Forgiveness
- Faith Like a Mustard Seed
- Duty

Raising Lazarus — 202
January, 30 – Perea to Bethany
- Lazarus' Illness Reported
- Disciples Fear Return
- Jesus Talks with Martha
- Jesus Talks with Mary
- Lazarus Raised

Council Plots Against Jesus — 206
February, 30 – Jerusalem

CHAPTER 22 – FINAL JOURNEY TO JERUSALEM

March, 30 - Border of Samaria — 209
- Ten Lepers
- Coming of the Kingdom of God

The Persistent Widow — 211
March, 30 – Galilee

The Pharisee and Tax Collector — 212
March, 30 – Galilee

Teaching on Divorce — 212
March, 30 – Through Perea

Jesus Blesses Children — 214
March, 30 – Perea

The Rich Ruler — 216
March, 30 – Perea
The Rich Ruler
Love of Possessions
Workers in the Vineyard

CHAPTER 23 – FORETELLING HIS DEATH

March, 30 – Judea — 221
Death Foretold
James and John's Request to be Great

Bartimaeus and Companion Healed — 223
March, 30 – Jericho

Parable of Money (Ten Minus) — 224
March, 30 – Jericho
Zachaeus
Money Usage – Ten Minas

Jesus Arrives at Bethany — 226
Friday, March 31, 30 – Bethany
Jesus Goes to Bethany
Mary Anoints Jesus
Plot to Kill Jesus

CHAPTER 24 – JESUS' TRIUMPHAL ENTRY

Sunday, April 2, 30 – Jerusalem — 229
Jesus Sends for Donkey
Triumphant Entry
Destruction of Jerusalem Foretold
Jesus' Popularity

Temple Cleansed — 232
Monday, April 3, 30 – Jerusalem
Barren Fig Tree
Temple Cleansed

Fig Tree Withered   233
    Tuesday, April 4, 30 – Road to Jerusalem

Authority Questioned   234
    Tuesday, April 4, 30 – Temple in Jerusalem

The Third Group of Miracles   235
    Tuesday – Temple
        The Parable of the Two Sons

Parable of the Vineyard   236

The Rejected Stone   237

The Parable of the Wedding   237

CHAPTER 25 – JESUS QUESTIONED   239

Jewish Rulers Ask About Taxes   239
    Tuesday – Temple

Sadducees Ask About the Resurrection   240
    Tuesday – Temple

The Greatest Commandment   241
    Tuesday – Temple

Jesus' Question that No One Could Answer   242
    Tuesday – Temple

CHAPTER 26 – JESUS' LAST PUBLIC TEACHINGS

    Tuesday – Temple
        Self-Righteousness   243
        Leaders
        Denunciation of Scribes and Pharisees
        Outward Appearances
        Persecution Condemned
        Jerusalem Lamented

The Widow's Mites   **246**
    Tuesday – Temple

Greeks See Jesus   **247**
    Tuesday – Temple
        Purpose of Jesus' Death
        Jesus Foretells that He Will Draw All People to Him
        Walk in the Light
        Disbelief Fulfills Prophecy
        Final Public Appeal

CHAPTER 27 – FUTURE SIGNS FORETOLD

    Tuesday - Temple and Mount of Olives   **251**
        Temple is to be Destroyed
        Jesus Tells of Future Signs

Second Coming of Christ Foretold   **254**
    Tuesday Evening – Mount of Olives
        Exact Time is Unknown
        Stay Ready
        The Faithful Servant
        Be Watchful

The Judgments   **257**
    Tuesday Evening – Mount of Olives
        Ten Virgins Parable
        Talents Parable
        The Judgment of Righteous Workers

Judas Makes His Bargain   **260**
    Wednesday, April 5, 30 – Mount of Olives
        Jesus Foretells of Crucifixion
        Judas' Bargain

CHAPTER 28 – JUDAS' BETRAYAL

Passover Preparation   263
Thursday Evening, April 6, 30 – Bethany
Preparations
A Servants Reward

Jesus Washes the Disciples' Feet   264
Thursday Evening – Upper Room
Jesus Explains Washing
Jesus Predicts His Betrayal

Judas' Betrayal   266
Thursday Evening – Upper Room
Betrayer Identified
Love One Another Commandment
Peter will Stumble
Be Wary of the World

CHAPTER 29 – THE LORD'S SUPPER   271

Thursday Evening – Upper Room

Farwell Teaching to the Disciples   272
Thursday Late Evening – Upper Room
Jesus Will Prepare a Place
Jesus in Almighty God
Holy Spirit Promised
Jesus Foretells Return
Disciples Relationship to Each Other
Disciples Relationship to the World
The Holy Spirit
Jesus' Warning
The Holy Spirit Promised
Jesus' Death and Resurrection Foretold
Prayer
Sayings Will be Made Clear

Emmanuel's Prayer   **280**
    Thursday Late Night – Upper Room
        Emmanuel's Glory and Authority
        Disciples in the World
        The Future Glory

CHAPTER 30 – GOING TO GETHSEMANE

    Thursday Night, Very Late – Mount of Olives
        Mount of Olives   **283**
        Final Prayers

Jesus is Betrayed   **284**
    Friday morning before dawn – Gethsemane

CHAPTER 31 – THER FIRST STAGE OF JESUS' TRIAL

Examination By Annas   **287**
    Friday Morning before dawn – Annas' House
        Peter's First Denial
        Jesus Before Annas

Jesus Condemned By Caiaphus and Sanhedrin   **288**
    Friday early morning, April 7, 30 –
        Caiaphas' Palace
        Peter's Denials
        Jesus in the Council Chambers Before the Sanhedrin

Judas Commits Suicide   **291**
    Early Friday Morning, April 7, 30

CHAPTER 32 – JESUS BEFORE PILATE 293
Early Friday Morning – Governor's Palace

Jesus Before Herod 295
Friday Morning – Herod's Palace

Jesus Before Pilate a Second Time 295
Friday Morning – Pilate's Palace
Jesus Scourged
Pilate Questions Jesus Again
Barabbas Released

CHAPTER 33 – JESUS IS CRUCIFIED

Jesus in Crucified 299
Friday, April 7, 30, 9AM to 3PM – Golgotha
The Road to Golgotha
Pilate's Inscription
Jesus in Crucified
Jesus is Mocked
Mary's Care is Arranged
Jesus Dies
The Earth is Shaken

Jesus is Buried 304
Friday afternoon, from 4 to 6 PM – Joseph's Tomb
Jesus Side is Pierced
Joseph Gets Jesus' Body
Guarding the Tomb – Saturday, April 8, 30

CHAPTER 34 – THE RESURRECTION

Sunday, April 9, 30 307
Jesus Rises
Women Come to the Tomb
Jesus Appears to the Women
The Guards are Silenced

Jesus on the Road to Emmaus   **310**
   Sunday, April 9, 30 – Road to Emmaus

Jesus Appears to Disciples   **312**
   Sunday, April 9, 30 & April 16, 30 – Jerusalem
     Jesus Appears
     Thomas Doubts

Jesus Appears at the Sea of Galilee   **314**
   April 23 to May 18, 30 – Sea of Galilee
     Jesus Gives the Miracle of Fish
     Jesus Cooks Breakfast
     Peter Forgiven

CHAPTER 35 – THE ASCENSION   317

Jesus Teaches   **317**
   April 23, 30 – Sea of Galilee

Additional Appearances By Jesus   **318**
   April 23 to May 18, 30 – Sea of Galilee and Jerusalem

The Great Commission   **319**
   April 23 to May 18, 30 – A Mountain in Galilee

The Ascension   **319**
   May 18, 30 – Mount Near Jerusalem

The Holy Spirit   **320**
     The Gospel's Purpose

The Gospel of Jesus Christ
As You've Never Read It Before!

The Gospel of Jesus Christ

by

Dr. Patrick Pierce

CHAPTER 1
THE FAMILY OF JESUS

LUKE 1:1-4

1. Since many have already written an account of the events which happened among us, based on those who were the eye-witnesses from the beginning and became servants of the Word handed it down to us, I have decided since I have carefully investigated all things from the beginning, to write it all out for you, Theophilus, your Excellency, an orderly account of them so you might know the exact truth about the things you have been taught.

BEFORE THE BEGINNING
JOHN 1:1-18

The Beginning - Heaven

2. In the beginning was the Word; and the Word was with Almighty God; and the Word was Almighty God. The Word was in the beginning with Almighty God. All things came into being by the Word; and there is nothing which exists that came into being without the Word. In the Word was life; and the life was the Light of all people; and the Light shines in the darkness; and the darkness cannot conquer It.

3. There came a man, sent from Almighty God, whose name was John. He came as a witness, in order to bear witness to the Light, that through him all might believe. He was not the Light himself, but his function was to bear witness to the Light.

4. That was the true Light, who in coming into the world, gives Light to every person. The Word was in the world, and the world was made by the Word, but the world did not know the Word. The Word came to It's own, and It's own did not receive the Word. But to all who received the Word, even to those who believe in the name of the Word, were given the right to become children of God. These were born not of blood, nor of the will of the flesh, nor of any person's will, but their birth was of Almighty God.

5. The Word became flesh, and dwelt among us, full of grace and truth; and we beheld the glory, glory like can only be received from Almighty God.

6. John was the Word's witness, and he cried out saying, "This is the One of whom I said, 'The One who comes after me has a higher place than I, because that One existed before I was born'."

7. Out of God's fullness all of us have received grace upon grace, because it was the law which was given through Moses; but grace and truth came through Jesus Christ. No one has ever seen Almighty God. It is the One and only, who is God, the One who is even a part of Almighty God, who has told us all about Almighty God.

JOSEPH AND MARY'S GENEALOGIES
MATTHEW 1:1-17; LUKE 3:24-38

8. LUKE 3: 24-38(MARY)	9. MATTHEW 1: 1-17(JOSEPH)
Heli *(Mary's Father)*	Jacob *(Joseph's Father)*
Matthat	Matthan
Levi	Eleazar
Melchi	Eluid
Jannai	Achim
Joseph	Zadok
Mattathias	Azor
Amos	Eliakim
Nahum	
Hesli	
Naggai	
Maath	
Mattathias	
Semein	
Josech	
Joda	
Joanan	Abiud
Rhesa	
Zerubbabel	Zerubbabel
Shealtiel	Shealtiel
Neri	
Melchi	Jechoniah

after the people had been taken away to Babylon. During the Babylonian captivity Jechoniah and his brother were the sons of

Addi		Josiah
Cosam		Amon
Elmadam		Manasseh
Er		Hezekiah
Joshua		Ahaz
Eliezer		Jotham
Jorim		Uzziah
Matthat		
Levi		
Simeon		
Judah		Joram
Joseph		Jehoshaphat
Jonam		Asa
Eliakim		Abijah
Melea		Rehoboam
Menna		
Mattatha		
Nathan		
	son of Uriah's wife	Solomon,
David		David, the king
Jesse		Jesse
Obed		Obed, son of Ruth
Boaz		Boaz, son of Rahab
Salmon		Salmon
Nahshon		Nahshon
Amminadab		Amminadab
Admin		
Ram		
Hezron		Hezron
Perez		Perez and Zerah,
	the sons of Tamar	

Judah
Jacob
Isaac
Abraham
Terah
Nahor
Serug
Reu
Peleg
Heber
Shelah
Cainan
Arphaxad
Shem
Noah
Lamech
Methuselah
Enoch
Jared
Mahalaleel
Cainan
Enosh
Seth
Adam
God

Judah
Jacob
Isaac
Abraham

So there are, in all, fourteen generations from Abraham to David, fourteen from David to the Babylonian captivity and fourteen from the Babylonian captivity to Christ.

CHAPTER 2
GOD'S MESSAGE OF JESUS

MARK 1:1

1. This is the beginning of the story of Jesus Christ and the Good News to all.

AN ANGEL COMES TO ZACHARIAS
LUKE 1: 5-25

September, 8 BC - Jerusalem

2. In the time when Herod was the king of Judea, there was a priest named Zacharias, who belonged to the priestly division of Abijah. His wife, Elizabeth, was also a direct descendent of Aaron. Both of them were good people before Almighty God, observing blamelessly all the commandments and ordinances of the Lord. But they had no child because Elizabeth was barren and both of them were very old.

3. When Zacharias was serving as priest before God, when his division was on duty, according to the custom of priestly duty, it fell to him by lot to go into the Temple of the Lord to burn the incense. The whole congregation of people was praying outside at the hour when the incense was offered.

4. And an angel of the Lord appeared to him, standing at the right side of the altar of incense. When Zacharias saw the angel he was startled and deeply afraid. The angel said to him, "Do not be afraid, Zacharias, because your request has been heard and your wife

Elizabeth will bear you a son and you will give him the name John. You shall have joy and delight and many will rejoice because of his birth for he will be great in God's sight. He must not drink wine or strong drink and, even from the time he is in his mother's womb, he will be filled with the Holy Spirit. He will turn many of the people of Israel to the Lord their God; and he will go before the Lord in the spirit and power of Elijah, to turn the hearts of the fathers to their children, and bring back the disobedient to the wisdom of the righteous to make ready a people prepared for the Lord."

5. Zacharias asked the angel, "How will I know that this is going to happen? I am an old man and my wife is also very old."

6. "I am Gabriel," the angel answered, "I stand before Almighty God, and I was sent to speak to you and to tell you this good news. And, hear this, you will be silent and unable to speak until the day these things happen, because you have not believed my words which will be fulfilled at the proper time."

7. The people were waiting for Zacharias, and they were surprised that he was lingering so long in the Temple. When he came out, he was not able to speak to them and they realized that he had seen a vision in the Temple. He kept making signs to them but he remained unable to speak.

8. When the days of his time of service were completed he returned to his own home. After these days Elizabeth, his wife, conceived, and she hid herself for five months. She said, "This is God's doing for me, for God has looked upon me and taken away my shame that I have suffered among the people."

GOD'S MESSAGE TO MARY
LUKE 1: 26-38

March, 7 BC - Nazareth

9. In the sixth month the angel Gabriel was sent from Almighty God to a town of Galilee called Nazareth, to a maiden who was engaged to a man named Joseph, who was a descendent of David. The maiden's name was Mary. The angel came in to her and said, "Greetings, highly favored one! The Lord is with you!"

10. Mary was deeply troubled by what the angel said and wondered what a greeting like that could mean. The angel said to her, "Do not be afraid, Mary, for you have found favor in Almighty God's sight. Believe this, you will conceive and you will give birth to a Son and you will give Him the name Jesus. He will be great, and He will be called the Son of the Most High, and the Lord God will give Him the throne of His forefather David; He will rule over the house of Jacob forever, and there will be no end to His kingdom."

11. Mary said to the angel, "How can this be since I am a virgin?"

12. The angel answered, "The Holy Spirit will come upon you and the power of the Most High will overshadow you, so the child who will be born will be called Holy, the Son of God. Know this also, Elizabeth, your relative, has also conceived in her old age, and this is now the sixth month for her who was called barren, because nothing is impossible with Almighty God."

13. Mary said, "I am the Lord's servant. Let it happen to me as you have said." Then the angel left her.

MARY VISITS ELIZABETH
LUKE 1: 39-45

March, 7 BC - Hill Country of Judea

14. After a few days Mary arose and hurried to the hill country, to a city of Judea, and went into the house of Zacharias and greeted Elizabeth.

15. When Elizabeth heard Mary's greeting, the baby leaped in her womb and Elizabeth was filled with the Holy Spirit. She lifted her voice and loudly exclaimed, "Blessed are you among women and blessed is the fruit of your womb. Why has this been granted to me, that the mother of my Lord should come to me? Believe this, when the sound of your greeting reached my ears, the baby in my womb leaped with joy. Blessed is she who believed that the things spoken to her from the Lord would be fulfilled."

MARY'S SONG OF PRAISE
LUKE 1: 46-56

March, 7 BC - Hill Country of Judea

16. Mary said,
    "My soul praises the Lord,
    My spirit rejoices in God my Savior,
    because God has remembered me,
        God's lowly servant!
    From now on all people
        will call me blessed.
    because of the great things
        Almighty God has done for me.
    God's name is Holy,
    God's mercy is shown to those
        who fear God,
    from generation to generation.
    God's arm has performed mighty deeds,
    God scattered the proud
        with all their plans,
    God brought down mighty rulers
        from their thrones,
        and lifted up the lowly,
    God filled the hungry with good things,
        But sent the rich away
        with empty hands.
    God kept the promises made
        to our ancestors,
    and came to the help of God's servants,
    remembering to show mercy
        to Abraham
    and to his descendants forever!"

Dr. Patrick Pierce

THE BIRTH OF JOHN THE BAPTIST
LUKE 1:57-66

June, 7 BC - Hill Country of Judea

17. When Elizabeth's time had come to have her baby, she gave birth to a son. When her neighbors and relatives heard that the Lord had shown great mercy on her, they rejoiced with her.

18. On the eighth day they went to circumcise the child and it was their intention to name him Zacharias after his father. But his mother said, "No, he must be named John."

They said to her, "There is no one among your relatives who has that name." They asked his father by signs what name he wished to name the child.

Zacharias asked for a writing tablet and wrote, "His name is John."

19. Immediately his mouth was opened and his tongue was loosed and he couldn't stop praising God. The neighbors were all filled with great wonder and surprise and all these events were talked about in all the hill country of Judea. Everyone who heard these things remembered them and said, "What will this child turn out to be, for the hand of the Lord is with him?"

ZACHARIAS' JOY AND PROPHESY
LUKE 1: 67-80

June, 7 BC - Hill Country of Judea

20. John's father Zacharias was filled with the Holy Spirit, and he spoke God's message saying.

> "Let us praise the Lord God Almighty!
>   For God has come to help God's people
>   and set them free.
> God has raised up a mighty strength for us,
>   a descendent of God's servant David.
> Long ago by God's holy prophets
>   God promised to save us
>   from our enemies,
>   and from the power of all who hate us.
> God would show mercy to our ancestors,
>   and remember God's sacred covenant.
> God made a solemn promise to
>   our ancestor Abraham,
>   and God vowed to rescue us
>   from our enemies,
>   and allow us to serve God without fear,
>   To be holy and righteous before God,
>   all the days of our life.

21. "You, my child, will be called a prophet of
    the Most High God.
  For you will go ahead of the Lord
    to prepare the way for the Lord
  To tell God's people that they will be saved,
    by having their sins forgiven.

> Our God is merciful and compassionate.
>> God will cause the bright
>> dawn of salvation
>> to rise on us,
> and shine from heaven on all those
>> who live in the dark
>> shadow of death,
> to guide our steps into
>> the way of peace."

GOD'S MESSAGE TO JOSEPH
MATTHEW 1:18-25

June, 7 B.C. - Nazareth

22. The birth of Jesus Christ happened this way:

Mary, His mother, was engaged to be married to Joseph; and, before they became man and wife, it was discovered that she was pregnant with a child through the Holy Spirit. Although Joseph, her betrothed husband, was a man who kept the law, he did not wish to publicly disgrace her, so he decided to divorce her secretly.

23. When he was planning this, an angel of the Lord came to him in a dream. "Joseph, son of David," said the angel, "Do not hesitate to take Mary as your wife, for that which has been conceived within her has come from the Holy Spirit. She will bear a son, and you will name Him Jesus, for it is He who will save His people from their sins."

24. All this has happened that what was spoken by the Lord through the prophet might be fulfilled, "Behold, a virgin will conceive

and bear a son, and they shall call his name Emmanuel," which is translated "God with us."

25. So Joseph woke from his sleep, and did as the angel had commanded him. He took Mary as his wife, but she remained a virgin until she gave birth to a son, and he named Him "Jesus."

CHAPTER 3
THE BIRTH OF JESUS

LUKE 2:1-7

October, 7 BC - Nazareth and Bethlehem

1. In those days a decree went out from Caesar Augustus that a census should be taken of the entire Roman Empire. The census first took place when Quirinius was governor of Syria, and everyone went to be registered, each man to his ancestral hometown.

2. So Joseph went up from Galilee, from the town of Nazareth, to Judea, to the town of David, which is called Bethlehem, because he belonged to the house and family of David, to register himself with Mary who was betrothed to him and was with Child.

3. When they arrived there, the time came for the baby to be born; and she gave birth to her first-born Son and wrapped Him in swaddling clothes and laid Him in a manger because there was no room for them in the inn.

THE SHEPHERDS AND THE ANGELS
LUKE 2:8-20

7 BC - Bethlehem

4. There were shepherds in the nearby fields keeping watch over their flocks at night. An angel of the Lord appeared to them and the glory of the Lord shone round them and they were very much

afraid. The angel said to them, "Do not be afraid, for behold, I bring you Good News of great joy, which will be for all people. For today, in Bethlehem, a Savior has been born for you, who is Christ the Lord. You will recognize Him by this sign. You will find the Baby wrapped in swaddling clothes and lying in a manger."

5. And suddenly there was with the angel a multitude of the army of Heaven praising God and saying.

> "Glory to God in the highest,
> and on earth peace
> to those with whom
> God is pleased."

6. When the angels had left them and gone into Heaven, the shepherds said to each other, "Come! Let's go across to Bethlehem and see this thing that has happened which the Lord has made known to us."

7. So they hurried off and discovered Mary and Joseph, and the Baby lying in a manger. When they had seen Him they told everyone what they had been told about this Child, and all who heard it were amazed at what was told them by the shepherds. But Mary treasured these things in her memory and in her heart kept wondering what they meant. So the shepherds returned glorifying and praising God for all that they had seen, just as it had been told to them.

JESUS IS NAMED AND PRESENTED IN THE TEMPLE
LUKE 2:21-39

October, 7 BC - Bethlehem to Jerusalem then to Nazareth

8. When the eight days necessary prior to circumcision had elapsed, He was named Jesus, the name given Him by the angel before He was conceived.

9. When the time of the purification ceremony, according to the Law of Moses had elapsed, they brought Him up to Jerusalem to present Him to the Lord. In accordance with the written Law, "Every first born male is to be consecrated to the Lord," and to make the sacrifice which the Lord's Law lays down, a pair of doves or two young pigeons.

Simeon's Joy

10. Now there was a man in Jerusalem called Simeon. This man was righteous and devout. He was waiting for the comforting of Israel and the Holy Spirit was upon him. He had received a message from the Holy Spirit that he would not see death until he had seen the Lord's Christ, the Anointed One. Moved by the Spirit he went into the Temple. When His parents brought in the Child Jesus, to do for Him the customary ceremonies directed by the Law, Simeon took Him into his arms and praised God saying:

11.   "Now, Lord, You have kept
       Your promise,
  and You may let Your servant
       go in peace.

> With my own eyes I have seen
> > Your Salvation,
> which You have prepared
> > in the presence of all peoples.
> A Light to reveal Your way
> > to the Gentiles,
> and bring glory to Your people."

12. His father and mother were amazed at what was said about Him. Simeon blessed them and said to Mary His mother, "Listen! This Child is appointed to cause the fall and rising of many in Israel and to be a sign which will meet much opposition. As for you, a sword will pierce through your soul, and this will happen that the inner thoughts of many hearts will be revealed."

Anna

13. There was a prophetess called Anna. She was the daughter of Phanuel and she belonged to the family of Acher. She was very old having lived with her husband ever since seven years after she came into womanhood, and now she was a widow eighty-four years old. She never left the Temple, and worshipped with fastings and prayers day and night. At that time she came up, and she began to give thanks to God and she kept speaking about Jesus to all those who were looking forward to the deliverance of Jerusalem.

When they had completed everything according to the Law of the Lord, they returned to Galilee to the town of Nazareth.

THE WISE MEN
MATTHEW 2:1-12

December, 6 BC and later - Bethlehem

14. After Jesus was born in Bethlehem in Judea, during the time when Herod was King, there came to Jerusalem Wise Men from the East. They said, "Where is the newly born King of the Jews? For we have seen His star in the East and have come to worship Him."

15. When King Herod heard this he was disturbed, and so was all Jerusalem with him. So he called together all the people's Chief Priests and Scribes of the Law, and asked them where the Christ was to be born.

16. They said to him, "In Bethlehem in Judea." For it is written by the prophets:

> "And you, Bethlehem, in the land of Judah,
>   are in no way the least among
>   the chief cities of Judah,
>   For out of you shall come forth a Ruler,
> who will be a Shepherd to
>   My people Israel."

17. Then Herod secretly called for the Wise Men and questioned them about the time when the star appeared. Then he sent them to Bethlehem saying, "Go and make every effort to find the Child. When you have found Him, send news to me, so I may go and worship Him also."

18. When they had listened to the king they went on their way. And the star, which they had seen rise in the East, led them on until it

came and stood over the place where the Child was. When they saw the star, they rejoiced and were overjoyed. They came into the house and saw the little Child with Mary, His mother, and they fell down and worshipped Him. Then they opened their treasures and offered gifts of gold, frankincense, and myrrh.

19. Having been given a warning from God in a dream, telling them not to go back to Herod, they returned to their own country by another route.

ESCAPE TO EGYPT
MATTHEW 2:13-18

6 BC to 2 BC - Bethlehem to Egypt

20. When they had gone, behold, an angel of the Lord appeared in a dream to Joseph and said, "Get up! Take the young Child and His mother, and flee into Egypt, and stay there until I tell you; for Herod is about to search for the Child, in order to kill Him."

21. So he got up and took the Child and His mother by night and left for Egypt, and he remained there until the death of Herod.

This happened that the word spoken by the Lord through the prophet might be fulfilled: "Out of Egypt I called my Son."

22. When Herod realized he had been tricked by the Wise Men, he gave orders and killed all the male children in Bethlehem, and in all the districts near by. He killed every child of two years and under, reckoning from the time when he had made his inquiries from the Wise Men.

23. Then the word which was spoken through Jeremiah the prophet was fulfilled:

> "A voice was heard in Rama,
>   Weeping and great mourning,
>   Rachel weeping for her children,
>   and she refused to be comforted,
>   because they were no more."

RETURN FROM EGYPT
MATTHEW 2:19-23

2 BC - Egypt to Nazareth

24. When Herod died, behold, the angel of the Lord appeared in a dream to Joseph in Egypt and said, "Rise , and take the Child and His mother, and go into the land of Israel, for those who sought the Child's life are dead." So he got up and took the Child and His mother, and went into the land of Israel.

25. When Joseph heard that Archelaus was king in Judea instead of his father Herod, he was afraid to go there. So, when he had received a message from God in a dream, he withdrew to the district of Galilee and he came and lived in a town called Nazareth. This happened so the word spoken through the prophets might be fulfilled: "He shall be called a Nazarene."

THE BOY JESUS IN THE TEMPLE
LUKE 2:40-52

April AD 5 - Nazareth and Temple in Jerusalem

26. And the Child grew and became strong, and He was filled with wisdom and God's grace was on Him.

27. Every year His parents went to Jerusalem for the feast of the Passover. When He was twelve years of age, they went up to the feast as was their custom. After the feast was ended and they were returning home, the Child Jesus stayed behind in Jerusalem but His parents were not aware of this. They thought He was in the caravan and when they had gone a day's journey, they looked for Him among their relatives and friends. When they did not find Him, they went back to Jerusalem, looking for Him all the time.

28. After three days they found Him in the court of the Temple sitting in the middle of the rabbis, listening to them and asking them questions. All who were listening were astonished at His understanding and His answers. When they saw Him they were amazed. His mother said to Him, "Child, why did You do this to us? Listen to me, Your father and I have been searching for You and have been very worried."

29. He said to them, "Why were you looking for Me? Didn't you know that I was bound to be in God's house and about Almighty God's business?" But they did not understand the meaning of what He said to them.

JESUS GROWING UP
AD 5 to 25 - Nazareth

30. So He went home with them to Nazareth and was obedient to them. His mother remembered all these things and thought about their meaning. And Jesus grew in wisdom and stature and in favor with God and all people.

CHAPTER 4
JOHN'S MINISTRY

MATTHEW 3:1-12; MARK 1:1-8; LUKE 3:1-18

AD 25 - Wilderness of Judea by Jordan River

1. In the fifteenth year of the reign of Tiberius Caesar, when Pontius Pilate was governor of Judea, and Herod was tetrarch of Galilee, and his brother Philip tetrarch of Ituraea and the district of Trachonitis, and Lysanias tetrarch of Abilene, in the high-priesthood of Annas and Caiaphas; the Word of God came to John, the son of Zacharias, when he was in the desert.

2. In those days John the Baptist began preaching in the wilderness of Judea saying, "Repent, the Kingdom of Heaven is at hand."

3. It was this man that was spoken of by Isaiah the prophet. He came into the country around Jordan, preaching a baptism of repentance for the forgiveness of sins. As it is written in the book of Isaiah:

"I send My messenger before You and
    he will prepare Your way for You.
The voice of one crying in the wilderness,
    'Prepare the way of the Lord,
    make the Lord's paths straight,
every valley shall be filled up,
every mountain and hill made level,
the crooked paths will be made straight,

and the rough ways made smooth,
and all people shall see God's
Instrument of Salvation!"

John Baptizes - Jordan River

4. This came true when John the Baptist came to the wilderness, wearing a garment made from camel's hair, and he had a leather belt around his waist, his food was locusts and wild honey, announcing a baptism which was a sign of repentance through which a person might find forgiveness for sins.

5. Then Jerusalem, the whole country of Judea and all the district around the Jordan went out to him, and they were baptized by him in the river Jordan, and, as they were baptized, they confessed their sins.

John Preaches Repentance

6. When he saw many of the Pharisees and Sadducees coming to his baptism he said to the crowds coming out to be baptized by him, "You brood of vipers! Who warned you to flee from the coming wrath? Produce fruit fit for repentance. Do not think or begin to say among yourselves, 'We have Abraham as our father.' For I tell you that God is able to raise up children of Abraham from these stones. The axe is already at the root of the trees. Therefore every tree which does not produce good fruit will be cut down, and thrown into the fire."

7. The crowds asked him, "What shall we to do?"

He answered them, "Anyone with two robes, give one to those who have none, and those with food do likewise." The tax-collectors came to be baptized and asked, "Teacher, what are we to do?" He said to them, "Collect no more than you are required to." The soldiers also asked him. "And we, what are we to do?" He said, "Treat no one with violence, do not accuse others falsely, and be content with your pay."

John Declares Christ Is At Hand

8. The people were waiting expectantly, and all were wondering in their minds if John could be the Christ. John answered them all, "I baptize you with water because you have repented, but the One who is coming after me is mightier than I. I am not fit to stoop down to loosen the strap of that One's sandals or carry the One's sandals. The One will baptize you with the Holy Spirit and with fire. The One's winnowing fork is in its hand to thoroughly cleanse its threshing floor, and the One will gather the wheat into its storehouse, but the One will burn the chaff with unquenchable fire that no one can put out."

So then urging the people with many other words, John preached the Gospel to them.

JOHN BAPTIZES JESUS
MATTHEW 3:13-17; MARK 1:9-11; LUKE 3:21-22

January AD 27 - Jordan River

9. Then Jesus came from Nazareth in Galilee to be baptized by John. But John tried to prevent Jesus saying, "It is I, who needs to be baptized by You, and are You coming to me?"

10. But Jesus answered him, "Let it now be so, for it is proper for us to do this to fulfill all righteousness." Then John consented.

11. When all of the people had been baptized, Jesus was also baptized by John in the Jordan; and as soon as Jesus was baptized while praying, John saw the Heavens opened unto Jesus; and the Holy Spirit of God descended in bodily form like a dove lighting upon Jesus. And a voice came from heaven, saying, "You are my only begotten the Beloved One, in You I am well pleased."

THE TEMPTATION OF CHRIST
MATTHEW 4:1-11; MARK 1:12-13; LUKE 4:1-13

February AD 27 - Judean Wilderness

Hunger Temptation

12. Jesus came back from the Jordan full of the Holy Spirit and the Spirit immediately led Jesus into the wilderness to be tempted by the devil. Jesus was in the wilderness forty days, and all of the time Jesus was being tested by Satan. The wild animals were Jesus' companions, and the angels helped Jesus. After Jesus had gone without food for forty days and forty nights, Jesus was hungry. So the devil tempter came and said to Jesus, "If you really are Emmanuel, tell these stones to become bread."

Jesus answered him, "It is written, 'Man shall not live by bread alone, but by every Word which proceeds from the mouth of God.'"

Display Power Temptation

13. Then the devil took Jesus to Jerusalem and set Jesus on the pinnacle of the Temple, and said to Jesus, "If you really are Emmanuel throw yourself down from here, for it is written, 'God has given the angels instructions, to take care of You, and they will lift You up lest You strike Your foot against a stone.'"

Then Jesus said to the devil, "It is also written, 'You shall not test the Lord your God.'"

Gain Power Temptation

14. Again the devil took Jesus to a very high mountain and showed Jesus all the kingdoms of the world and their glory, and said to Jesus, "I will give You all this power and the glory of all these things if You will fall down and worship me because it has all been handed over to me, and I can give it to whomever I wish."

Then Jesus answered the devil, "Be gone, Satan! For it is written, 'You shall worship the Lord your God, and God alone shall you serve.'" So when Jesus had gone through all of the temptations, the devil left Jesus alone for a time, and angels came and attended to Jesus.

Dr. Patrick Pierce

THE WITNESS OF JOHN
LUKE 3:23; JOHN 1:19-34

February AD 27 - Bethany across Jordan

John Explains His Ministry

15. This is the witness of John, when the Jews sent priests and Levites from Jerusalem to ask him, "Who are you?"
    He stated definitely, "I am not the Messiah."
    So they asked him, "Who are you then? Are you Elijah?"
    "I am not," he replied.
    "Are you the promised Prophet?"
    "No," he answered.

16. So they asked him, "Who are you? Tell us, so we can give an answer to those who sent us. What claim do you make for yourself?"
    He said, "I am the voice of one crying in the wilderness, 'Make straight the way of the Lord!' as Isaiah the prophet said."

17. Now they had been sent by the Pharisees, and they asked him, "If you are neither the Messiah, nor promised prophet, why do you baptize?"

18. John answered, "I baptize with water, but there is One coming after me, the straps whose sandals I am not worthy to undo." These things happened at Bethany, on the other side of the Jordan, where John was baptizing.

19. On the next day, John saw Jesus coming towards him, and said, "See! The Lamb of God, who takes away the sin of the world! This is the One whom I said to you, 'There is the One who is coming after me, who surpasses me because this One was before me.' Even I did not know the One, but the reason I came baptizing with water was that the One might be revealed to Israel."

Jesus Begins Public Ministry

20. When Jesus began the ministry Jesus was about thirty years old.

21. Then John gave this witness, "With my own eyes, I saw the Spirit coming down from Heaven, as it might have been a dove, and the Spirit remained on Jesus. I did not know Jesus, but it was God who sent me to baptize with water who said to me, 'The One on whom you see the Spirit come down and remain on is the One who baptizes with the Holy Spirit.' I saw this happen, and I testify that this is Emmanuel."

CHAPTER 5
JESUS' FIRST PUBLIC ACTS

JESUS MAKES HIS FIRST DISCIPLES
JOHN 1:35-42

Spring AD 27 - At Bethany across Jordan

1. The next day John was again standing with two of his disciples, and looked at Jesus as Jesus walked. He said, "The Lamb of God!" And the two disciples heard him say this and followed Jesus.

Jesus turned and saw the two disciples following Him. "What are you looking for?" Jesus asked.

2. They said to Jesus, "Teacher, where are You staying?"

Jesus replied, "Come and see." They came and saw where Jesus was staying, and stayed with Jesus that day. It was about four in the afternoon.

3. Andrew, Simon Peter's brother, was one of the two who heard what John had said about Jesus, and who had followed Jesus. The first thing in the morning, he went and found his brother, Simon. "We have found the Messiah," he said to him. (The Word Messiah means the same as the word Christ). He brought him to Jesus.

4. Jesus looked at him and said, "You are Simon, Jonas' son. You shall be called Cephas." Cephas is the same name as Peter and means a rock.

PHILIP AND NATHANAEL
JOHN 1:43-51

Next Day - Galilee

5. The next day Jesus decided to leave for Galilee, and there Jesus found Philip. Jesus said to him, "Follow me!" Now Philip came from Bethsaida, which was the town from which Andrew and Peter came.

6. Philip found Nathanael and said to him, "We have found the One about whom Moses wrote in the Law, and about whom the prophets also wrote. I mean Jesus of Nazareth, the son of Joseph."

Nathanael said to him, "Can anything good come out of Nazareth?"

"Come and see!" Philip replied to him.

7. When Jesus saw Nathanael coming towards Him, Jesus said, "See, a true Israelite! A man in whom there is nothing false!"

Nathanael said to Jesus, "How do You know me?"

8. Jesus answered, "Before Philip called you, I saw you when you were under the fig tree."

"Teacher," answered Nathanael, "You are the Emmanuel! You are the King of Israel!"

9. Jesus answered, "Do you believe because I told you, 'I saw you under the fig tree?' You will see greater things than that." Jesus said to him, "This is the truth I tell you, you will see the Heavens opened and angels of God ascending and descending on Emmanuel."

JESUS' FIRST PUBLIC MIRACLE
WATER INTO WINE
JOHN 2:1-12

Spring, AD 27 - Cana in Galilee

10. Two days after this was a wedding in Cana, and Jesus' mother was there. Jesus and the Disciples were invited to the wedding. When the wine had run short, Jesus' mother said to Jesus, "They have no more wine."

11. Jesus said to her, "Dear woman, let me do this in My own way. My time has not yet come."
Jesus' mother said to the servants, "Do whatever Jesus tells you to do."

12. There were six stone water pots standing there which were used for the Jewish purifying custom, and each of them could hold about twenty to thirty gallons. Jesus said to them, "Fill the water pots with water." They filled them up to the top. Jesus said to them, "Draw from them now, and take what you draw to the Master of the banquet." They did so.

13. When the Master of the banquet had tasted the water which had become wine, he did not know where it came from, but the servants who had drawn the water knew, he called the bridegroom and said to him, "Everyone first brings out the good wine, and then, when they have drunk their fill, he brings out the inferior wine. You have kept the good wine until now."

14. Jesus did the first of Jesus' signs in Cana of Galilee, and revealed Jesus' glory, and Jesus' disciples believed on Jesus as the Christ.

After this Jesus went down to Capernaum with Jesus' mother, Jesus' brothers and Jesus' Disciples, and they stayed there for a while.

JESUS CLEANSES THE TEMPLE
JOHN 2:13-25

April 9, AD27 - Jerusalem

15. The Jewish Passover was near and Jesus went up to Jerusalem. In the Temple courts Jesus found those selling oxen and sheep and doves, and the money-changers sitting at their tables. Jesus made a whip of cords and drove them all out of the Temple, and the sheep and oxen as well. Jesus scattered the coins of the exchangers and overturned their tables. Jesus said to those selling doves, "Take these away and stop making God's house a house of trade."

16. Jesus' Disciples remembered that there is a scripture written, "Zeal for Your house will consume Me."

17. Then the Jews demanded of Jesus, "What sign do You show us to justify Your acting in this way?"

Jesus answered, "Destroy this Temple and in three days I will raise it up."

18. Then Jews said, "It has taken forty-six years to build this Temple, and are You going to raise it up in three days?" But Jesus was speaking about Jesus' body. So when Jesus was raised from the dead,

Jesus' disciples remembered that Jesus had said this, and they believed the Scripture and on the words which Jesus spoke.

19. While Jesus was in Jerusalem, at the Passover Festival, many believed in the Christ as they saw the signs that Jesus did; but Jesus would not trust them, because Jesus knew all people, and Jesus had no need that anyone should testify about other people for Jesus knew well what was in human nature.

JESUS TALKS TO NICODEMUS
JOHN 3:1-21

April, AD 27 (Passover) - At Jerusalem

20. Now, there was a man who was of the Pharisees named Nicodemus, a member of the Jewish ruling council. He came to Jesus by night and said to Him, "Teacher, we know that You are a teacher who has come from God, for no one can do these signs which You do unless God is with that One."

21. Jesus answered him, "This is the truth I tell you, unless a person is reborn from above, the person cannot see the Kingdom of God."

Nicodemus said to Jesus, "How can a man be born when he is old? Surely he cannot enter into his mother's womb a second time and be born?"

22. Jesus answered, "This is the truth I tell you, unless a person is born of water and the Spirit, the person cannot enter into the Kingdom of God. That which is born from the flesh is flesh, and that which is born of the Spirit is spirit. Do not be surprised that I said to you, 'You must be

born again from above.' The wind blows where it will, and you hear the sound of it, but you do not know where it comes from and where it goes. So it is with everyone who is born of the Spirit."

Nicodemus answered, "How can these things happen?"

23. Jesus answered, "Are you the man regarded as the teacher of Israel, and you do not understand these things? This is the truth I tell you, we speak what we know, and we bear witness to what we have seen, but you do not receive our witness. If I have spoken to you of earthly things and you do not believe Me, how will you believe Me if I speak to you about Heavenly things. No one has gone up to Heaven, except the One who came down from Heaven, I mean, Emmanuel.

24. "And as Moses lifted up the serpent in the wilderness, so Emmanuel must be lifted up, that everyone who believes may have eternal life.

25. "For God so loved the world that God gave the only begotten One so that whoever believes should not perish but have eternal life.

26. "For God did not send Emmanuel into the world to condemn the world, but that the world might be saved through Emmanuel. Whoever believes in Emmanuel is not condemned, but whoever does not believe is condemned already, because they have not believed in the Emmanuel. And this is the reason for this condemnation, the Light is come into the world and people loved the darkness rather than the Light, for their deeds were evil. Everyone whose deeds are evil hates the Light, and does not come to the Light, for fear that their deeds will be exposed. But whoever puts the truth into action

comes to the Light, that their deeds may be seen clearly, because they are done in God."

JOHN'S SECOND TESTIMONY
JOHN 3:22-36

Summer, 27 - Judea and Aenon

27. After these things Jesus and Jesus' disciples went to the district of Judea. Jesus spent some time there with them and was baptizing.

John was baptizing at Aenon, near Salem, because there was much water there. The people kept coming to Jesus and being baptized, for John had not yet been thrown into prison.

28. A discussion arose between some of John's Disciples and the Jews about purification. So they came to John and said to him, "Teacher, the One who was with you on the other side of Jordan, the One to whom you bore witness, look, that One is baptizing and they are all coming to the One."

29. John answered, "A person can receive only what is given to that person from Heaven. You yourselves can testify that I said, 'I am not the Anointed One of God,' but, 'I have been sent before the One.'

30. "The One who has the bride is the bridegroom. But the friend of the bridegroom who stands and listens for Him, rejoices at the sound of the bridegrooms voice. And then my joy is complete. Jesus must increase, but I must decrease. The One who comes from above is above all, he who is of the earth is from the earth and speaks of the earth. The One who comes from Heaven is above all.

31. "It is of what the One has seen and heard that the One bears witness, and no one receives the One's witness. Whoever has received his witness sets his seal on the fact that God is true. The One whom Almighty God sent speaks the words of Almighty God, for the One gives the Spirit without limit. Almighty God loves Emmanuel and has given all things into Emmanuel's hand. Whoever believes in Emmanuel has eternal life. Whoever does not believe in Emmanuel will not see life, but the wrath of Almighty God rests upon them."

CHAPTER 6
TRIP THROUGH SAMARIA

JESUS LEAVES JUDEA
MATTHEW 4:12; MARK 1:14a; LUKE 3:19-20; JOHN 4:1-4

Summer, 27 – Judea

1. But, when Herod the tetrarch was rebuked by John concerning the matter of Herodias, his brother Philip's wife, and concerning all the other wicked things he had done, he added this also to everything else and he locked up John in prison.

2. When Jesus heard that John had been delivered into the hands of the authorities and put in prison, Jesus also learned that the Pharisees had heard that Jesus was making and baptizing more disciples than John (although it was not Jesus Himself who was in the habit of baptizing but Jesus' disciples), Jesus quit in Judea and went away again to Galilee.

THE SAMARITAN WOMAN
JOHN 4:5-42

Summer, 27 - Samaria

3. Now Jesus had to pass through Samaria.

Jesus came to a town of Samaria, called Sychar, which is near the piece of ground which Jacob gave to Joseph, his son, and Jacob's well was there. So Jesus, tired from the journey, was sitting by the well. It was about midday. There came a woman of Samaria to draw water. Jesus said to her, "Give Me a drink." For Jesus' Disciples had gone away into the town to buy provisions.

4. So the Samaritan woman said to Jesus, "How is it that You, who are a Jew, ask a drink from me, a Samaritan woman?" (For there is no familiarity between Jews and Samaritans)

5. Jesus answered her, "If you knew the gift that God is offering you, and Who it is saying to you, 'Give Me a drink,' you would have asked the One, and the One would have given you living water."

6. The woman said to Jesus, "Sir, you have no bucket to draw with and the well is deep. Where does this living water that You have come from? Are You greater than our father Jacob who gave us this well, and who himself drank from it with his children and his cattle?"

7. Jesus answered her, "Everyone who drinks of this water will thirst again, but whoever drinks of the water that I will give, will never thirst again. But the water I will give will become a well of water within, springing up to give eternal life."
The woman said to Jesus, "Sir, give me this water, so that I will not thirst again, and so that I will not have to come here to draw water."

8. Jesus said to her, "Go, call you husband, and come back here."

The woman answered, "I have no husband."
Jesus said to her, "You spoke well when you said, 'I have no husband.' For you have had five husbands, and the one you now have is not your husband. This is the truth that you have told."

9. The woman said to Jesus, "Sir, I see that You are a Prophet. Our ancestors worshipped in this mountain and You say Jerusalem is the place where we ought to worship."

10. Jesus said, "Woman, believe Me, the hour is coming when you will worship Almighty God neither in this mountain nor in Jerusalem. You do not know what you worship. We do know what we worship, because the world's salvation has it's origin among the Jews. But the hour is coming and is now here, when the true worshippers will worship Almighty God in spirit and in truth, for it is worshippers like that who Almighty God is looking for. God is Spirit, and those who worship God must worship in spirit and in truth."

11. The woman said to Jesus "I know that the Messiah, the One who is called Christ, is coming. When the One comes, the Messiah will declare all things to us."
Jesus said to her, "I, who am speaking to you, am the One."

Spiritual Food

12. Upon this Jesus' Disciples came up; and they were amazed that Jesus was talking to a woman, but no one said, "What are You looking for?" or, "Why are You talking to her?"

13. So the woman left her water pot, and went to the town and said to the people, "Come and see a person who told me all the things that I have done! Can this be the Anointed One of God?" They came out of the town and came out to Jesus.

14. Meanwhile Jesus' Disciples asked Jesus, "Teacher! Eat something!"

Jesus said to them, "I have food that you do not know about."

Jesus' Disciples were saying to each other, "Surely someone couldn't have given Jesus something to eat?"

15. Jesus said to them, "My food is to do the will of God who sent Me and to complete God's work. Do you not say, 'Four more months, and the harvest will come?' Listen, I say to you, lift up your eyes and look at the fields, because they are already ripe for harvesting. The harvester receives wages and stores up fruit for eternal life, so that the one who sows and the one who harvests may rejoice together. In this case it is true, 'One sows and another harvests.' I have sent you to harvest a crop which your labor did not produce. Others have labored, and you have entered into their labors."

16. Many of the Samaritans from the city believed in Jesus, because of the woman's story, for she testified, "This One told me all things that I have done." So when the Samaritans came to Jesus, they asked Jesus to stay with them, and Jesus stayed there two days. And many more believed when they heard Jesus' word, and they said to the woman, "No longer do we believe because of what you said. We have listened to Jesus ourselves and we know that this One is really the Savior of the World."

RETURN TO GALILEE
LUKE 4:14; JOHN 4:43-45

Summer, 27 - Galilee

17. After two days Jesus left there and returned in the power of the Spirit to Galilee. Jesus declared that a Prophet has no honor in his own country. But when Jesus came into Galilee, the Galileans welcomed Jesus, because they had seen all that Jesus had done at Jerusalem at the Feast, for they too went to the Feast.

JESUS' TEACHINGS
MATTHEW 4:17; MARK 1:14b-15; LUKE 4:15

Summer, 27 - Galilee

18. From that time Jesus began to proclaim God's message announcing the Good News about God saying, "Repent, for the Kingdom of God of the Heavens is near. Believe the Good News."

19. The story of Jesus spread throughout the whole countryside. Jesus kept on teaching in their synagogues and Jesus was held in high regard by all.

JESUS HEALS THE OFFICIAL'S SON
JOHN 4:46-54

Autumn, 27 - Cana

20. So Jesus came again to Cana in Galilee, where Jesus had made the water into wine. Now there was a certain royal official

whose son was ill in Capernaum. When this man heard that Jesus had come from Judea into Galilee, he went to Jesus and asked Jesus to come down and heal his son, for he was going to die.

21. Jesus said to him, "Unless you see signs and wonders you will not believe."

The royal official said to Jesus, "Sir, come down before my child dies."

22. Jesus said to him, "Go your way! Your son lives!"
The official believed the word which Jesus spoke to him, and started on his way home. While he was still on the way down, his slaves met him and said, "Your son lives!" So he asked them at what hour his condition had improved. They told him, "Yesterday, at one o'clock in the afternoon, the fever left him." The father knew that was the hour at which Jesus said to him, "Your son lives!" And he and his whole household believed.
This is the second miracle which Jesus did after Jesus had come from Judea into Galilee.

JESUS' HOME IN CAPERNAUM
MATTHEW 4:13-16

Autumn, 27 - Capernaum

23. Leaving Galilee Jesus came and made Jesus' home in Capernaum, which is on the lake side, in the districts of Zebulun and Naphtali. This was done to fulfill what was spoken through Isaiah the prophet, when he said, "Land of Zebulun, land of Naphtali, by the way of the sea, beyond Jordan, Galilee of the Gentiles, the people who sat

in darkness have seen a great Light, and the Light has risen for those who sat in the land and in the shadow of death."

JESUS CALLS FOUR
MATTHEW 4:18-22; MARK 1:16-20; LUKE 5:1-11

Autumn, 27 - Capernaum

Peter and Andrew

24. While Jesus was walking beside the Sea of Galilee, Jesus saw two brothers, Simon, who was called Peter, and Andrew, his brother, casting their nets into the sea, for they were fishermen. And Jesus said to them, "Follow Me, and I will make you fishers of people."

James and John

25. Jesus went on from there a little further and saw two other brothers, James, Zebedee's son, and John, his brother, who were in their boat with Zebedee their father mending their nets. Jesus called them as soon as Jesus saw them.

Catching Fish Miracle

26. Jesus was standing on the shore of the Sea of Galilee with the crowds pressed in on Jesus to listen to the Word of God. Jesus saw two boats close to the shore, the fishermen had disembarked from them and were washing their nets. Jesus got in one of the boats, which belonged to Simon, and asked him to push out a little way from the shore. Jesus sat down and continued to teach the crowds from the boat.

When Jesus stopped speaking, Jesus said to Simon, "Push out into the deep water and let down your nets for a catch."

27. Simon answered, "Master, we have worked hard all night long and we caught nothing; but, if You say so, I will let down the nets."

28. When they had done so they caught such a large number of fish that their nets began to be torn, so they signaled to their partners in the other boat to come and help them. They came and they filled both the boats so full they began to sink.

29. When Simon Peter saw this, he fell at Jesus' knees and said, "Leave me, Lord, because I am a sinful man." He and all who were with him were amazed at the number of fish they had caught. It was the same with James and John, Zebedee's sons, who were partners with Simon.

Jesus said to Simon, "From now on you will be catching people."

30. So they brought the boats to land, and they immediately left everything, their father Zebedee and the boat with the hired servant, and went and followed Jesus.

JESUS DRIVES OUT A DEVIL
MARK 1:21-28; LUKE 4:31-37

Autumn, 27 - Capernaum

31. So Jesus came down to Capernaum, a town in Galilee, and early on the Sabbath day Jesus went into the Synagogue and began to

teach, and they were amazed at Jesus' teaching, for Jesus taught them like One who had authority, and not as the experts in the law.

32. There was a man in the synagogue possessed by a spirit of an unclean demon. He shouted, "What have we to do with You, Jesus of Nazareth? Have you come to destroy us? I know who You are, the Holy One of God."

33. Jesus rebuked him saying, "Be silent, and come out of him."

34. When the unclean spirit had thrown him down in a convulsion in their midst, it came out of him and it did him no harm. They were all so astonished and they started asking each other, "What message is this? This is a new teaching. Jesus gives orders to unclean spirits with authority and they obey Jesus." And the story of Jesus went out everywhere over the whole region of Galilee.

HEALING PETER'S MOTHER-IN-LAW
MATTHEW 8:14-17; MARK 1:29-34; LUKE 4:38-41

Autumn, 27 - Capernaum

35. Jesus left the synagogue and they quickly went, along with Peter and John, into the house of Simon and Andrew. Peter's mother-in-law was lying in bed ill suffering from a high fever. They spoke to Jesus and urged Him to do something for her. Jesus went up to her and stood over her and rebuked the fever, took her by the hand and raised her up, and the fever left her. She got up and began to wait on them.

36. When evening had come and the sun had set, all who had any who were ill with all kinds of sicknesses brought them to Jesus;

they brought many who were possessed by evil spirits, and Jesus laid hands on each one of them and Jesus cast out the spirits with a word, and all those who were ill were healed.

37. This happened that the saying spoken through the Prophet Isaiah might be fulfilled, "He took our weaknesses and carried our sins."

38. The whole city had gathered together at the door; and Jesus healed many who were ill of various diseases and cast out demons, crying out saying, "You are the One of God."

39. And Jesus rebuked them and forbade the demons to speak, because they knew that Jesus was the Anointed One.

CHAPTER 7
PREACHING IN GALILEE

MATTHEW 4:23-25; MARK 1:35-39; LUKE 4:42-44

Fall to Winter, 27 - Galilee

1. Very early in the morning while it was still dark, Jesus rose and went out. Jesus went to a deserted place and there He was praying. When day broke Simon and his friends found Him and said to Him, "They are all searching for You."

Jesus said to them, "Let us go somewhere else, to the nearby villages, that I may proclaim the Good News there too, for that is why I came."

2. The crowds kept looking for Jesus and they tried to keep Him so He would not leave them. He went to their synagogues and made a tour all over Galilee, teaching and proclaiming the Good News of the Kingdom. As He went, healing all kinds of diseases and ailments among the people, and the report of His activities went out all over Syria. So they brought to Him all those were ill, those who were in the grip of the most varied diseases and pains, those who were possessed by demons, those who were epileptics, and those who were paralyzed; and He healed them. And large crowds followed Him from Galilee, the Decapolis, Jerusalem, Judea, and the region across Jordan.

JESUS HEALS A LEPER
MATTHEW 8:2-4; MARK 1:40-45; LUKE 5:12-16

Early, 28 - Galilee

3. While Jesus was in one of the towns, behold a man who had a severe case of leprosy saw Jesus and came to Him. He fell on his face before Jesus, asking Jesus to help him, saying, "Lord, if you are willing, You are able to cleanse me."

4. Jesus was moved with compassion and stretched out His hand and touched him saying, "I am willing, be cleansed."
Immediately the leprosy left him and he was cleansed. Jesus sent him away at once with a strong order. "See to it that you tell no one about this, but go and show yourself to the priest, and make an offering for your cleansing just as Moses commanded for proof to them."

5. But he went away and began to tell the story and spread it everywhere. As a result it was not possible for Jesus to come into any town openly, but He had to stay outside in the lonely places. But He would slip away into the wilderness and pray. Yet the people kept coming to Him from everywhere.

JESUS HEALS A PARALYTIC
MATTHEW 9:1-8; MARK 2:1-12; LUKE 5:17-26

AD 28 - Capernaum

6. One day afterward, Jesus got on the boat and crossed over to the other side and came back to Capernaum and was teaching, the

news got around that He was in a house. Such crowds gathered that there was no longer any room left, not even outside the door. So He was speaking the Word to them. Sitting and listening were Pharisees and experts in the law who had come from every village in Galilee and from Judea and Jerusalem. And the power of the Lord was with Him to enable Him to heal them.

7. Now, behold, a group arrived with four men carrying a man on a bed who was paralyzed. They were trying to carry him in to set him before Jesus. When they could find no way to carry him in because of the crowd, they climbed up on to the roof and they let him, bed and all, down through the tiles which they removed right into the middle in front of Jesus.

8. When Jesus saw their faith, He said to the paralyzed man, "Courage young man, your sins are forgiven."

Emmanuel's Authority

9. Some of the experts in the law, Scribes and Pharisees who were sitting there, were debating among themselves and began to raise questions. They said, "Who is this who insults God and is blaspheming? Who can forgive sins but God alone?"

10. Jesus at once knew in His Spirit that this reasoning was being thought in their minds, and Jesus said to them, "Why do you reason evil thoughts in your minds? Which is easier to say, 'Your sins are forgiven you,' or to say, 'Get up, lift your bed, and walk?'"

11. Just to let you see and know that Emmanuel has authority on earth to forgive sins, He said to the paralyzed man, "I say to you, Get up! Take your bed, and go home."

12. And at once he stood up in front of them and took up the bed on which he had been lying and went home glorifying God. When the crowds saw this they were filled with fear, they were all astonished, and they glorified God, because God had given such power to Jesus. They said, "We have seen amazing things today that we have never seen before."

THE CALL OF MATTHEW
MATTHEW 9:9; MARK 2:13-14; LUKE 5:27-28

AD 28 - Capernaum

13. After that Jesus went out again to the lake side and the whole crowd came to Him and He went on teaching them. And as He walked along, He saw a man, a tax collector, called Levi or Matthew, the son of Alphaeus, sitting at his tax-collector's table. He said to him, "Follow Me!"

He arose and left everything and followed Him.

JESUS HEALS A LAME MAN ON THE SABBATH
JOHN 5:1-18

April, 28 - Jerusalem

14. After this there was a feast of the Jews, and Jesus went up to Jerusalem. In Jerusalem, near the Sheep gate, there is a bathing pool with five porches, which is called in Hebrew, Bethzatha. In these porches there lay a crowd of people who were ill, blind and lame and whose limbs were withered. There was a man there who had been ill for thirty-eight years. When Jesus saw him lying there, and since He knew that he had already been there a long time, He said to him, "Do you want to get well?"

15. The sick man answered, "Sir, I have no one to put me into the pool when the water is stirred up, so, while I am on the way, another gets down before me."

Jesus said to him, "Get up! Lift your bed and walk!" And the man was made well instantly, and he took up his bed and walked.

16. Now, it was the Sabbath on that day, so the Jews said to the man who had been cured, It is the Sabbath and it is not permissible for you to carry your bed."

But he answered them, "He who made me well was the One who said to me, 'Lift your bed and walk.'"

17. They asked him, "Who is the One who said to you, 'Lift your bed and walk'?"

But the man who had been healed did not know who He was, for Jesus had slipped away while there was a crowd in the place.

18. Afterwards Jesus found him in the Temple and said to him, "Look! You have been made well. Sin no more or something worse may happen to you!"

The man went away and told the Jews that it was Jesus who had made him well. Because of this the Jews were out to persecute Jesus, because He had done these things on the Sabbath. But Jesus answered them, "Almighty God continues to work until now, and so do I continue to work."

19. Because of this the Jews tried even harder to find a way to kill him, because not only was He breaking the Sabbath, but He spoke of being of God, making Himself equal with Almighty God.

Dr. Patrick Pierce

THE AUTHORITY OF EMMANUEL
JOHN 5:19-29

Jerusalem

20. Jesus gave them this answer, "This is the truth I tell you, Emmanuel cannot do anything which proceeds only from that One. Emmanuel can only do that which Almighty God has been seen doing. In whatever way Almighty God does, Emmanuel likewise does in the same way, for Almighty God loves Emmanuel and has shown Emmanuel everything that Almighty God does. And Almighty God will show Emmanuel greater works than these, so that you will be amazed. For, as Almighty God raises the dead and makes them alive, so also Emmanuel makes alive those whom Emmanuel wishes. Neither does Almighty God judge anyone, but Almighty God has given all judgment to Emmanuel, that all may honor Emmanuel, as they honor Almighty God. Anyone who does not honor Emmanuel does not honor Almighty God who sent Emmanuel."

21. "This is the truth I tell you, whoever listens to My word and believes on Almighty God who sent Me has eternal life, and is not on the way to judgment, but has crossed from death to life."

22. "This is the truth I tell you, the hour is coming and now is when the dead will hear the voice of the One of God, and those who hear will live. For, as Almighty God had life in God's self, so Almighty God has given to Emmanuel to have life in God's self, and Almighty God has given Emmanuel authority to execute all judgment, because Emmanuel is the One. Do not be amazed at this, for the hour is coming when everyone in their graves will hear this voice, and will come forth, those who have done good

works will come out to a resurrection of life, but those who have done evil will come out to a resurrection of judgment."

WITNESS TO JESUS
JOHN 5:30-47

Jerusalem

23. "I can do nothing on my own initiative. As I hear, I judge, and My judgment is just, because I do not seek My own will, but the will of Almighty God who sent Me.

24. "If I bear witness about Myself, My witness need not be accepted as true, but there is another who bears witness about Me, and I know that the witness which that one bears about Me is true. You sent inquirers to John, and he gave witness to the truth, but the witness which I receive is not from any person, but I say these things that you may be saved. He was the lamp which burns and shines and for a time you were willing to enjoy his light. But I have a greater witness than John's. The works which Almighty God has given to Me to accomplish, the very works which I do, are evidence about Me to prove that Almighty God has sent Me. And Almighty God who sent Me has borne witness of Me. You have never heard Almighty God's voice, nor have you ever seen Almighty God's form. You do not have Almighty God's Word dwelling in you, because you do not believe in the One whom Almighty God sent. You search the Scriptures, because you think that in them you have eternal life. It is these that bear witness of Me, yet you refuse to come to Me that you may have life.

25. "I receive no glory from people, but I know you that you do not have the love of God in you. I came in Almighty God's

name, and you did not receive Me. If others shall come in their own name, you will receive them.

26. "How can you believe when you receive glory from one another, and you do not seek the glory that comes from the One and Only God? Do not think that I will accuse you before Almighty God. You have an accuser, it is Moses, in whom you set your hopes. If you had believed in Moses, you would have believed in Me, for he wrote about Me. But if you do not believe in his writings, how will you believe My words?"

PLUCKING GRAIN ON THE SABBATH
MATTHEW 12:1-8; MARK 2:23-28; LUKE 6:1-5

May, 28 - Road from Jerusalem to Galilee

27. At that time Jesus went through the fields on a Sabbath. His disciples were hungry and began to pick some heads of grain as they made their way along, rubbing them in their hands and eating them.

28. When some of the Pharisees saw this, they said to Him, "Look! Your disciples are doing what is unlawful to do on the Sabbath. Why are you doing what is illegal to do on the Sabbath?"

29. Jesus answered, "Haven't you read what David did when he and his friends were in need and hungry? Haven't you read how he went into the house of God, when Abiathar was High Priest, and took and ate the loaves of consecrated bread and gave them to his friends, although it is not legal for any person to eat them except the priests? Or haven't you read in the Law that the priests profane the Sabbath and yet remain blameless? I tell you

that something greater than the Temple is here. But, if you had known the meaning of the saying, 'It is mercy that I desire, and not sacrifice,' you would not have condemned the innocent." He said to them, "The Sabbath was made for people and not people for the Sabbath. So Emmanuel is the Lord even of the Sabbath."

HEALING MAN WITH A WITHERED HAND
MATTHEW 12:9-14; MARK 3:1-6; LUKE 6:6-11

Early Summer, 28 - Galilee, Capernaum

30. He left there and on another Sabbath went into the synagogue again and was teaching, and there was a man there whose right hand was withered. The Scribes and Pharisees were watching Him closely to see if He would heal him on the Sabbath day, so that, if He did, they might be able to accuse Him. So they asked Him, "Is it permitted to heal on the Sabbath?"

31. But He knew well what they were thinking. He said to the man with the withered hand, "Stand up and come out into the middle of the congregation." He said to them, "What person will there be among you who will have sheep, and if the sheep falls into a pit on the Sabbath day, will not take hold of it, and lift it out? How much more valuable is a man than a sheep? So then, it is permitted to do a good thing on the Sabbath day." Jesus said to them, "Here is a question for you, is it legal to do good on the Sabbath day or to do evil? To save a life or to destroy it?"

32. But they remained silent. He looked around at them with anger, for He was distressed at the hardness of their hearts. He then said to the man, "Stretch out your hand!"

33. He stretched it out, and his hand was restored, sound as the other. The Pharisees went out immediately and were furious, they discussed with each other what they could do to destroy Jesus and began to plot with Herod's officers against Jesus, with a plan to kill Him.

HEALING OF MULTITUDES
MATTHEW 12:15-21; MARK 3;7-12

Early summer, 28 - Sea of Galilee

34. Because Jesus knew this, He withdrew from there to the lake side with His disciples, and a great multitude from Galilee followed Him. And from Judea, from Jerusalem, from Idumaea, from the region across the Jordan, and from the territory around Tyre and Sidon, there came a great crowd of people for they heard about the great things He was doing. He healed many of them, and He gave them strict orders not to tell who He was.

35. This happened to fulfill the word through Isaiah which says, "Look, My Servant, whom I have chosen! My beloved One in whom My soul finds delight! I will put My Spirit upon Him, and He will tell the nations what justice is. He will not strive, nor cry aloud, nor will anyone hear His voice in the streets. He will not break the crushed reed, and He will not put out the smoking wick, till He leads justice to victory, in His name the nations will put their hope."

36. He told His disciples to have a boat ready for Him because of the crowd, so they would not crush Him, for He healed many, and the result was that all who were suffering from afflictions pressed upon Him to touch Him. And whenever the unclean spirits saw Jesus, they flung themselves down before Him

and crying, "You are Emmanuel." Many times He sternly forbade them to tell the people of Him.

JESUS CHOOSES TWELVE APOSTLES
MATTHEW 10:1-4; MARK 3:13-19; LUKE 6:12-16

Summer, 28 - Near Capernaum

37. In these days Jesus went out to a mountain to pray, and spent the whole night praying to God. When morning came, He called His disciples and invited to His service the people of His choice. From them He chose twelve, whom He called apostles, that they might be with Him, and that He might send them out to act as His ambassadors, and to have power to cast out demons.

NAMES OF THE TWELVE APOSTLES
38.

Matthew & Mark	Luke	Acts
Simon, called Peter	Peter	Peter
Andrew, Peter's brother	Andrew	Andrew
James, the son of Zebedee	James	James
John, brother of James	John	John
Philip	Philip	Philip
Bartholomew	Bartholomew	Bartholomew
Thomas	Thomas	Thomas
Matthew	Matthew	Matthew
James, son of Alphaeus	James	James
Simon, the Cananaean	Simon, the Zealot	Simon, the Zealot
Thaddaeus	Judas, son of James	Judas, son of James
Judas Iscariot	Judas Iscariot	

CHAPTER 8
THE SERMON ON THE MOUNT

MATTHEW 5:1-2; LUKE 6:17-20a

Summer, 28 - Near Capernaum

INTRODUCTORY STATEMENTS

1. He came down with them and stood with them on the plain; and there was a crowd of His disciples there, and a large crowd of people from all Judea and Jerusalem and from the coastal district of Tyre and Sidon, who had come to listen to Him and to be healed from their diseases; and those who were distressed by unclean spirits were healed and the whole crowd went out from Him, and He healed all.

2. And when He saw the great crowd, He went up on the mountain side; and after He had sat down, His disciples came to Him. He looked at His disciples and opening His month He began to teach them saying.

BEATITUDES (PROMISES TO JESUS' FOLLOWERS)
MATTHEW 5:3-12; LUKE 6:20b-26

3.   "Blessed are the poor in spirit,
        for theirs is the kingdom of heaven.
    Blessed are they who mourn,
        for they shall be comforted.

4. Blessed are the meek,
>for they shall inherit the earth.
>Blessed are they who hunger and thirst,
>>for they shall be filled.
5. Blessed are the merciful,
>for they shall obtain mercy.
>Blessed are the pure in heart,
>>for they shall see God.
6. Blessed are the peacemakers,
>for they shall be called children of God.
>Blessed are they who are persecuted
>>for righteousness sake,
>>for theirs is the Kingdom of Heaven.
7. Blessed are you who are poor,
>for yours is the Kingdom of God.
>Blessed are you who are hungry now,
>>for you shall be satisfied.
>Blessed are you who weep now,
>>for you shall laugh.

8. "Blessed are you when people shall insult you, persecute you, and shall say all manner of evil against you falsely, for My sake, Emmanuel.

"Rejoice and be glad, because your reward will be great in heaven. This is how they persecuted the prophets before you.

9. "But woe to you who are rich,
>for you are receiving
>>your comfort in full now.
>Woe to you who are well fed now,
>>for you shall be hungry.

10. Woe to you who laugh now,
>> for you shall mourn and weep.
> Woe to you when all people speak well of you,
>> for in the same way their ancestors used to treat the false prophets."

INFLUENCE AND DUTIES OF JESUS' FOLLOWERS
MATTHEW 5:13-16
Luke 14:34-35

Salt

11. Jesus said, "You are the salt of the earth. But if salt becomes tasteless, what can make it salty again? It is fit for neither the land nor manure pile. It is thrown out, and can only be thrown out to be trampled underfoot by people. Whoever has ears to hear, let them hear."

Light

12. "You are the light of the world. A city built on a hill cannot be hidden. No one lights a lamp to put it under a basket, but to put it on the lamp stand where it gives light to everyone in the house. Let your light shine before people in such a way that they may see your good works and glorify your Almighty God who is in Heaven."

Dr. Patrick Pierce

JESUS' TEACHINGS AND THE OLD TESTAMENT
MATTHEW 5:17-48; LUKE 6:27-30, 32-36

The Law:

13. "Do not think that I came to destroy the Law or the Prophets, I have not come to destroy them but to fulfill them. This is the truth I tell you, until heaven and earth pass away, not the smallest letter or the smallest part of any letter shall pass away from the Law, until all is accomplished. So then, whoever breaks one of the least of these commandments, and teaches others to do so, shall be called least in the Kingdom of Heaven, but whoever keeps them and teaches others to keep them, will be called great in the Kingdom of Heaven. For I tell you, that you will not enter into the Kingdom of Heaven, unless your righteousness surpasses that of the Scribes and Pharisees.

Killing:

14. "You have heard that it was said by the people of old, 'You shall not kill, and whoever kills is guilty before the judgment court. But I say to you that everyone who is angry with another of God's children is guilty before the judgment court; and whoever says to another of God's children, 'You good for nothing idiot!' is guilty of the judgment in the supreme court; and whoever says to another of God's children, 'You fool!' is guilty to be cast into hell fire.

Giving:

15. "So then, if you bring your gift to God's place, and you then remember that your heavenly brother has something against you,

leave your gift there before God's place and go, and first be reconciled to your brother, and then come and offer your gift.

Debts:

16. "Get on good terms with your opponent while you are still on the road with them in order that your opponent may not hand you over to the judge, and the judge hand you over to the court officer, and you be put into prison. This is the truth I tell you, if that happens, you will not come out until you have paid the last debtor's cent.

Adultery:

17. "You have heard that it has been said, 'You must not commit adultery.' But I say to you that everyone who looks at an another with sexually lust for them has already committed adultery with them within their heart.

Temptation:

18. "If your right eye makes you stumble, tear it out and throw it away, for it is better that one part of your body should be destroyed than that your whole body be thrown into Hell. If your right hand makes you stumble, cut it off and throw it away from you, for it is better for you that one part of your body should be destroyed than that your whole body should go to Hell.

Divorce:

19. "It has been said, 'Whoever divorces their spouse shall give them a bill of divorcement.' But I say to you that everyone who

divorces their spouse for any cause other than unchastity causes them to commit adultery, and anyone who marries a person who has been so divorced commits adultery.

Oaths:

20. "Again, you have heard that it was said by the people of old, 'You shall not make an oath falsely, but you shall fulfill your oath to the Lord.' But I say to you, make no oath at all, neither by Heaven, for it is the throne of God, nor by the Earth, for it is the footstool of God's feet, nor by Jerusalem, for it is the city of the Great King, nor by your head, for you cannot make one hair black or white. But when you say, 'Yes,' let it be Yes; and when you say, 'No,' let it be No. Anything which goes beyond that has its source in evil.

Retaliation:

21. "You have heard that it has been said, 'An eye for an eye, and a tooth for a tooth.' But I tell you not to resist the one who is evil; but if anyone hits you on the right cheek, turn the other to them also; and if anyone wants to obtain judgment against you for your shirt, give them your coat also; and if anyone shall force you to go one mile, go with them two miles. Give to them who ask you, and do not turn away from them who want to borrow from you, and do not demand it back.

Love Enemies:

22. "You have heard that it has been said, 'You shall love your neighbor, and you shall hate your enemy.' But I say to you, love your enemies, do good to those who hate you, bless those who curse you, and pray for those who persecute you and mistreat you, so that you

may become the children of Almighty God who is in Heaven; for God makes the sun to rise on the evil and the good, and sends rain on the righteous and the unrighteous. If you love those who love you, what reward can you expect? Don't even the tax collectors do that? Even sinners love those who love them.

23. "If you are kind to those who are kind to you, what credit is there in that? Even sinners do that. If you lend to those from whom you expect to receive, what credit is that to you? Even sinners lend to sinners in order to get as much back again. But you must love your enemies, and do good, and lend expecting nothing in return. Your reward will be great and you will be the children of the Most High, because God is kind both to thankless and wicked people. Be merciful as your Almighty God in Heaven is merciful."

GIVING
MATTHEW 6:1-4

24. "Beware of practicing your deeds publicly, in order to be seen by people. If you do, you have no reward with your Almighty God who is in Heaven.

25. "So, when you give, do not sound a trumpet before you, as the hypocrites do in the synagogues and in the streets, that they may be praised by people. This is the truth I tell you, they have their reward in full. But when you give offerings to God, your left hand must not know what your right hand is doing, so that your offering to God may be in secret, and your Almighty God who sees what happens in secret will give you your full reward.

Dr. Patrick Pierce

PRAYER
MATTHEW 6:5-8

26. "And when you pray, you must not be like the hypocrites, for they like to pray standing in the synagogues and on the street corners , so that they may be seen by people. This is the truth I tell you, they have their reward in full. But when you pray, go into your private room and shut the door, and pray to your Almighty God who is in secret, and your Almighty God who sees what happens in secret will give you your full reward.

27. "When you pray, do not use meaningless repetition, as the Gentiles do, for their idea is that they will be heard because of their many words. So then, do not be like them, for your Almighty God knows the things you need before you ask God.

THE LORD'S PRAYER
MATTHEW 6:9-15

28. "So then, pray in this way:
Expanded Literal Greek Translation
"Our Father, who art in Heaven
   "Almighty God, our source and creator, who is through the universe
Hallowed be thy name.
   Blessed and worshiped be Your Name.
Your kingdom come
   Let Your Kingdom come now and always,
Your will be done *same*
On earth as it is in Heaven
   On earth, in our lives through us as it is in Your Kingdom.
Give us this day our daily bread,
   Please give us each day what we need daily to live,

And forgive our debts
>*And forgive us our debts to You,*

As we forgive our debtors.
>*In the same way as we forgive the debts owed to us.*

And lead us not into temptation,
>*Keep us clear of temptations and trials,*

But deliver us from evil.
>*But save and protect us from evil and the Evil One.*
>Amen

29. "For, if you forgive others their failures, your Heavenly God will forgive you also, but if you do not forgive others their failures, neither will your God forgive your failures.

FASTING
MATTHEW 6:16-18

30. "When you fast, don't put on a sad face, as the hypocrites do, for they neglect their appearance so everyone can see that they are fasting. This is the truth I tell you, they have received their reward in full. But when you fast, groom your head and wash your face, so to others you do not look as if you were fasting, but to your Almighty God who is in secret, and your Almighty God, who sees what happens in secret, will give you your full reward.

POSSESSIONS
MATTHEW 6:19-24

Spiritual Treasures:

31. "Do not lay up for yourselves treasures upon earth, where moth and rust destroy them, and where thieves break in and steal. But lay up for yourselves treasures in heaven, where moth and rust do not

destroy, and where thieves do not break in and steal. For where your treasure is, there will your soul be also.
Spiritual Insight:

32. "The light of the body is the eye. So then, if your eye is clean and pure the whole body will be full of light, but if your eye is bad your whole body will be full of darkness. If then, the light which is in you is darkness, how great is that darkness!

Two Masters:

33. "No one can serve two masters, for either the one will be hated and the other will be loved, or one will be cleaved to and the other despised. You cannot serve both Almighty God and material possessions.

JUDGING
MATTHEW 7:1-6; LUKE 6:37-42

34. "Do not judge others, in order that you may not be judged; for with the standard of judgment that you judge you will be judged, and with the measure you measure to others it will be measured to you.

"Do not condemn, and you will not be condemned yourselves; grant pardon, and you will be pardoned.

Giving:

35. "Give, and it will be given to you; full measure, pressed down, shaken together, and running over, pouring over into your lap, because the standard you measure out it will be measured to you in return."

Choosing Teachers:

36. Jesus spoke a parable to them, "Surely a blind person cannot lead a blind person? If they try will not both fall into the ditch? The pupil cannot advance beyond the teacher, but everyone after they are fully trained will be like their teacher.

Dealing with Your Own Problems First:

37. "Why do you look at the speck that is in one of God's children's eyes and never notice the log that is in your own eye? Or, how can you say to your spiritual brother, 'Let me take out the speck that is in your eye,' when you yourself do not notice the log in your own eye? You hypocrite! First take the log out of your own eye and then you will see clearly to remove the speck that is in your brother's eye.

World's Treatment of Heavenly Truths:

38. "Do not give what is holy to the dogs, and do not throw your pearls before pigs, lest they trample upon them with their feet, and turn and attack you viciously.

PRAYER
MATTHEW 7:7-11

39.   "Ask and keep on asking,
      and it will be given you;
   Seek and keep on seeking,
      and you will find;
   Knock and keep on knocking,
      and it will be opened to you.

> For everyone who keeps on asking,
>> always receives;
> And whoever keeps on seeking,
>> always finds;
> And whoever keeps on knocking,
>> it will be opened.

40. "What person is there, who, when their children ask for bread, will give them a stone? Or, if they will ask for a fish, will give them a serpent? If, then you, who are of this world, know how to give good gifts to your children, how much more will your God who is in Heaven give what is good to those who ask God?

THE GOLDEN RULE
MATTHEW 7:12; LUKE 6:31

41. "Therefore, the way you want others to treat you, treat them the same way; for this is the Law and the prophets.

FALSE PROPHETS
MATTHEW 7:13-23; LUKE 6:43-45

42. "Go in through the narrow gate, for wide is the gate and broad is the road that leads to destruction, and there are many who go in through it. Narrow is the gate and hard is the way that leads to life, and those who find it are few.

43. "Beware of false prophets, who come to you in sheep's clothing, but are ravenous wolves inwardly.

44. "You will recognize them by their fruits. People do not gather grapes from thorn bushes, or figs from thistle bushes. So every good tree produces good fruit, but every bad tree produces bad fruit. A good tree cannot produce bad fruit, nor can a rotten tree produce fine fruit. Every tree which does not produce good fruit is cut down and thrown into the fire. So then you will recognize them by their fruits.

Good Fruit:

45. "The good person produces good from the treasure of their own spirit. The evil person produces evil fruit from the evil. The mouth speaks out of whatever fills the spirit.

46. "Not everyone who says to me, 'Lord, Lord,' will enter into the Kingdom of Heaven, but whoever does the will of Almighty God who is in Heaven. Many will say to Me on that day, 'Lord, Lord, did we not prophesy in Your name and in Your name did we not cast out devils, and in Your name did we not do many great things?' Then will I declare to them, 'I never knew you. Depart from Me you doers on lawlessness.'"

BUILD ON A ROCK
MATTHEW 7:24-29; LUKE 6:46-49

47. Jesus said, "So then, everyone who comes to Me and hears these words of Mine and does them is like a wise person who built a house who dug deep down into the earth and laid the foundation upon the rock. And the rain came down, and the rivers swelled, and wind blew, and the flood rose and the river dashed against the house but it could not shake it and did not fall, for it was well founded upon the rock.

48. "But everyone who hears these words of Mine and has not done what I say is like a foolish person who built a house on top of the sand without any foundation. And the rain came down, and the rivers swelled, and the winds blew, and the river dashed against the house, and it collapsed, and its fall was great."

49. And when Jesus had ended these words, the people were amazed at His teaching, for He was teaching them as One who had authority, and not as the Scribes.

CHAPTER 9
GALILEAN JOURNEYS

HEALING CENTURION'S SERVANT
MATTHEW 8:1, 5-13; LUKE 7:1-10

Summer, 28 - Capernaum

1. When Jesus had completed all His teachings and had come down from the mountainside, great crowds followed Him. He went to Capernaum. A centurion's servant who was highly regarded was going to die. When he heard about Jesus he went and sent some Jewish elders to Him and asked Him to come and save his servant's life, appealing to Him, "Lord, my servant lies at home paralyzed, suffering terribly." They came to Jesus and urged Him to come saying. "He is a man who deserves that you should do this for him, for he loves our nation and has himself built us our synagogue."

2. He said, "I will come and heal him." So Jesus went with them. When He was not far from the house the centurion sent friends to Him saying, "Lord, do not trouble Yourself further. I am not worthy that You should come under my roof; nor do I count myself fit to come to You; but, only speak a word, and my servant will be cured. For I, too, am a man under orders with soldiers under me, and I say to one, 'Go,' and he goes; and to another, 'Come,' and he comes; and I say to my servant, 'Do this,' and it is done."

3. When Jesus heard this He was amazed at him. He turned and said to the crowd who was following Him, "This is the truth I tell you, not even in Israel have I found so great a faith. I tell you that many

will come from the east and west and will dine with Abraham and Isaac and Jacob in the Kingdom of Heaven; but the children of the kingdom will be cast into outer darkness, there will be weeping and gnashing of teeth in that place."

4. And Jesus said to the centurion, "Go your way, let it be done to you as you have believed." And those who were sent returned to the house and found the servant completely cured that very hour.

JESUS RAISES WIDOW'S SON
LUKE 7:11-17

Summer, 28 - Nain in Galilee

5. After that, Jesus went to a city called Nain; and His disciples and a great crowd accompanied Him on the journey. When He came near the gate of the city a man who had died was being carried out to be buried. He was his mother's only son, and she was a widow and there was a sizeable crowd of townspeople with her.

6. When the Lord saw her He felt compassion for her, and said to her, "Do not weep!" He went up and touched the coffin and those who were carrying it stood still. He said, "Young man, I say to you, rise!" And the dead man sat up and began to speak. And He gave him back to his mother.

7. And fear gripped all of them. They glorified God saying, "A great prophet has been raised up amongst us," and, "God has graciously visited God's people." This story about Him went out all over Judea and all the surrounding countryside.

MESSENGERS FROM JOHN
MATTHEW 11:2-30; LUKE 7:18-35

Summer, 28 - Galilee

8. John's disciples told him about all these things. When John, while in prison, had heard about the things that the Anointed One of God was doing, he called two of his disciples and sent them to the Lord saying, "Are you the Expected One who is come, or are we to look for another?"

9. When they arrived the men said the Him, "John, the Baptizer, has sent us to You. Are You the One who is to come," he asks, "or must we go on looking for another?"

10. At that time He cured many of their diseases, afflictions and evil spirits, and to many blind people He gave the gift of sight. And He answered and said to them, "Go back and report to John what you have heard and seen. The blind receive their sight, the lame walk, the lepers are cleansed, and the deaf hear, the dead are raised up, the poor are receiving the Good News. And blessed is the person who keeps from taking offense over Me."

Jesus Praises John:

11. When John's messengers had left, Jesus began to say to the crowds concerning John, "What did you go out into the desert to see? A reed shaken by the wind? But what did you go out to see? A man dressed in soft good clothes? Look, those who wear splendid clothes and live in luxury are in grand houses. But what did you go out to see? To see a prophet? Indeed it was, I tell you, and one who is more than a

prophet. This is the one about whom it is written, 'Behold, I send my messenger before You who will prepare Your way before You.'

12. "This is the truth I tell you, among those born of woman there is no greater person than John the Baptizer. But the least in the Kingdom of God and Heaven is greater than he." When all of the people and the tax-collectors heard this they called God righteous for they had been baptized with John's baptism. But the Pharisees and Scribes rejected God's purpose for themselves because they were not baptized by John.

13. "From the days of John the Baptist until now, the Kingdom of Heaven suffers violence and violent people take it by force. For up to John all the prophets and the Law prophesied; and if you care to accept it, he himself is Elijah who was to come. Whoever has ears to hear let them hear."

Jesus and John Rejected:

14. "But to what will I compare this generation? They are like children sitting in the market place who call to other children and say:
>We have played instruments for you,
>>and you did not dance.
>
>We have sung for you a funeral song,
>>and you did not weep.

15. "For John, the Baptizer, came neither eating bread nor drinking wine, you and they say, 'The man is mad and has a demon!' Emmanuel came eating and drinking, you and they say, 'Look, a gluttonous man and a wine-drinker, the friend of tax-collectors and sinners.' But wisdom is justified and shown to the right by its deeds."

Penalty of Rejection:

16. Then He began to reprove the cities in which most of His miracles had been done, because they did not repent. "Woe to you Chorazin! Woe to you Bethsaida! For, if the miracles which occurred in you had occurred in Tyre and Sidon, they would have repented in sackcloth and ashes long ago. But I tell you, it will be more tolerant for Tyre and Sidon in the Day of Judgment than for you! And you Capernaum, will not be exalted will you? You will go down to Hell, for if the miracles which happened in you had occurred in Sodom it would have remained to this day. But I tell you, it will be more tolerant for the land of Sodom in the Day of Judgment, than for you."

Revelation of Truth:

17. At that time Jesus answered and said, "I thank you, Almighty God, Lord of Heaven and Earth, that You have hidden these things from the wise and intelligent, and have revealed them to babes. Even so, Almighty God, for this it was Your will in Your sight. All things have been delivered to Me by Almighty God; and no one really knows Emmanuel except Almighty God, nor does anyone know Almighty God except Emmanuel, and anyone to whom Emmanuel will reveal God.

Rest for the Weary:

18. "Come to Me, all who are weary and heavy-laden, and I will give you rest. Take My yoke upon you, and learn from Me, for I am gentle and humble in spirit, and you will find rest for your souls; for My yoke is easy and My load is light."

Dr. Patrick Pierce

JESUS' FEET ANOINTED
LUKE 7:36-50

Fall, 28 - Galilee

19. One of the Pharisees invited Jesus to dine with him. He entered the Pharisee's house and reclined at the table, and behold there was a woman in the city who was a sinner and when she learned that He was reclining at the table in the Pharisee's house, she bought an alabaster vial of perfume and stood behind Him, at His feet, weeping. She began to wash His feet with her tears, and she wiped them with the hair of her head; kissing His feet and anointing them with the perfume. Now when the Pharisee, who had invited Him saw this, he said to himself, "If this Man was a prophet, He would have known who and what kind of person this woman is who is touching Him, for she is a sinner."

20. Jesus answered him, "Simon, I have something to say to you."

He said, "Teacher, say it."

21. "There were two people who were in debt to a certain money lender. One owed him $2000, and the other $2. When they were unable to repay, he graciously forgave the debt of both. Who then will love the lender more?"

Simon, answered and said, "I suppose the one whom was forgiven more."

22. He said to him, "Your judgment is correct." He turned to the woman and said to Simon, "Do you see this woman? I

entered your house, you gave Me no water for My feet, but she has washed My feet with her tears, and wiped them with her hair. You gave Me no kiss, but she, since the time I came in, has not ceased kissing My feet. You did not anoint My head with oil, but she has anointed My feet with perfume. For this reason I tell you, her sins, which are many, are forgiven for she loved much, but the one to whom little is forgiven loves little."

23. He said to her, "Your sins have been forgiven."

Those who were reclining at the table with Him began to say to themselves, "Who is this who even forgives sins?"

He said to the woman, "Your faith has saved you. Go in peace."

JOURNEYS AROUND GALILEE
LUKE 8:1-3

Fall, 28 - Galilee

24. Soon after that, Jesus traveled through the country, town by town, and village by village, preaching the Kingdom of God. The Twelve were with Him, as were certain women who had been cured from evil spirits and illnesses. There was Mary, who is called Mary Magdalene, from whom seven demons had come out and Joanna, the wife of Dhuza, Herod's steward, and Susanna and many others who were contributing to their support out of their private resources.

Dr. Patrick Pierce

BLASPHEMOUS ACCUSATIONS
MATTHEW 12:22-37; MARK 3:20-30; LUKE 11:14-23

Fall, 28 - Galilee

Accusations and Answers:

25. Jesus entered a house, and again a crowd collected so they could not even eat bread. When His own people heard what was going on, they went out to restrain Him, for they said, "He has taken leave of His senses."

26. Then there was brought to Him a man possessed by a demon who was blind and dumb; Jesus cast out the dumb demon and cured him, so that the dumb man spoke and saw and the crowd was amazed. "Surely," they said, "this cannot be the Son of David?"

27. The experts in the law from Jerusalem came down. But when they heard it, the Pharisees said, "The only way in which this man casts out demons, is by the help of Beelzebub, the ruler of the demons." Others, trying to put Him to the test, sought a sign from Heaven from Him.

28. Jesus called them and when He saw what they were thinking, Jesus said to them by way of illustrations. "How can Satan cast out Satan? Every kingdom divided against itself cannot stand and is laid waste; and any city, or house divided against itself will not stand. If Satan casts out Satan, Satan is divided against Satan. How then shall Satan's kingdom stand? Satan is finished.

29. "You must answer that question because you say that I cast out demons by the help of Beelzebub. If I cast out demons by the

power of Beelzebub, by whose power do your sons cast them out? You have become your own judges. They do cast them out, and therefore they convict you of hypocrisy by the charge which you accuse Me of. But, if I cast out demons by the Spirit of God, the finger of God, then the Kingdom of God has come upon you.

30. "When a strong man, fully armed, guards his own house, his property is safe. But when a stronger man than he comes and conquers him, he will take the armor he trusted, and will divide his property. Or, how can anyone enter into the house of a strong man, and seize his property unless he first binds the strong man? Then he will plunder, and seize his house.

31. "Whoever is not with Me is against Me, and whoever does not gather with Me scatters.

Blasphemy:

32. "This is the truth I tell you, every sin and blasphemy will be forgiven people, I mean all the insulting things that they say; but whoever blasphemes the Holy Spirit will not be forgiven, and whoever shall speak a word against Emmanuel, it shall be forgiven them, but whoever shall speak against the Holy Spirit, it shall not be forgiven them, either in this world or in the world to come. They have made themselves guilty of the sin that not even eternity can wipe out."

This He said because they were saying, "He has an unclean spirit."

Good and Bad Fruit:

33. "Either make the tree good and it's fruit good, or make the tree bad and it's fruit bad. For the tree is known by its fruit. You brood of vipers, how can you who are evil speak good things? For it is what fills the soul that the mouth speaks. The good person brings out good things from the good treasure; and the evil person brings out evil things from the treasure. I tell you, that every careless word which people shall speak, they shall render account for it in the day of judgment. For by your words you will be justified and by your words you will be condemned."

THE DEMAND FOR A MIRACLE
MATTHEW 12:38-45; LUKE 11:24-36

Same day - Galilee

34. As the crowds were beginning to increase, then the Scribes and Pharisees answered Him saying, "Teacher, we want to see a sign from You."

35. But He answered and said to them, "It is an evil, unfaithful generation which seeks a sign yet no sign was given to it but the sign of Jonah the prophet. For, as Jonah was in the belly of the whale three days and three nights, so Emmanuel will be in the heart of the earth for three days and three nights. Just as Jonah was a sign to the people of Nineveh so Emmanuel will be to this generation. At the judgment the people of Nineveh will be witnesses against this generation, and they will condemn it, because they repented at the preaching of Jonah, and behold, something greater than Jonah is here. The Queen of the South will rise up in judgment with this generation, and will condemn it,

because she came from the ends of the earth to hear the wisdom of Solomon, and behold, something greater than Solomon is here!

Need for God's Spirit of Light:

36. "When an unclean spirit goes out of a person, it goes through waterless places, seeking rest. And when it does not find it, it says, 'I will go back to my house, from which I came out.' So when it comes and finds the house empty, swept and in perfect order, then it goes and brings with it seven other spirits more evil than itself, and they go in and live there. So the last state of that person is worse than the first; so it will be with this evil generation."

37. When He was speaking, a woman in the crowd raised her voice and said, "Blessed is the womb that bore You, and the breasts at which You nursed."

He said, "Rather, blessed are those who hear the Word of God and observe it.

38. "No one lights a lamp and puts it in a cellar or under a basket, but on a lamp-stand, so that those who enter may see the light. The lamp of the body is your eye. When your eye is clear your whole body is full of light; but if the eye is bad, the whole body is full of darkness. Then watch out that the light in you may not be darkness. If then, your whole body is full of light, without any part in darkness, it will be wholly light as when the lamp with its ray gives you light."

JESUS' MOTHER AND BROTHERS
MATTHEW 12: 46-50; MARK 3:31-35; LUKE 8:19-21

Same day - Galilee

Spiritual Kinship:

39. While He was still speaking to the crowd, look, His mother and His brothers came to Him, and they could not contact Him because of the crowd. They stood outside and sent someone in with a message to Him, for they were seeking an opportunity to speak to Him. The crowd was sitting around Him. He was given the message, "Look, Your mother and Your brothers are standing outside and they want an opportunity to speak to You."

40. He looked around at those who were sitting in a circle around Him and answered the man who had spoken to Him, "Who is My mother? And who are My brothers?" And He stretched out His hand towards His disciples. "See look," He said, "My mother and My brothers are those who hear the Word of God and do it. Whoever does the will of Almighty God in heaven is My brother, sister and mother."

CHAPTER 10
START OF PARABLES

DINING WITH SCRIBES & PHARISEES
INWARD STATE AND LEGALISM
LUKE 11:37-54

Fall, 28 - Galilee

Hypocrisy Condemned:

1. After Jesus had spoken, a Pharisee asked Him to dine with him. He came in and reclined at the table. The Pharisee was surprised when he saw that He did not first ceremonially wash His hands before He ate. The Lord said to him, "Now you Pharisees clean the outside of the cup, but inside you are full of robbery and wickedness. You Fools! Did not the One who made the outside make the inside also? But give that which is within as charity, and then all things are clean for you.

2. "But woe to you Pharisees! Because you give tithes of mint and rue and every herb yet disregard justice and the love of God. These are the things you ought to have done without omitting the others. Woe to you Pharisees! Because you love the front seats in the synagogue and respectful greetings in the market places. Woe to you! Because you are like concealed tombs, and people who walk over them are unaware of it."

One of the lawyers said to Him in reply, "Teacher, when You talk like that, You are insulting us."

Lawyers Condemned:

3. But Jesus said, "Woe to you lawyers too! Because you weigh people down with burdens hard to bear while you yourselves do not lay a finger on the burdens. Woe to you! Because you build tombs of the prophets whom your ancestors killed! So you are witnesses that you agree with the deeds of your ancestors, because it was they who killed them and you build their tombs. Because Almighty God in God's wisdom said, 'I will send them prophets and apostles and some of them they will kill and some they will persecute, so that the blood of all the prophets, shed from the foundation of the world may be charged against this generation, from the blood of Abel to the blood of Zacharias who perished between the altar and the house of God.'

Yes, I tell you, it will be charged against this generation. Woe to you lawyers! Because you have taken away the key of knowledge, you did not enter in yourselves and you hindered those who were trying to enter."

4. As Jesus went away from them, the Scribes and Pharisees began to be very hostile and to question Him closely on many subjects, plotting against Him, to catch Him in something He might say.

HYPOCRISY AND ANXIETY
PARABLE OF RICH MAN'S POSSESSIONS
LUKE 12:1-3, 11-50, 54-59;
MATTHEW 6: 25-34

Fall, 28 – Galilee

Hypocrisy:

5. Under these circumstances, after the people had been gathered together in so many thousands, that they stepped on each other, Jesus began to say first of all to His disciples, "Beware of the leaven of the Pharisees, which is hypocrisy. But there is nothing covered up which will not be unveiled, and hidden which shall not be known. Accordingly, whatever you have said in the dark shall be heard in the light, and what you have whispered in the inner room will be proclaimed on the housetops.

6. "When they bring you before synagogues and rulers and the authorities, do not worry how you will defend yourself or about what you will say, for the Holy Spirit will teach you in the same hour what you ought to say."

Greed:

7. Someone in the crowd said to Jesus, "Teacher, tell my brother to divide the inheritance with me."

But He said to him, "Man, who appointed Me a judge or an arbitrator over you?" He said to them, "Beware and be on your guard against every form of greed, for not even when one has an abundance does his life come from the possessions."

Worldly Possessions:

8. He told them a parable saying. "The land of a certain rich man grew good crops. He began thinking, 'What will I do, because I have no room to store my crops?' So he said, 'This is what I will do. I will tear down my barns and build larger ones, and I will gather all my corn and all my goods there; and I will say to my soul, "Soul, you have many goods laid up for many years to come. Take your rest, eat, drink and enjoy yourself."'

9. "But God said to him, 'You Fool! This night your soul is required from you; and the things you prepared, who will own them all?' So are the persons who store up treasure for themselves and are not rich towards Almighty God."

Trust God:

10. Jesus said to His disciples, "For this reason I tell you, do not worry about your life, about what you are to eat, or what you are to drink; and do not worry about your body, about what you are to wear. Is not your life more than food, and your body more than clothes? Look at the birds of the air, and see that they do not sow, or reap, or gather things into store-houses, and yet your Heavenly God feeds them. How much more valuable are you than the birds? Which of you, by worrying, can add a few days to your own life span? If then, you cannot do the littlest thing, why worry about the other things?

11. "And why do you worry about clothes? Observe how the lilies of the field grow. They do not toil or spin, but I tell you that

not even Solomon in all his glory was clothed like one of these. If God so clothes the grass of the field, which exists today and which is thrown into the furnace tomorrow, shall God not cloth you much more, O You of little faith?

12. Do not worry then saying, 'What are we to eat?' or 'What are we to drink?' or 'What are we to wear?' Do not keep worrying. The gentiles in the nations of the world seek for all these things but your Almighty God knows that you need them.

13. But seek first God's Kingdom and God's righteousness and all these things will come to you in addition. So then, do not worry or be afraid little flock about tomorrow, tomorrow will take care of itself and Almighty God will give you the Kingdom. Each day's troubles are enough for that day.

Your Treasures:

14. "For where your treasure is, there your heart will be also.

15. "Be dressed ready for service and keep your lamps burning."

Watchfulness:

16. "Be dressed in readiness and your lamps burning. Be like people waiting for their master to return from the wedding feast, so that, when he comes and knocks, they will immediately open the door to him. Blessed are those servants whom the master will find on the alert when he comes. This is the truth that I tell you, that he will gird himself, have them recline at the table, and will come and serve them.

Whether he comes in the second or even the third watch and finds them so, blessed are those servants. Know this, that if the head of the house knew at what time the thief would come he would not have allowed his house to be broken into. So you too must be ready, for Emmanuel comes at an hour you do not expect."

Peter said, "Lord, are you speaking this parable to us or to everyone else as well?"

17. The Lord said, "Who, then, is the faithful and wise steward, whom the master will put in charge of the servants, to give them their ration of food at the right time? Blessed is the servant whom the master finds acting like this when he comes. I tell you truly that he will put him in charge of all his possessions. But if that servant says in his heart, 'My master will be delayed a long time in coming,' and begins to beat the servants both men and women, and to eat and drink and get drunk, the master of that servant will come on a day when he is not expecting him and at an hour he does not know, and will cut him in pieces and assign him a place with the unbelievers.

18. "That servant who knew the will of his master, and who failed to have things ready, and to act in accordance with that will, will be beaten with many lashes. But he who did not know, even if he did things that deserved a beating, will receive only few. To everyone who has been given much from them much will be required; and to whom they entrusted much, of them, they will ask the more.

Division:

19. "I came to cast fire upon the earth. And how I wish it were already kindled! But I have a baptism to undergo, and I am distressed until it is accomplished!"

20. Jesus also said to the crowd, "When you see a cloud rising in the west, immediately you say, 'Rain is coming.' And so it happens. When you feel the south wind blowing, you say, 'It will be a hot heat.' And so it happens. You hypocrites! You know how to analyze the appearance of the earth and the sky. But why can't you analyze the present?

21. "Why do you not on your own initiative judge what is right? When you are going with your adversary to appear before the magistrate, make an effort to come to an agreement with him on the way, in order that he may not drag you before the judge, and the judge will hand you over to the officer, and the officer throw you into prison. I tell you, you will not come out from there until you have paid the last debtor's cent."

REPENTANCE REQUIRED
PARABLE OF THE BARREN FIG TREE
LUKE 13:1-9

Fall, 28 - Galilee

Repent or Perish:

22. At this time some present told Jesus about the Galileans whose blood Pilate had mingled with their sacrifices.

And He answered and said to them, "Do you think, that these Galileans were sinners above all the Galileans, because this happened to them? I tell you, No! But unless you repent you will all likewise perish. Or, do you think that those eighteen on whom the tower in Siloam fell and killed them, were worse debtors than all those who dwell in Jerusalem? I tell you, No! But unless you repent you will all likewise perish."

Penalty for Fruitlessness:

23. Jesus spoke this parable, "A man had a fig-tree planted in his vineyard. He came looking for fruit on it and did not find any. He said to the vineyard keeper, 'Look, for three years I have come looking for fruit on this fig-tree without finding any. Cut it down! Why should it use up the ground?' He answered him, 'Let it alone this year, too, until I dig round about it and fertilize it, and if it bears fruit next year, good; but if not, cut it down.'"

CHAPTER 11
FIRST GROUP OF PARABLES

MATTHEW 13:1-2; MARK 4:1-2; LUKE 8:4

Fall, 28 - Sea of Galilee

Introduction

1. On that day, when Jesus went out of the house, He began to teach by the lake side. A large crowd gathered to hear Him. Such large crowds gathered from every city that He had to go on a boat and sit in it on the lake. The whole crowd stood on the land facing the lake. Jesus taught them many things in parables and teaching.

THE SOWER
MATTHEW 13:3-23; MARK 4:3-25; LUKE 8:5-18

Fall, 28 - Sea of Galilee

The Sower

2. He said, "Look! The sower went out to sow seed. As he sowed, some seed fell along the roadside, it was walked on and the birds came and ate it. Other seed fell upon rocky ground where it did not have much soil; and it sprang up immediately, because it had no depth of soil, but when the sun rose, it was scorched, and it withered away, because it had no root. Other seed fell in the middle of thorns and the thorns grew up along with it and crowded in on it until they choked it out, and it did not yield any fruit. And other seed fell on

good soil; and, as it grew up and grew greater, it yielded fruit and bore as much as thirty fold and sixty fold and a hundred fold."

As He told the story He said, "The ones who have ears to hear, let them hear."

Purpose of Parables

3. When Jesus was alone, the disciples came with His own circle of people, and asked about the parables and what they meant. They said to Him, "Why do You speak to them in parables?"

4. He said to them, "To you is given knowledge of the secrets of the Kingdom of God, which only a disciple can know and understand. But to those who are outside, it has not been so given. For it will be given to those who already have, and they will have an overflowing knowledge. But from those who have not, what they have will be taken away. It is for that reason that I speak to them in parables, for although they see, they perceive not the meaning of things; and although they can hear, they do not hear or understand, lest at any time they should turn and be forgiven.

5. "There is being fulfilled Isaiah's prophecy which says, 'You will hear, but you will not understand; and you will look, but you will not see; for the soul of God's people has grown fat, and they hear dully with their ears, and their eyes are smeared, lest at any time they should see with their eyes, and hear with their ears, and understand with their soul, and turn, and I will heal them. But blessed are your eyes for they see, and your ears because they hear.'

6. "This is the truth I tell you, many prophets and righteous people longed to see things that you are seeing, and did not see them, and to hear the things that you are hearing, and did not hear them."

Sower Explained

7. "Don't you understand this parable?" He said to them. "How then will you understand all the parables? Listen then to the meaning of the parable of the sower. What the sower is sowing is the Word of the Kingdom of God.

"The kind of people represented by the situation in which the seed fell by the side of the road, are those who hear the Word of the Kingdom, and do not understand it. Immediately Satan comes, and takes away the Word that was sown in their heart so that they may not believe and be saved.

"Just so, the kind of people represented by the case in which the seed was sown on the rocky ground are those, who, whenever they hear the Word, immediately receive it with joy. But they have no root in themselves. They believe for a time but they are temporary and are at the mercy of the moment, and so, when trials, trouble and persecution happen because of the Word, they immediately stumble and fall away.

"Then there are the others who are represented by the case in which the seed was sown among thorns. These are the people who hear the Word, go their way, but the cares and the anxieties of this world and the deceptive attractions of wealth and the desires for pleasures of this life enter into them and choke the life out of the Word, and it never gets a chance to bear fruit.

"The kind of people who are represented by the case in which the seed fell on good ground are those who hear, keep hold of it in a soul that is good, and understand it. They indeed bear fruit and produce some a hundred fold, some sixty fold, some thirty fold.

Pay Attention to What You Hear

8. "There is nothing secret or hidden that will not be brought into the open; nothing is done that it should be hidden away, but that it should lie open for all to see. Take care, then, if people have ears to hear let them hear; for to those who have, it will be given; and from those who have not, there shall be taken away even what they think they have."

9. This was another of Jesus' sayings;

> "Pay attention to what you hear!
> What you get depends on what you give.
> What you give you get back,
>   only more so."

THE SEED GROWING BY ITSELF
MARK 4:26-29

10. He said to them, "The Kingdom of God is like a person who casts seed upon the ground and goes to bed for the night and wakes up the next day, and the seed sprouts and grows, and he does not know how it does it. The soil produces crops by itself, first the shoot, then the head, then the mature grain in the head. When the crop allows it, immediately reaping starts, for the time to harvest has come."

THE WEEDS
MATTHEW 13:24-30; 36-43

The Weeds

11. Jesus presented another parable to them saying, "The Kingdom of Heaven may be compared to a man who sowed good seed in his field. When the man slept, his enemy came and sowed weeds among the wheat, and went away. When the wheat grew, and began to produce grain, then the weeds appeared also. The servants of the landowner came to him and said, 'Sir, did you not sow good seed in your field? From where then did it get the weeds?' 'An enemy has done this,' he said to them. The servants said to him, 'Do you wish us to go and gather the weeds?'

"But he said, 'No, for if you gather the weeds you may root up the wheat at the same time. Allow both to grow together until the harvest; and at the time of the harvest I will say to the reapers, First gather the weeds and bind them into bundles for burning. But gather the wheat into my storehouse.'"

The Weeds Explained

12. When He had sent the crowds away, He went into the house. His disciples came to Him saying, "Explain to us the parable of the weeds in the field."

He answered, "The one who sows the good seed is Emmanuel, and the field is the world. As for the good seed, these are the children of the Kingdom; the weeds are the children of the evil one. The enemy who sowed them is the devil. The harvest is the end of this age; the reapers are angels.

13. "Just as the weeds are gathered and burned with fire, so will it be at the end of this age. Emmanuel will send God's angels, and they will gather out of the Kingdom all causes of offense, and all those who act lawlessly, and will throw them into the furnace of fire; and in that place there will be weeping and gnashing of teeth. Then the righteous will shine forth as the sun in the Kingdom of their Almighty God. Who has ears, let them hear."

MUSTARD SEED AND LEAVEN
MATTHEW 13:31-35; MARK 4:30-34
Luke 13:18-21

The Mustard Seed

14. Jesus presented another parable to them saying, "How shall we find something with which to compare the Kingdom of God's Heaven, or what parable will we use to represent it? The Kingdom of Heaven is like a grain of mustard seed, which a man took and sowed in his garden or field. When it is sown upon the ground, it is the smallest of all seeds. But when it is full grown, it is larger than all the garden plants, and becomes a tree, so the birds of the air come and nest in its branches."

Leaven

15. Again Jesus spoke another parable to them, "The Kingdom of Heaven is like leaven, which a woman took and mixed in three measures of meal, until it was all leavened."

16. It was with many parables that Jesus spoke all these things to them, according to their ability to hear it. He did not speak to them without a parable so what was spoken through the prophets might be

fulfilled, "I will open my mouth in parables. I will utter things which have been hidden since the foundation of the world." But He explained the meaning of everything privately to His own disciples.

TREASURE, PEARL AND THE NET
MATTHEW 13:44-53

Treasure

17. "The Kingdom of Heaven is like a treasure hidden in a field. A man found it, and hid it; and, as a result of his joy over it he goes and sells everything that he has and buys the field.

Pearl

18. "Again, the Kingdom of Heaven is like a merchant seeking fine pearls. When he found a very valuable pearl, he went and sold everything he had, and bought it.

The Net

19. "Again, the Kingdom of Heaven is like a net cast into the sea, which gathered fish of every kind. When it was full, they hauled it up on to the shore, and sat down, and collected the good contents into containers, but threw the useless contents away. So it will be at the end of the age. The angels will come, and they will separate the wicked from the righteous, and they will cast them into the furnace of fire. There will be weeping and gnashing of teeth there.

20. "Have you understood all these things?"

They said to Him, "Yes."

And He said to them, "That is why every Scribe, who has become a disciple of the Kingdom of Heaven, is like a householder who brings out of the store house things new and old."

When Jesus had finished these parables, He left there.

CHAPTER 12
HEALINGS & MIRACLES

TEACHING ON SACRIFICE
MATTHEW 8:18-22; LUKE 9:57-62

1. When on that day, evening had come as they were journeying along the road, Jesus saw the large crowd around Him. A Scribe said to Jesus, "Teacher, I will follow You wherever You go."

Jesus said to him, "The foxes have holes; the birds of the air have nests; but Emmanuel has nowhere to lay His head."

2. He said to another of His disciples, "Follow Me!"

That one said, "Lord, let me go first and bury my father."

He said to that one, "Follow Me, and let the dead bury their dead; but as for you, go everywhere and tell the news of the Kingdom of God."

3. Another one said to Him, "Lord, I will follow You; but let me first say good-bye to those at home."

Jesus said, "No person who puts their hand to the plough and looks back is the right kind of person for the Kingdom of God."

Dr. Patrick Pierce

JESUS CALMS THE SEA
MATTHEW 8:23-27; MARK 4:35-41; LUKE 8:22-25

Same day - Sea of Galilee

Calms Sea

4. And when He got into the boat, His disciples followed Him. So they left the crowds and took Him, just as He was, in the their boat. And there were other boats with Him.

So they set sail and as they sailed He fell asleep. A violent storm came upon the lake, so that the boat was covered by the waves. The waves beat upon the boat, so that the boat began to fill and was at the point of being swamped, and He was in the stern sleeping on a pillow.

5. They came to Him and woke Him. "Teacher, Master, Lord," they said, "don't You care that we are perishing? Save us!"

He said to them, "Why are you so frightened, you of little faith?" Then He arose from sleep and rebuked the wind and sea saying, "Be silent! Be calm!" The wind ceased and it was perfectly calm.

6. The people were amazed, and they said to each other, "Who can this be? What kind of man is this? He gives orders even to the winds and the sea, and they obey Him."

EVIL SPIRITS ORDERED OUT
MATTHEW 8:28-34; 9:1; MARK 5:1-21; LUKE 8:26-40

Fall, 28 - Gerges, now called Khersa

7. They came to the other side of the lake to the district of the Gerasenes, which is across the sea from Galilee. When Jesus had gotten out of the boat immediately two demon possessed men from the tombs of the town met Him. These men lived among the tombs and were fierce, so that no one was able to pass by the road. For a long time they had gone unclothed. No one had ever been able to bind them with a chain, because they had often been bound with shackles and chains, and the chains had been torn apart by them and the shackles broken into pieces; and no one was strong enough to subdue them. Constantly, night and day, in the tombs and in the hills, they kept shrieking and cutting themselves with stones.

8. They saw Jesus when He was still a long way away, and they ran and knelt before Him. They shouted, "What have You and I to do with each other, Jesus, Emmanuel of the Most High God? In Almighty God's name, I beg You, do not torture us before the proper time." For Jesus had said to them, "Unclean spirit, come out of the man!"

9. "What is your name?" He asked.

"Legion is my name," he said, "for we are many." And they begged Jesus not to order them to depart to the abyss. There was a herd of pigs there, feeding on the mountain side. The demons said, "If you cast us out, send us into the herd of pigs."

10. And Jesus permitted them and said to them, "Begone." The demons came out of the men and entered into the pigs and the herd of about two thousand rushed down the cliff into the lake and were drowned.

And the men who were feeding the pigs saw what happened. They fled and told what had happened to the town and the country.

11. And look, the whole town came out to meet Jesus. They came to Jesus and found the men from whom the demons had gone out sitting at Jesus' feet, clothed and in their right mind and they became frightened. Those who had seen what had happened told them how the demon possessed men had been cured; and the whole crowd from the Gerasene countryside asked Jesus to get out of their region, because they were very much afraid.

12. As Jesus was getting into the boat, one man who had been demon possessed begged Him to be allowed to go with Him. He sent him away and said to him, "Go back to your own people, and tell them the story of all that God has done for you." So he went away and proclaimed throughout the whole town all that Jesus had done for him.

Jesus embarked on the boat, and crossed to the other side, and came to His own town.

The Gospel of Jesus Christ

MATTHEW'S FEAST
MATTHEW 9:10-17; MARK 2:15-22; LUKE 5:29-39

Late, 28 - Capernaum

Eating with Sinners

13. Matthew had a big reception and feast for Him in his house. Jesus was reclined at the meal in Matthew's house, and a crowd of tax collectors and sinners who were their friends sought His company and sat down at the table with Jesus and His disciples. When the experts in the law, who belonged to the school of the Pharisees, and the Scribes saw that He was eating in the company of sinners and tax-collectors, they complained and said to the disciples, "Why do you and your Teacher eat and drink with tax collectors and sinners?"

14. Jesus heard them and answered, "It is not those who are healthy who need a doctor, but those who are sick. Go and learn what the saying means, 'It is compassion I desire, and not sacrifice.' I did not come to call the righteous, but sinners to repentance."

Fasting

15. The disciples of John often fasted and prayed as did the Pharisees. So they came to Jesus and said, "John's disciples fast frequently and pray. So do the disciples of the Pharisees, but Your disciples eat and drink and do not fast?"

16. Jesus said to them, "Surely the bridegroom's attendants cannot mourn and fast while the bridegroom is with them? So long as they have the bridegroom they do not fast. But the days will come when someday the bridegroom will be taken away from them, and then they will fast."

The Patch

17. He spoke a parable to them, "No one sews a patch of new, unshrunken cloth on to an old garment. If they do, the new patch used to fill the old tears the garment apart, and the tear is worse than ever.

Wine Skins

18. "No one puts new, still fermenting, wine into old wine skins. If they do the wine will burst the wine skins and the wine will be lost as well as the wineskins. But new wine must be put into new skins, and both are preserved. No one who drinks fully aged wine wishes for new wine, for they say, 'The old is good.'"

JAIRUS' DAUGHTER HEALED
MATTHEW 9:18-26; MARK 5:22-43; LUKE 8:41-56

Same day as last - Capernaum

Jairus Asks Jesus to Heal

19. While He was saying these things, look, a man called Jairus, one of the officials of the synagogue, came to Him; and when he saw Jesus, he bowed down at His feet in worship. He pled with Jesus, "My daughter is dying. Come and lay Your hands on her, that she may be cured and live." He had an only daughter who was about twelve years of age.

20. Jesus went away with him and so did His disciples. As He went the crowd pressed around Him and were following Him, and pushing in upon Him on all sides.

Woman Touches Garment

21. Now there was a woman who was suffering from a hemorrhage which had lasted for twelve years. She had endured many things at the hands of many doctors; she had spent everything she had and it had not helped but had gotten worse. When she heard the stories of Jesus, she came up behind Him in the crowd, and she touched the edge of His robe, for she said to herself, "If I only touch His clothes, I will be cured." And immediately the flow of blood was stopped, and she felt in her body that she was healed from her illness.

22. Jesus immediately knew Himself that the power which issued from Him had gone forth; and at once, in the middle of the crowd, He turned and said, "Who touched My clothes?"

23. When they denied that they had done so, Peter and his companions said, "Master, the crowds are all around You and pressing in on You, what's the point of saying, 'Who touched Me?'"

24. Jesus said, "Someone has touched Me, for I know that power has gone out of Me." He kept looking around to see who had done this. The woman was terrified and trembling and saw that she could not hide. She knew what had happened to her. She came, trembling, and fell down before Him and told Him the truth why she had touched Him, and that she had been immediately cured.
25. He said to her, "Courage, daughter! Your faith has cured you! Go in good health, and be healed of the affliction. Go in peace." And the woman was cured from that hour.

Jesus Raises Daughter

26. While He was still speaking, messengers came from the synagogue official's house. "Your daughter is dead," they said. "Why bother the Master anymore?"

Jesus overheard this message being spoken. He said to the official of the synagogue, "Don't be afraid!" Only believe! Just have faith and she will be cured."

27. He allowed no one to accompany Him except Peter, James and John, James's brother. They came to the house of the synagogue official and saw the uproar. They were all weeping and wailing, and they saw the flute players.

28. He said to them, "Why are you making a commotion and weeping? Stop weeping, for she is not dead but asleep." And they laughed at Him because they were sure she was dead. "Leave us," He said, "for the girl is not dead, but is asleep." He put them all out, and He took with Him the father of the little girl, and the mother and His own friends, and went into the room where the little girl was. He took hold of her hand, and said to her, "Child, I say to you, Arise! Her spirit returned and immediately she arose and walked around. He told them to give her something to eat! They and her parents were amazed and He gave them orders that no one should know about this. And the news of this went out into the whole country.

The Gospel of Jesus Christ

HEALING BLIND MEN
MATTHEW 9:27-34

Fall, 28 - Capernaum

Two Blind Men Healed

29. And as He passed on from there, two blind men followed Him, crying out saying. "Have mercy on us, Son of David."

After He came into the house, the blind men came to Him and Jesus said to them, "Do you believe that I am able to do this?"

"Yes, Lord," they said.

30. Then He touched their eyes and said, "Be it done to you according to your faith." And their eyes were opened. And Jesus sternly warned them, "See, let no one know of this." But they went out and spread the news of Him all over the country.

Mute Healed

31. As they were going out, look, they brought to Him a mute man who was demon possessed; and when the demon was cast out of him, he spoke.

The crowds were amazed saying, "Nothing like this was ever seen in Israel."

But the Pharisees said, "He casts out the demons by the power of the demons."

CHAPTER 13
REJECTION AND
JOHN BEHEADED

JESUS REJECTED IN NAZARETH
MATTHEW 13:54-58; MARK 6:1-6; LUKE 4:16-31

January, 29 - Nazareth

Rejected in Home Town

1. Jesus left Capernaum and came to Nazareth, His home town, and His disciples went with Him. As was His custom, He went into the synagogue on the Sabbath day to teach.

2. The book of the prophet Isaiah was given to Him. He opened the book and found the passage where it is written,

> "The Spirit of the Lord is upon Me,
>   because He has anointed Me to bring
>   the Good News to the poor.
> He has sent Me to proclaim
>   release to the captives, and
>   recovery of sight to the blind,
>   to set free those who are downtrodden,
>   to proclaim the favorable year of the Lord."

3. He closed the book and handed it back to the attendant and sat down; and the eyes of all in the synagogue were fixed on Him. He began to say to them, "Today this scripture has been fulfilled in your eyes."

4. His teaching was such that they were astonished. And they said, "Where did this man get these powers? And how can such wonderful things happen through His hands? Is this not the Son of the carpenter? Is not His mother called Mary? And are James, Joseph, Simon and Judas not His brothers? Are His sisters not here with us? Where did He get all these things?" And, they were offended by Him.

5. Jesus said to them, "You are bound to quote a proverb to Me, 'Physician, heal yourself; we have heard about all that happened in Capernaum; do the same things in Your home country.'"

6. He said, "This is the truth that I tell you, no prophet is welcomed or has honor in his home country. In truth I tell you there were many widows in Israel in the days of Elijah, when the sky was shut up for three years and six months and when there was a great famine over all the land. And to none of them was Elijah sent, but he was sent to the widow Zerephath, in the land of Sidon. And there were many lepers in Israel in the times of Elisha the prophet; and none of them were healed, but only Naaman the Syrian."

Attempt to Kill Jesus

7. The people in the synagogue were filled with anger as they listened to these things, and they rose up and cast Him out of the town. They took Him to the brow of the hill on which their town had been built, in order to throw Him down the cliff; but He slipped through the crowd and went on His way.

He did not do many miracles there, because of their unbelief, except that He laid His hands on a few sick people and healed them.

He was amazed by their unwillingness to believe. Jesus came down to Capernaum, a town in Galilee.

JESUS SENDS THE TWELVE APOSTLES
MATTHEW 9:35-38; 10:1,5-42; 11:1; MARK 6:7-13; LUKE 9:1-6; 12:4-10,51-53

January, 29 - Galilee

Workers Needed

8. Jesus made a tour of all of the towns and villages, teaching in synagogues, and proclaiming the Good News of the Kingdom, and healing every kind of disease and every kind of illness.

When He saw the crowds, He was moved with compassion, for they were distressed and downcast, like sheep without a shepherd.

9. Then He said to His disciples, "The harvest is great, but the workers are few. Therefore, pray to the Lord of the harvest to send out workers for God's harvest."

Apostles Instructed

10. Jesus called His twelve apostles to Him and gave them power and authority over demons, to cast them out and to heal every kind of disease and every kind of sickness. Jesus sent out these twelve in twos and He sent them out to proclaim the Kingdom of God, and to cure those who were ill.

11. He instructed them to take nothing for their journey except a staff, but to wear sandals and, He said, "You must not put on two

coats. Do not enter into any city of the Samaritans, but go rather to the sheep of the house of Israel who have perished.

12. "As you go make this proclamation, 'The Kingdom of Heaven in near.' Heal the sick, raise the dead, cleanse the leper, cast out demons. Freely you have received, freely give.

"Do not set out to get gold or silver or bronze for your purses; do not take a bag for the journey, not two coats, nor shoes, nor a staff. The workman deserves sustenance.

13. "When you enter into any city or village, make inquiries as to who in it is worthy, and stay there until you leave. When you come into a household, give your greetings to it. If the house is worthy, let your peace come upon it; if it is not worthy, let your peace return to you. If anyone will not receive you, and will not listen to your words, as you leave that house or that city, shake off the dust of it from your feet, to bear witness to the fact that they were guilty of such conduct. This is the truth I tell you, it will be easier for the land of Sodom and Gomorrah on the day of judgment than for that city.

Apostles Warned

14. "Look, I send you out as sheep in the midst of wolves. Therefore, be shrewd as serpents, and innocent as doves.

"Beware of people! For they will hand you over to the courts, and they will beat you in their synagogues. You will be brought before rulers and kings for My sake, that you make your witness to them and to the Gentiles. But when they hand you over, do not worry how you are to speak, or what you are to say. What you are to speak will be given to you in that hour, for it is not you who speaks, but the Spirit of your Almighty God who speaks in you.

15. "Brother will hand over brother to death, and father will hand over child. Children will rise up against parents, and cause them to be put to death; and you will be hated by all on account of My name. But the one who endures to the end will be saved.

16. "When they persecute you in one city, flee into another. This is the truth I tell you, you will not finish your tour of the cities of Israel, until Emmanuel shall come.

17. "The disciple is not above the teacher nor is the slave above the master. It is enough for the disciple to be as the teacher, and the servant to be as the master. If they have called the master of the house of Beelzebul, how much more shall they call the member of that household.

18. "Do not fear them; for there is nothing covered that will not be revealed. What I tell you in the darkness, speak in light. What you hear whispered in your ear, proclaim on the housetops.

Fear God

19. "I tell you, My friends, do not be afraid of those who kill the body and who after that are not able to do anything further. But I will warn you whom you are to fear: Fear the One who after that One has killed you has authority to destroy the soul and body and cast you into Hell. Yes, I tell you, fear that One!

God Loves Even Sparrows

20. "Are not five sparrows sold for two cents? And yet not one of them is forgotten and will not fall to the ground without Almighty God's knowledge. But as for you, even the hairs of your head are all numbered. So then do not be afraid, you are of more value than many sparrows.

Confess Emmanuel

21. "I say to you, whoever confesses Me before others, that one Emmanuel will confess before the angels and Almighty God who is in Heaven; but whoever denies Me before others, I will deny before the angels and Almighty God who is in Heaven. If anyone speaks a word against Emmanuel it will be forgiven, but the one who blasphemes the Holy Spirit will not be forgiven.

Conflict Over Jesus

22. "Do not think that I came to bring peace on the earth;
I did not come to bring peace,
    but a sword of division.
From now on a house of five people
    will be divided.
Three against two,
    and two against three.
For I came to set
    children against their parents,
    father against son,
    son against father,
    and a daughter against her mother,

and a daughter-in-law
against her mother-in-law;
and a person's enemies shall be
the members of their own household.

23. "Whoever loves father and mother
more than they love Me
is not worthy of Me;
and whoever does not
take up their cross and follow after Me
is not worthy of Me.
Whoever finds their life
will lose it;
and whoever loses their life
for My sake shall find it.

24. Whoever receives you, receives Me; and whoever receives Me, receives Almighty God who sent Me. Whoever receives a prophet in the name of the prophet will receive a prophet's reward; and whoever receives a righteous person in the name of the righteous person will receive a righteous person's reward. And whoever in the name of a disciple gives one of these little ones even a drink of cold water, this is the truth I tell you, they will not lose their reward."

25. And when Jesus had completed His instructions to the twelve apostles, He left them to go on teaching in their towns. So they went out through all the villages to preach that people should repent; and they cast out many demons, and anointed many sick people with oil and healed them.

Dr. Patrick Pierce

HEROD BEHEADS JOHN
MATTHEW 14:1-12; MARK 6:14-29; LUKE 9:7-9

March, 29 - Jerusalem

26. At that time King Herod the tetrarch heard the news about Jesus, for His name was known everywhere, and about the things which were going on. He did not know what to make of them, because it was said by some, "John the Baptizer has risen from the dead. That is why these wonderful powers work through Him." Others said, "It is Elijah;" and others, "One of the prophets of old."

27. But Herod tried to see Him and said to his servants, "This is John the baptizer, whom I beheaded, risen from the dead." For Herod had sent and had John arrested and bound in prison because of the affair of Herodias, his brother Philip's wife, whom he had married. For John had said to Herod, "It is not right for you to have your brother's wife."

28. Herodias set herself against him and wanted to kill him, but she could not succeed in doing so, for Herod was afraid of John. He wished to kill John, but he was afraid of the crowd, for they regarded him as a prophet, and because he knew he was a righteous and holy man, he kept him safe. When Herod listened to John he did not know what to do, and yet he found a certain pleasure in listening to him.

29. But a day of opportunity came, when on his birthday, Herod was giving a banquet to his courtiers and to his captains and to the leading men of Galilee. Herodias's daughter came in and danced before them in public and she pleased Herod and those who were reclining at the table with him. The King gave an oath to the maiden,

"Ask me for anything you like and I will give it to you." He swore to her, "Whatever you ask me for, I will give you, even up to half of my kingdom."

30. She went out and said to her mother, "What am I to ask for myself?"

Her mother urged her on and said, "John the Baptizer's head."

At once she hurried in to the king and made her request, saying, "I wish, that right now you give me the head of John the Baptizer on a plate."

31. The king was grief-stricken, but because of the oath, and because of his guests, he did not wish to break his word to her. So immediately the king sent the executioner with orders to bring his head. The executioner went away and beheaded him in prison. And brought his head on a plate and gave it to the girl, and the girl gave it to her mother. When his disciples heard about it, they came and took his body, and laid it in a tomb. Then they went and told Jesus about it.

APOSTLES RETURN
MATTHEW 14:13; MARK 6:30-32; LUKE 9:10; JOHN 6:1

April, 29 - Bethsaida

32. When the apostles returned, they came together again to Jesus. They told Him all that they had done and taught. He said to them, "Come by yourselves to a deserted place, and rest a while," for there were many coming and going and they could not find time even to eat. So they went away in a boat across the Sea of Galilee, that is, the Sea of Tiberias and withdrew privately to a deserted place called Bethsaida.

Dr. Patrick Pierce

FEEDING FIVE THOUSAND
MATTHEW 14:14-21; MARK 6:33-44; LUKE 9:11-17; JOHN 6:2-13

Spring, 29 - Bethsaida

33. Now many saw them going and recognized them; and when the crowd found out where He was they followed Him on foot from all the towns and went on ahead of them. The large crowd was following Him, because they were watching the signs which He did on those who were ill.

When Jesus disembarked He saw a large crowd and welcomed them. He had compassion for them, because they were like sheep who had no shepherd. He began to heal their sick and teach them about the Kingdom of God.

34. Jesus went up into a hill and was sitting there with His disciples. The Passover, the Feast of the Jews, was near. When it was late He said to Philip, "Where are we to buy bread for these to eat?" He was testing Philip when He said this, for He knew what He was going to do.

Philip answered Him, "Seven pounds worth of bread is not enough to give each of them to eat."

35. The twelve came to Him and said, "Send the crowd away, that they may go to the surrounding villages and countryside and find some place to stay and buy themselves something to eat because here we are in a deserted place."

36. He said to them, "You give them something to eat."

They said to Him, "Are we to go and buy six month's wages worth of loaves and so give them something to eat?"

37. "How many loaves have you?" He said to them, "go and see!"
One of His disciples, Andrew, Simon Peter's brother, said to Him, "There is a boy here who has five barley loaves and two small fish. But what use are they among so many?"

38. Jesus said, "Bring them here to Me." He ordered them to make them all sit down in groups on the green grass. So they sat down in sections of hundreds and fifties.

39. He took the five loaves and two fishes, and looked up to heaven and blessed them, and broke the loaves and gave them to the disciples to serve the people with them. And He divided up the two fishes among them all. They all ate until they were satisfied. He said to the disciples, "Collect the broken pieces that are left over, so that nothing may be wasted." So they collected, and they filled twelve baskets with the broken pieces of bread and what was left of the fishes.

40. The number of those who ate was about five thousand men, apart from women and children. So when the men had seen the sign which had been done, they said, "Truly, this is the prophet who is come into the world."

Dr. Patrick Pierce

JESUS WALKS ON WATER
MATTHEW 14:22-36; MARK 6:45-56; JOHN 6:14-21

Spring, 29 - Galilee

41. Jesus, aware that they were going to seize Him to make Him king, withdrew again to the mountain alone. He made the disciples get into the boat and to go on ahead to the other side to Capernaum, until He could send away the crowds. When He had dismissed the crowd, He went up into the mountain by Himself to pray.

42. By this time the boat was in the middle of the sea in the waves, and Jesus was alone upon the land. He saw that they were worn out as they rowed, for the wind was against them. About three o'clock in the morning, He came to them walking on the sea. It looked like He was about to pass them, but when they saw Him walking on the water they thought it was a ghost, and they cried out in terror, for they all saw Him and they were terrified.

43. He spoke to them immediately and said, "Courage! It is I, don't be afraid."

Peter got down from the boat and walked on the water to come to Jesus. But, when he saw the wind, he was afraid; and, when he began to sink, he cried out, "Lord save me!"

44. Immediately Jesus stretched out His hand and grasped him and said, "Oh you of little faith! Why did you begin to have doubts?"

And when they got into the boat, the wind died down. They were completely amazed, because they did not understand what the miracle of the loaves meant; their minds were closed. Those in the boat knelt in worship of Him, saying, "Truly You are the One of God."

45. When they had crossed over, they came to land at Gennesaret. When the men of that place recognized Him, they sent the news that He had come to the surrounding countryside, and they brought to Him all those who were ill, and begged Him to let them only touch the edge of His robe; and all who touched Him were healed.

CHAPTER 14
THE BREAD OF LIFE

JOHN 6:22-71

Spring, 29 - Sea of Galilee

1. On the next day, the crowd that was standing on the far side of the sea, saw that there had been only one boat, and that Jesus had not gone into the boat with His disciples, but that the disciples had gone away alone. But some boats from Tiberias came near the place where they had eaten the bread, after the Lord had given thanks. So when they saw that Jesus was not there, nor His disciples, they got into the boats, and came to Capernaum, looking for Jesus.

2. When they found Him on the other side of the sea, they said to Him, "Teacher, when did You get here?"

Jesus answered, "This is the truth I tell you, you are looking for Me, not because you saw signs, but because you ate of the loaves until you were filled. Do not work for the food which perishes, but for the food which lasts, and gives eternal life; which Emmanuel will give you; for Almighty God has set God's seal upon Emmanuel."

3. They said to Him, "What will we do, that we may do the works of God?"

Jesus answered, "This is the work of God, that you believe on the One God has sent."

4. They said to Him, "What sign are You going to perform that we may see it and believe in You? What is Your work? Our ancestors ate the manna in the wilderness. As it is written, 'God gave them bread from Heaven to eat.'"

Jesus said to them, "This is the truth I tell you, Moses did not give you bread from heaven, but Almighty God gives you the real bread from Heaven. For the bread of God is the One who comes down from Heaven, and gives life to the world."

5. They said to Him, "Sir, always give us that bread."

Jesus said to them,
"I am the bread of Life.
Whoever comes to Me will never be hungry;
whoever believes in Me will never thirst.
But, as I have told you,
you can see Me and still you do not believe.
All that Almighty God gives Me will come to Me,
and whoever comes to Me
I shall not turn them away;
because I have come from Heaven,
not to do My own will,
but to do the will of the One who sent Me.

6. Now the will of Almighty God who sent Me
is that I should lose nothing
of all that God has given to Me,
and that I should raise it up on the last day.

Yes, it is Almighty God's will
that whoever sees Emmanuel and
    believes in Emmanuel
shall have eternal life,
and that I shall raise them up on the last day."

Jews Challenge Jesus

7. So the Jews were murmuring about Him, because He said, "I am the bread which came down from Heaven." They were saying, "Is this not Jesus, the son of Joseph, whose father and mother we know? How can He now say, 'I have come down from Heaven?'"

Jesus answered, "Stop complaining to each other."

8. "No one can come to Me
unless they are drawn by Almighty God
    who sent Me,
and I will raise them up at the last day.
It is written in the prophets:
They will all be taught by God,
and to hear the teachings of Almighty God,
and learn from it,
is to come to Me.

9. "No one has seen Almighty God,
except the One who comes from God;
Emmanuel has seen Almighty God.
I tell you the truth,
everyone who believes has eternal life.

10. "I am the bread of life.
Your ancestors ate the manna in the desert
and they are dead;
but this is the bread that comes down from Heaven,
so that a person may eat it and not die.
I am the living bread
which has come down from Heaven.
Anyone who eats this bread will live forever;
and the bread that I shall give
is my flesh, for the life of the world."

Jews Question Eating Flesh

11. Then the Jews started arguing with one another saying, "How can this man give us His flesh to eat?"

Jesus replied,

12. "I tell you the truth,
if you do not eat the flesh of Emmanuel
and drink Emmanuel's blood,
you will not have life in you.
Anyone who eats My flesh and drinks My blood
has eternal life,
and I shall raise them up on the last day.

13. "For My flesh is true food
and My blood is true drink.
Whoever eats My flesh and drinks My blood
abides in Me
and I live in them.

14. "As I, who am sent by the living
Almighty God on a mission
I draw life from Almighty God,
likewise whoever eats Me will draw life from Me.
This is the bread come down from heaven;
not like the bread our ancestors ate;
they are dead,
but anyone who eats this bread will live forever."

He said these things when He was teaching in the synagogue at Capernaum.

Offended Disciples Leave

15. When they had heard this discourse many of His disciples said, "This word is difficult! Who is able to listen to it?"

Jesus knew that His disciples were murmuring about this, so He said to them, "Does this cause you to stumble? What then if you were to see Emmanuel ascending to where Emmanuel formerly was?

16. "It is the Spirit who gives life; the flesh is of no help. The words that I have spoken to you are spirit and are life. But there are some who do not believe." For Jesus knew from the beginning who they were, who did not believe, and who it was who was going to betray Him. He said, "No one can come to Me, except it has been granted to Emmanuel by Almighty God to do so."

After this many of His disciples turned back and would not walk with Him anymore.

Peters Affirms Belief

17. Jesus said to the twelve, "Surely You do not want to go away, do you?"
Simon Peter answered Him, "Lord, to whom will we go? You have the words of eternal life; and we have believed and we have come to know that You are the Holy One of God."

18. Jesus answered them, "Did I not choose you twelve, and one of you is a devil?" He meant Judas, the son of Simon Iscariot, for he was going to betray Him, and was one of the twelve.

JESUS DISREGARDS TRADITION
MATTHEW 15:1-20; MARK 7:1-23; JOHN 7:1

Spring, 29 - Capernaum

19. After these things Jesus walked in Galilee, for He did not wish to walk in Judea, because the Jews were seeking to kill Him.

There gathered around Jesus the Pharisees, and some of the experts in the law who had come from Jerusalem. They saw that some of His disciples ate their bread with ceremonially unclean hands which had not had the prescribed washings; for the Pharisees, and all the Jews who hold to the traditions of the elders, do not eat unless they wash their hands, using the fist as the law prescribes, and when they come in from the market-place they do not eat unless they immerse their whole bodies; and there are many other traditions which they observe which relate to the prescribed washings of cups and pitchers and vessels of bronze.

20. So the Pharisees and the experts in the law asked Him. "Why do Your disciples transgress the traditions of the elders? They do so transgress, because they do not wash their hands before they eat bread."

21. Jesus answered them, "Why do you transgress God's commandment, because of your tradition? For God said, 'Honor your father and your mother,' and 'He who curses his father and mother, let him die;' but you say, 'Whoever says to his father and mother, Whatever help you might otherwise have received from me is a gift dedicated to God,' will certainly not honor his father and his mother, and is yet guiltless. You have nullified the commandment of God through your tradition. You hypocrites.

22. "Isaiah was right when he prophesied about you hypocrites, as it is written,

> 'These people honor Me with their lips,
> but their heart is far from Me.
> They worship Me in vain,
> their teachings are but rules taught by people.'

"While you hold fast the tradition of men you abandon the commands of God."

Uncleanliness

23. Jesus called the crowd to Him and said to them, "Listen to Me everyone and understand. Nothing which goes into a person's mouth from outside can make the person unclean; but it is what comes out of a person's mouth which makes the person unclean."

24. When He came into the house, away from the crowd, His disciples said, "Do you know that when the Pharisees heard you, they were offended by it?"

He answered them, "Every plant that My Almighty God has not planted will be rooted up. Leave them alone. They are blind guides. If the blind leads the blind, both of them fall into the ditch."

25. Peter said to Him, "Tell us what this illustration means."

He said, "Are you even yet without understanding? Do you not understand that everything that goes into a person from outside cannot make them unclean, because it does not go into their heart, but into their stomach, and then out of their bodies? (The effect of this saying is to make all foods clean. And to eat with unwashed hands does not make a person unclean.)

26. He continued, "What comes out of a person is what makes them 'unclean.' For from within, out of persons' hearts, come evil thoughts, sexual immorality, theft, murder, adultery, greed, malice, deceit, lewdness, envy, slander, arrogance and folly. All these evils come from inside and make a person 'unclean.'"

HEALING A WOMAN'S DAUGHTER
MATTHEW 15: 21-28; MARK 7:24-30

After Passover, 29 - Near Tyre

27. And Jesus left, and went into the regions of Tyre and Sidon. He went into a house and He did not want anyone to know about it, but He could not be there without people knowing it. When a Canaanite woman from that area whose daughter had an unclean spirit

heard about Him, she immediately came there and fell at His feet. The woman was a Greek, a Syrophoenician by birth. She cried, "Have compassion upon me, Son of David! My daughter is suffering terribly from a demon." But He answered her not a word.

28. His disciples came and asked Him, "Send her away, for she is crying out after us."

Jesus answered, "I was sent only to the lost sheep of Israel."

She came and knelt before Him. "Lord," she said, "help me!"

29. Jesus answered, "First of all you must let the children eat their fill; it is not right to take the bread that belongs to the children and throw it to the dogs."

"True sir," she answered, "but even the dogs below the table eat some of the bits of bread that the children throw away."

30. He said to her, "Woman, you have great faith. Your request is granted."

She went home and found the child lying upon her bed, restored to health and the demon gone.

THE DEAF STAMMERER HEALED
MATTHEW 15:29-38; MARK 7:31-37; 8:1-9

Summer, 29 - Sea of Galilee

Man Healed

31. Then Jesus left the regions of Tyre and went through Sidon down to the Sea of Galilee, through the regions of the Decapolis. He went up into the mountain, and was sitting there; and they brought a man who was deaf and could hardly talk, and they asked Him to lay

His hands on him. He took him aside from the crowd by Himself. He put His fingers into his ears, and He spit and touched his tongue. Then He looked up to heaven, and sighed, and said to him, "Ephatha!" Which means, "Be opened!" And his ears were opened, and his tongue was loosed, and he spoke plainly.

32. He commanded them to tell no one, but the more He insisted the more they told the story of what He had done. People were completely amazed. "He has done all things well," they said. "He made the deaf hear and the dumb speak."

Many Healed

33. Great crowds came to Him, bringing with them people who were lame, blind, deaf and crippled, and laid them at His feet, and He healed them. The crowd was amazed when they saw the mute speaking, the maimed made well, the lame walking, the blind seeing; and they praised the God of Israel.

Four Thousand Fed

34. Jesus called His disciples to Him and said, "My heart has compassion for the crowd, because they have stayed with Me now for three days, and they have nothing to eat. If I send them away to their homes still fasting, they will faint on the road; and some of them have come from a distance."

His disciples answered Him, "Where could anyone get bread to satisfy them in a desert place like this?"

35. He asked them, "How many loaves have you?"
They said, "Seven."

36. He ordered the crowd to sit down on the ground. He took the seven loaves and gave thanks for them and broke them, and gave them to His disciples to set before the people. So they set them before the crowd, and they had a few small fishes. So he blessed them and told them to set them before them too. So they ate until they were completely satisfied. They gathered up what remained over of the broken pieces in seven baskets.

Those who ate were four thousand men, apart from women and children. So He sent the multitudes away.

PHARISEE'S TEST
MATTHEW 15:39-16:12; MARK 8:10-26

Summer, 29 - Magadan

Pharisee's Test

37. Immediately He got into a boat with His disciples and went to the border of Magadan to the district of Dalmanutha.

The Pharisees and Sadducees came to Him, trying to put Him to the test, asking Him questions. They asked Him to show them a sign from Heaven.

38. He answered them, "Why does this generation look for a sign? When evening comes, you say, 'It will be fine weather, because the sky is red.' And early in the morning you say, 'It will be stormy today, because the sky is red and threatening.' You know how to interpret the appearance of the sky, but you cannot interpret the signs of the times. A wicked and adulterous generation looks for a sign. No sign will be given to it except the sign of Jonah."

The Gospel of Jesus Christ

He sent them away and He again got in the boat, and crossed to the other side.

Warning about Leaders

39. When the disciples came to the other side, they had forgotten to take bread with them, except for one loaf they had with them in the boat. Jesus said to them, "Be on your guard against the leaven of the Pharisees and Sadducees."

They argued amongst themselves, "He must be saying this because we did not bring bread."

40. Jesus knew what they were thinking and said, "Why are you arguing among yourselves, you of little faith, because you have no bread?" Do you not yet understand, and do you not remember the five loaves of the five thousand, and how many baskets you took up?"

They replied, "Twelve."

"And do you not remember the seven loaves of the four thousand, and how many baskets full you took up?"

They answered, "Seven."

41. How is it that you do not understand that it was not about bread that I spoke to you? Beware of the leaven of the Pharisees and Sadducees!" Then they understood that He did not tell them to beware of the leaven that is in bread, but the teaching of the Pharisees and Sadducees.

Blind Man Healed

42. They came to Bethsaida; and they brought a blind man to Him and asked Him to touch him. He took the blind man's hand and took him outside the village. He spat into his eyes and laid His hands on him, and asked him, "Do you see anything?"

He looked up and said, "I see men, but I see them walking looking like trees."

43. Again He laid His hands on his eyes. He gazed intently, and his sight was restored and he saw everything clearly. He sent him away to his home. He said, "Don't go into the village."

CHAPTER 15
PASSION FORETOLD

PETER'S CONFESSION
MATTHEW 16:13-20; MARK 8:27-30; LUKE 9:18-21

Summer, 29 - Caesarea Phillippi

1. Jesus and His disciples went into the region of Caesarea Phillippi. He asked His disciples, "Who do people say that Emmanuel is?"

They said, "Some say John the Baptist, others Elijah, others Jeremiah, or one of the prophets."

2. He said to them, "But what about you, who do you say that I am?"

Simon Peter answered, "You are the Anointed One, the One of the Living God."

3. Jesus answered him, "Blessed are you, Simon son of Jonah, because this world has not revealed this to you, but Almighty God who is in Heaven. And I tell you that you are Peter, and on this rock I will build My Church, and the gates of Hell will not overcome it. I will give you the keys of the Kingdom of Heaven; and whatever you bind on earth will remain bound in heaven; and whatever you loose on earth will remain loosed in heaven."

He gave orders to His disciples to tell no one that He was Almighty God's Anointed One, the Christ.

Dr. Patrick Pierce

PASSION FORETOLD
MATTHEW 16:21-28; MARK 8:31-38; 9:1; LUKE 9:22-27

Summer, 29 - Caesarea Phillippi

Suffering Foretold

4. From that time Jesus began to explain to His disciples that Emmanuel must go to Jerusalem, and suffer many things by the elders and Chief Priests and Scribes, and that He must be killed and on the third day be raised to life again. He told them this plainly. Peter took Him, and began to urge Him, "God forbid that this should happen to You! This must never happen to You!"

He turned and said to Peter, "Get behind Me, Satan! You are putting a stumbling block in My way. Your ideas are not Almighty God's but this world's."

Burden of Discipleship

5. Then He called the crowd to Him together with His disciples, and said to them, "If anyone wants to come after Me, let them deny themselves, and they must sacrifice their own desires and preferences, and then follow only Me. Whoever seeks to save their life shall lose it; and whoever loses their life for My sake and the Gospel shall save it. What profit is it for a person to gain the whole world and to forfeit their life? For what is a person to give in exchange for their life?

6. "Whoever is ashamed of Me and My words in this adulterous and sinful generation, Emmanuel shall also be ashamed of them. For Emmanuel will come with Emmanuel's glory and the glory

of Almighty God, with God's holy angels, and then Emmanuel will judge each person in accordance with their deeds.

7. "This is the truth I tell you, there are some of those who are standing here who will not taste death, until they see the Kingdom of God come with power.

THE TRANSFIGURATION
MATTHEW 17:1-13; MARK 9:2-1; LUKE 9:28-36

Summer, 29 - Mount Hermon

8. Six days after saying this, Jesus took Peter and James and John, his brother, and brought them by themselves to a high mountain to pray. While He was praying He was transfigured before them. The appearance of His face shone like the sun, and His clothing become radiantly white as light, such that no bleach on earth could have made them so white.

9. And look, two men were talking with Him, who were Moses and Elijah. They appeared in glory, and they talked about the departure which He was going to accomplish in Jerusalem.

Peter and His friends were very sleepy. When they were fully awake they saw His glory, and the two men standing with Him.

10. When they were going to leave Him, Peter said to Jesus, "Master, it is good for us to be here. So let us make three tabernacles, one for You and one for Moses, and another for Elijah." He said this and did not know what he was saying, for they were very much amazed.

11. As he said this, a bright cloud came and overshadowed them and they were afraid as they entered the cloud. There came a

voice out of the cloud saying, "This is My beloved One, My chosen One, in whom I am well pleased! Listen to the One!" When the disciples heard that, they fell on their faces and were very much afraid.

12. When the voice had spoken, they immediately looked around and saw no one except Jesus alone with them. Jesus came and touched them and said, "Rise, and do not be afraid."

13. As they were coming down the mountain, Jesus gave them strict instructions, "Tell no person about what you have seen until Emmanuel has been raised from the dead."

They kept faithful to His word and asked among themselves, what this saying about rising from the dead could mean. They asked Jesus, "Why then do the Scribes say that Elijah must come first?"

14. He answered, "It is true that they say that Elijah is to come and will restore all things. And yet how is it written about Emmanuel that Emmanuel must suffer many things and be treated with contempt? But, I say to you, Elijah, also has come, and they did not recognize him and they treated him as they wished, even as it is written about him." Then the disciples understood that He spoke to them about John the Baptizer.

HEALING DEMONIC BOY
MATTHEW 17: 14-21; MARK 9:14-29; LUKE 9:37-43

Summer, 29 - Caesarea Phillippi

15. On the next day, when they had come down from the mountain to the other disciples, they saw a large crowd gathered around them, and the experts in the law in discussion with them. As soon as the people saw Jesus the crowd was amazed and ran to greet Him.

He asked them, "What are you discussing among yourselves?"

16. And a man from the crowd shouted in answer. He came and fell at His feet and said, "Teacher, have compassion on my son, for he is my only child. He is an epileptic and a spirit seized him and he suddenly shouts out; the spirit convulses him until he foams at the mouth; he shakes and suffers severely and is wasting away. I brought him to your disciples and begged them to cast out the spirit but they could not do it."

17. Jesus answered, "O faithless and perverse generation! How long will I be with you? How long am I to bear you? Bring him to Me!"

They brought him to Jesus. When he saw Jesus, the spirit immediately sent the boy into a convulsion, and he fell to the ground, and rolled about, foaming at the mouth.

18. Jesus asked his father, "How long has this been happening to him?"

He said, "He has been like this since he was a child. Often it throws him into the fire and into the water for it is out to destroy him. But if You can, let Your heart be moved with compassion, and help us."

19. Jesus said to him, "You say, 'If You can.' All things are possible to those who believe."

Immediately the father of the boy cried out, "I do believe. Help me overcome my unbelief."

20. When Jesus saw that the crowd was running to the scene, He rebuked the unclean spirit saying, "Spirit of dumbness and deafness, I order you, come out of him, and don't go into him again."

When it had cried and violently convulsed him it came out, and he became like a dead person, so that many said, "He is dead." But Jesus took him by the hand, and raised him up, and he stood up and He gave him back to his father. Everyone was astonished at the majesty of God.

21. When He had gone into the house, and they were by themselves, His disciples asked Him, "Why were we not able to cast out the demon?"

Jesus said to them, "Because you have little faith. This is the truth I tell you, if you have faith as small as a mustard seed you can say to the mountain, 'Be moved from here to over there' and it will move. So nothing will be impossible to you. This kind of faith," He said to them, "can come out only by prayer and fasting."

DEATH FORETOLD AGAIN
MATTHEW 17:22-23; MARK 9:30-32; LUKE 9:44-45

Summer, 29 - Galilee

22. When they left there they went through Galilee, and Jesus did not want anyone to know where He was for He was teaching the disciples. While they were all wondering at the things He was doing, He said to His disciples, "Let these words be always in your mind, Emmanuel is going to be delivered into the hands of men, and they will kill Him, and when He is killed, after three days He will rise again."

But they did not understand what He said, and they were afraid to ask Him what He meant.

JESUS PAYS TEMPLE TAX
MATTHEW 17:24-27

Late summer, 29 - Capernaum

23. When they came to Capernaum, the collectors of the half-shekel Temple tax came to Peter and said, "Doesn't your teacher pay the tax?"

Peter said, "Yes, He does."

24. When he had gone into the house, before he could speak, Jesus said to him, "What do you think, Simon? From whom do earthly kings collect tax and tribute? From their own people or from strangers?"

Then Peter said, "From strangers."

25. Jesus said to him, "So then the people are free, but so as not to set a stumbling-block in anyone's way, go to the sea, and cast a fishing line in it, and take the first fish which you catch, and when you have opened its mouth, you will find a shekel. Take it and give it to them for My tax and yours."

CHAPTER 16
GOD'S FAMILY

AMBITION VERSUS CHILDLIKENESS
MATTHEW 18:1-14; MARK 9:33-50; LUKE 9:46-50

Autumn, 29 - Capernaum

1. They came to Capernaum. When Jesus was in the house He asked them, "What were you arguing about on the road?" They remained silent, for on the road they had been arguing with each other about who was to be greatest. So Jesus sat down, and called the Twelve, and said to them, "If anyone wishes to be first, they must be the very last, and the servant of all."

2. "Who, then," they said, "is the greatest in the Kingdom of Heaven?"

Jesus called a little child and set him before them, and taking him in His arms said, "This is the truth I tell you, unless you become as children, you will not enter into the Kingdom of Heaven. Whoever humbles themselves as this child, they are the greatest in the Kingdom of Heaven. Whoever," He said to them, "receives one of these little children in My name, receives Me; and whoever receives Me, receives Almighty God who sent Me."

Stumbling Blocks to Children

3. "And whoever puts a stumbling-block in the way of one of these little ones, who believe in Me, it is better for them that a

large millstone should be hung about their neck, and be drowned in the open sea.

"See that you do not despise one of these little ones; for, I tell you their angels in Heaven always see the face of Almighty God who is in Heaven.

Lost Sheep

4. "What do you think? If a man has a hundred sheep, and one of them wanders away, will he not leave the ninety-nine, and go out to the hills and look for the one that wandered off? And if he finds it, this is the truth I tell you, he rejoices more over it than over the ninety-nine who never wandered away. In the same way it is not the will of Almighty God that any of these little ones should be lost.

World's Stumbling Blocks

5. "Woe to the world because of its stumbling blocks! For it is inevitable that stumbling blocks come; but woe for the person by whom the stumbling block comes.

6. "If your hand proves a stumbling block to you, cut it off. It is better for you to enter life maimed than to go away to Hell with two hands, to the eternal fire. And if your foot is a stumbling block to you, cut it off. For it is better for you to enter life lame than to be cast into Hell with two feet. And if your eye proves a stumbling block to you, cast it away. For it is better for you to enter into the Kingdom of God with one eye than to be cast into Hell with two eyes, where the worm does not die and the fire is never quenched.

7. "Everyone must be salted with fire,
Salt is good, but,
if the salt has become saltless,
How can you make it salty again?

Have salt in yourselves,
and so be at peace with each other."

Works in Jerusalem

8. John said to Jesus, "Teacher, we saw a man casting out demons in Your name, and we tried to stop him because he is not one of our group."

Jesus said, "Don't stop him. There is no one who can do a miracle in My name and say anything bad about Me. For whoever is not against us, is for us."

SIN AND FORGIVENESS IN GOD'S FAMILY
MATTHEW 18:15-35

Autumn, 29 - Capernaum

Disputes in God's Family

9. "If another of God's children sins against you, go, and try to convince them of their error alone. If they listen to you, you have gained back your brother or sister. If they will not listen to you, take one or two more who know the sin with you, so that every fact may be confirmed by the mouth of two or three witnesses. If the offender refuses to listen to them, tell it to the Church. And if the one refuses to listen to the Church, let that one be to you as one of the world's and a tax-collector.

Disciple's Authority

10. "This is the truth I tell you, whatever you bind on earth will be bound in Heaven; and whatever you loose on earth will be loosed in Heaven.

"Again, I tell you, that if two of you agree on earth about anything that they may ask, it shall be done for them by Almighty God who is in Heaven. For where two or three are assembled together in My name, there I am in their midst."

Peter Asks About Forgiveness

11. Then Peter came and said to Him, "Lord, how often will my brother or sister sin against me, and I forgive them? Up to seven times?"

Jesus said to him, "I tell you not up to seven times, but up to seventy times seven. That is why the Kingdom of Heaven can be compared to a king who wished to settle accounts with his servants.

Parable of Servant's Debt

12. "When he began to settle them there was one debtor brought to him who owed ten thousand talents. But, since he was unable to pay, his master ordered him to be sold, together with his wife and children, and all his possessions, and payment to be made. The servant fell on his face saying, 'Have patience with me, and I will repay you everything.' The master of the servant felt compassion, and forgave him the debts.

13. "But when that servant went out, he found one of his fellow servants, who owed him a hundred denarii. He caught hold of him and seized him by the throat and said, 'Pay what you owe.' The fellow-servant fell down and begged him, 'Have patience with me, and I will pay you everything.' But he refused. Rather, he went away and flung him into prison, until he should pay what was owed.

14. "So, when his fellow servants saw what had happened, they were very distressed; and they reported all that had happened to their master. Then the master summoned him, and said to him, 'You wicked servant! I forgave you all that debt when asked me. Ought you not to have had mercy on your fellow-servant, as I had mercy on you?' And his master was angry with him and handed him over to the torturers, until he should pay all that was owed.

15. "Even so shall Almighty God do to you, if each of you do not forgive God's children from your hearts."

JESUS ADVISED TO GO TO JUDEA
JOHN 7:2-10

September, 29 - Capernaum

16. The festival of the Jews which is called the Feast of Tabernacles was near. So His brothers and sisters said to Him, "Leave here and go to Jerusalem so Your disciples also may see the works that You do. For no one does things in secret, when he wishes to draw public attention to himself. Since You can do these things show Yourself to the world." For even His brothers and sisters did not have faith in Him.

17. So Jesus said to them, "My time is not yet at hand, but your time is always ready. The world cannot hate you, but it hates Me because I testify about it that it's deeds are evil. Go up to the festival yourselves. I am not yet going up to the festival, because My time has not yet come." When He had said these things to them He stayed in Galilee. However, after his brothers and sisters had left for the festival, He went also, not publicly, but in secret.

THE JOURNEY TO JERUSALEM
LUKE 9:51-56

October, 29 - Through Samaria

18. And it came about when the days for His ascension were approaching, that He resolutely set His face to go to Jerusalem. He sent messengers on ahead.

When they had gone and entered a village of the Samaritans to make ready for Him; and the Samaritans refused to receive them because He was journeying with His face toward Jerusalem.

19. When His disciples, James and John, learned of this they said, "Lord, would You like us to order fire to come down from Heaven and destroy them?"

He turned to them and rebuked them; and said, "You do not know what kind of spirit you are of; for Emmanuel did not come to destroy people's lives but to save them." And they went on to another village.

CHAPTER 17
JESUS TEACHES IN THE TEMPLE

JOHN 7:11-52

October, 29 - Jerusalem

1. The Jews searched for Him at the festival, and were saying, "Where is He?" And there were many heated arguments about Him among the crowd. Some said, "He is a good man." But others said, "No, far from it, He is leading the people astray." But no one spoke about Him openly because of their fear of the Jews.

Temple Teaching

2. But in the middle of the festival, Jesus went to the Temple and began to teach. The Jews were amazed saying, "How can this man know so much when He is uneducated?"

3. Jesus answered them:

"My teaching is not from Myself:
It comes from the One who sent Me;
and if anyone is prepared to do God's will,
they will know whether My teaching is from God
or whether My doctrine is My own.

4. When a person's doctrine is their own
they are hoping to get honor for themselves;
but when they are working for the honor

of the One who sent them,
then they are love
and there is no wickedness in them.

Did not Moses give you the Law?
And yet not one of you keeps the Law!

5. "Why do you try to kill Me?"

The crowd answered, "You are mad! Who is trying to kill You?"

6. Jesus answered them, "I have done only one deed and you all marvel. Moses gave you circumcision (not that it had its origin in Moses, it came down from your ancestors) and you circumcise a boy on the Sabbath. If a boy can be circumcised on the Sabbath, without breaking the law of Moses, are you angry at Me for making the entire person whole on the Sabbath? Stop judging by appearances, and make your judgment just."

People Talk About Jesus

7. So some of the people of Jerusalem said, "Is not this the man whom they are trying to kill? And look! He is speaking publicly, and they say nothing to Him! The authorities really do not know that this is the Christ, do they? But He cannot be because we know where He comes from. When the Anointed One of God comes no one knows where He comes from."

8. So Jesus, as He taught in the Temple, cried out, "So you know Me? And you know where I come from. But it is not on My own

authority that I have come; but Almighty God who sent Me is real, and you do not know God. But I know Almighty God, because I have come from God, and it was Almighty God who sent Me."

9. So they would like to find a way to arrest Him; but no one laid a hand upon Him, because His hour had not yet come.

Many of the crowd believed in Him. "When the Anointed One of God comes," they said, "surely He cannot do greater signs than this man has done?"

Guards Sent to Arrest Jesus

10. The Pharisees heard the crowds carrying on these discussions about Him, and the Chief Priests and Pharisees sent officers to arrest Him.

So Jesus said, "For a little while longer I am to be with you, and then I go back to God who sent Me. You will search for Me and you will not find Me. You cannot come where I am."

11. So the Jews said to each other, "Where is this man going to go that we will not find Him? Surely He is not going to go to the Jews who are dispersed among the Greeks and teach the Greeks? What can the statement of His mean, 'You will search for Me and you will not find Me, and You cannot come where I am'?"

Spiritual Drink

12. On the last day, the great day of the festival, Jesus stood and cried out saying, "If anyone thirsts, let him come to Me and drink.

As the scripture says, 'Whoever believes in Me, rivers of living water shall flow from their innermost being.'"

13. But this He spoke about the Spirit, whom those who believed in Him were to receive. For as yet the Spirit was not given because Jesus was not yet glorified.

People Divided

14. When they heard these words some of the crowd said, "This is really the promised Prophet." Others said, "This is the Anointed One of God." But some said, "Surely the Anointed One of God does not come from Galilee? Does the scripture not say that the Anointed One of God is a descendant of David, and that He is to come from Bethlehem, the village where David used to live?" So there was a division of opinion in the crowd because of Him. Some of them would have liked to arrest Him, but no one laid hands on Him.

Nicodemus Advised

15. So the officers came to the Chief Priests and the Pharisees. They said to them, "Why did you not bring Him here?"

The officers answered, "Never did a man speak the way He speaks."

16. So the Pharisees answered, "Surely you too have not been led astray? No one of the authorities or Pharisees have believed in Him! But this crowd which is ignorant of the law and is accursed believes in Him!"

17. Nicodemus (the man who came to Him before) said to them, for he was one of them, "Surely our law does not condemn a man unless it first hears a statement of the case from him, and has first-hand information about what he is doing?"

They answered him, "Surely you too are not from Galilee? Search and see that no prophet arises from Galilee."

THE ADULTERESS
JOHN 7:53-8:11

October, 29 - Jerusalem

18. And each of them went to their own home, but Jesus went to the Mount of Olives. Early in the morning He was again in the Temple, and all the people came to Him. He sat down and began teaching them.

19. The Scribes and Pharisees brought a woman arrested for adultery. They set her in the midst and said to Him, "Teacher, this woman was caught committing adultery, in the very act. Now in the law Moses commanded us to stone a woman like this. What do you say?" They were testing Him when they said this, so that they might have some grounds on which to accuse Him.

20. But Jesus stooped down and wrote with His finger on the ground. When they persisted in asking Him, He straightened Himself and said to them, "Let the person among you who is without sin be the first to cast a stone at her." And again He bent down and wrote with His finger on the ground.

21. One by one those who had heard what He said went out, beginning with the older ones. So Jesus was left alone, and the woman where she had been. Jesus straightened up and said to her, "Woman, where are they? Has no one condemned you?"

She said, "No one, Lord."

22. Jesus said, "I am not going to condemn you either. Go, and from now on, sin no more."

JESUS ARGUES WITH THE JEWS
JOHN 8:12-59

October, 29 - Jerusalem

Light of the World

23. So Jesus spoke to them saying, "I am the Light of the world. Whoever follows Me will not walk in darkness, but they will have the Light of life."

24. So the Pharisees said to Him, "You are bearing witness about Yourself. Your witness is not true."

Jesus answered and said to them, "Even if I bear witness about Myself, My witness is true; because I know where I came from and where I am going. But you do not know where I came from and where I am going. You people judge according to the world. I do not judge anyone. But if I do judge, My judgment is true, because I am not alone in My judgment, but I and Almighty God who sent Me. It is written in your law, that the witness of two persons is to be accepted as true. I bear witness about Myself, and Almighty God who sent Me also bears witness about Me."

25. They said to Him, "Where are your parents?"

Jesus answered, "You know neither Me nor Almighty God. If you had known Me you would know Almighty God also.

26. He spoke these words in the treasury while He was teaching in the Temple; and no one seized Him, because His hour had not yet come.

Unbelief

27. So He said to them again, "I am going away, and you will search for Me, and you will die in your sin. You cannot come where I am going."

So the Jews said, "Surely He is not going to kill Himself, because He is saying, 'You cannot come where I am going?'"

28. He said to them, "You are from below, but I am from above. You are of this world, but I am not of this world. I said to you that you will die in your sins. For if you will not believe that I am who I am, you will die in your sins."

29. They said to Him, "Who are You?"

Jesus said to them, "What have I been saying to you from the beginning. I have many things to say to you, and many judgments to deliver to you; but God who sent Me is true, and I speak to the world what I have heard from Almighty God."

They did not know that it was about Almighty God that He was speaking to them.

30. So Jesus said to them, "When you lift up Emmanuel, then you will know that I am the One, and that I do nothing on My own authority, but that I speak these things as Almighty God has taught Me. And God who sent Me is with Me. God has not left Me alone, because I always do the things that are pleasing to God." As He said these things, many believed in Him."

Spiritual Freedom

31. Jesus said to the Jews who had come to believe in Him, "If you remain in My word, you are truly My disciples; and you will know the truth, and the truth will make you free."

32. They answered Him, "We are the descendants of Abraham and we have never been slaves to anyone. How do you say, 'You will become free'?"

Jesus answered them, "This is the truth I tell you, everyone who commits sin is the slave to sin. The slave does not remain in the house forever, Emmanuel does remain forever. If Emmanuel shall make you free, you will be really free.

33. "I know that you are the descendants of Abraham, but you are trying to kill Me, because there is no place in you for My word. I speak what I have seen in the presence of Almighty God. So you must do what you have heard from Almighty God."

Abraham's Children

34. "Our father is Abraham," they answered.

Jesus said to them, "If you are the children of Abraham, do the deeds of Abraham. But as it is, you are trying to kill Me, a man who has spoken the truth to you, truth which I heard from God. Abraham did not do this. As for you, you do the works of your Lord."

35. They said to Him, "We were born of no adulterous union. We have one Lord, even God."

36. "If God was your Lord," said Jesus, "you would love Me. For it was from God that I came forth and have come here. I had nothing to do with My own coming, but it was God who sent Me. Why do you not understand what I am saying? The reason is that you are unable to hear My word. You belong to your Lord, the devil, and it is the evil desires of your Lord that you wish to do. The devil was a murderer from the very beginning, and never took a stand in the truth, because the truth is not in the devil. When the devil speaks falsehood it is from the devil's own nature, because the devil is a liar and the creator of lies. But because I speak the truth, you do not believe in Me. Who of you can convict Me of sin? If I speak the truth, why do you not believe in Me? Whoever is of God hears God's words. That is why you do not hear, because you are not of God."

Eternal Existence

37. The Jews answered, "Are we not right in saying that You are a Samaritan, and that you have a devil?"

Jesus answered, "It is not I who have a devil. I honor Almighty God, but you dishonor Me. I do not seek My own glory. There is One who seeks and judges.

38. "This is the truth I tell, if anyone keeps My word, they will not see death forever."

The Jews said to Him, "Now we are certain that You are mad. Abraham died and so did the prophets, yet You are saying, 'If anyone keeps My word, they will not taste of death forever.' Surely You are not greater than our father Abraham who did die? And the prophets died too. Who are You making Yourself out to be?"

39. Jesus answered, "It is Almighty God Who glorifies Me, Who, you claim, is your God, and yet you know nothing about God. But I know God. If I were to say that I do not know God, I would be a liar, like you. But I know God and I keep God's word. Abraham your ancestor rejoiced to see My day; and he saw it and was glad."

40. The Jews said to Him, "You are not yet fifty years old, and have You seen Abraham?"

Jesus said to them, "This is the truth I tell you, before Abraham, I Am."

So they picked up stones to throw at Him, but Jesus hid Himself and left the Temple.

CHAPTER 18
JESUS TEACHES

JESUS HEALS A BLIND MAN
JOHN 9:1-41

October, 29 - Jerusalem

1. As Jesus was passing by, He saw a man who was blind from birth. "Teacher," His disciples said to Him, "who was it who sinned that he was born blind, this man or his parents?"

"It was neither, he nor his parents who sinned," answered Jesus, "but it happened that the works of God might be displayed. We must do the works of God who sent Me while day lasts; the night is coming when no one can work. While I am in the world, I am the Light of the world."

2. When He had said this He spat on the ground, and made clay from the spittle, and He smeared the clay on his eyes and said to him, "Go, wash in the Pool in Siloam." (The word "Siloam" means "sent.") So he went away and washed, and came back seeing.

3. So the neighbors and those who formerly saw him as beggar, said, "Is this not the man who sat begging?"

Some said, "It is he." Others said, "It is not him, but it is someone like him."

The man himself said, "I am he."

4. They said to him, "How then have your eyes been opened?"

He answered, "The man they call Jesus made clay and smeared it on my eyes, and said to me; Go to the Pool of Siloam and wash.' So I went and washed, and I received sight."

They said to him, "Where is this Man you are talking about?"

He said, "I don't know."

Pharisees Question Miracle

5. They brought the man who had been blind to the Pharisees. The day on which Jesus had made the clay and opened his eyes was the Sabbath day. So the Pharisees asked him again how he had received his sight.

He said to them, "He put clay on my eyes; and I washed, and now I can see."

6. So some of the Pharisees said, "This man is not from God, because He does not observe the Sabbath." But others said, "How can a man who is a sinner perform such signs?" And there was a division of opinion among them. So they said to the blind man, "What is your opinion about Him, since He opened your eyes?"
He said, "He is a prophet."

7. Now the Jews refused to believe that he had been blind and had become able to see, until they called the parents of the man who had become able to see, and asked them, "Is this your son? And do you say that he was born blind? How, then, can he now see?"

8. His parents answered, "We know that this is our son; and we know that he was born blind; how he has now come to see we do not know; or who it was who opened his eyes we do not know. Ask himself, he is of age and can answer his own questions." His parents said this because they were afraid of the Jews; for the Jews had already agreed that if anyone acknowledged Jesus to be the Anointed One of God, they should be excommunicated from the synagogue. That is why his parents said, "He is of age. Ask him."

9. A second time they called the man who had been blind. "Give the glory to God," they said. "We know that this Man is a sinner."

The man answered, "Whether He is a sinner or not, I do not know. One thing I do know, I used to be blind and now I can see."

10. "What did He do to you?" they said. "How did He open your eyes?"

He answered them, "I have already told you, and you did not listen. Why do you want to here the story all over again? Surely you don't want to become His disciples?"

11. They reviled him and said, "You are His disciple. We are Moses's disciples. We know that God spoke to Moses; but as for the Man, we do not know where He comes from."

12. The man answered, "It is an amazing thing that you do not know where He comes from, and yet He opened my eyes. We know that God does not listen to sinners. But if a person is a God-fearing person and does God's will, God hears them. Since the

beginning of time no one has ever heard of anyone who opened the eyes of a person born blind. If this Man was not from God, He could not have done anything."

They said to him, "You were entirely born in sins, and are you trying to teach us?" And they ordered him to get out.

Jesus Reveals He is Emmanuel

13. Jesus heard that they had put him out, so He found him and said to him, "Do you believe in Emmanuel?"

He answered Him, "But who is He, Sir, that I might believe in Him?"

14. Jesus said to him, "You have both seen Him, and He is the One talking with you."

"Lord," he said, "I believe." And he knelt before Him.

15. Jesus said, "It was for judgment that I came into this world that those who do not see might see, and that those who see might become blind."

Some of the Pharisees who were with Him heard this and said, "Surely, we are not blind?"

Jesus said to them "If you were blind, you would have no sin. But since you say, 'We see,' your sin remains."

THE GOOD SHEPHERD
JOHN 10:1-21

October, 29 - Jerusalem

The Sheep

16. Jesus said, "This is the truth I tell you; whoever does not enter the sheepfold through the door, but climbs in some other way, is a thief and a robber. But whoever comes in through the door is the shepherd of the sheep. The keeper of the door opens the door to him; and the sheep hear his voice; and he calls his own sheep by name and leads them out. Whenever he puts his own sheep out, he walks in front of them; and the sheep follow him, because they know his voice. But they will not follow a stranger, but they will flee from him, because they do not know the voice of strangers."

The Gate to the Fold

17. Jesus spoke this parable to them, but they did not know what He was saying to them.

> "I tell you most solemnly,
> I am the door of the sheepfold.
> All others who have come
> are thieves and robbers;
> but the sheep did not listen to them.
>
> I am the door.
> Anyone who enters through Me will be safe;
> they will go freely in and out
> and be sure of finding pasture.

The thief comes
only to steal and kill and destroy.
I have come so that they may have life
and have it in full abundance.

The Good Shepherd

18. "I am the good shepherd;
the good shepherd is the one
who gives his life for his sheep.

　　The hired man, since he is not the shepherd
and the sheep do not belong to him,
abandons the sheep and runs away
as soon as he sees a wolf coming,
and then the wolf attacks and scatters the sheep;
this is because he is only a hired man
and has no concerns for the sheep.

　　I am the good shepherd;
I know My own
and My own sheep know Me
just as Almighty God knows Me
and I know Almighty God;
and I lay down My life for My sheep.

19. "And there are other sheep I have
that are not of this fold
and these I must bring in.
They too will listen to My voice,
and they will become one flock,
and there will be one shepherd.

20.   "Almighty God loves Me,
because I lay down My life
in order that I may take it up again.
No one takes it from Me;
I lay it down of My own free will,
and as it is in My power to lay it down,
so it is in My power to take it up again;
and this is the command
I have been given by Almighty God."

People Divided

21. There was again a division among the Jews because of these words. Many of them said, "He has an evil spirit, and He is mad. Why do you listen to Him?" Others said, "These are not the words of a man possessed by an evil spirit. Can a man with an evil spirit open the eyes of the blind?"

THE MISSION OF THE SEVENTY
LUKE 10:1-24

October, 29 - Judea

Seventy Sent

22. After these things the Lord appointed seventy others and sent them out in twos ahead of Him into every town and place where He intended to go.

23. He said to them, "The harvest is great but the workers are few. Ask then the Lord of the harvest to send out workers for the harvest. Go! Look, I am sending you out as sheep in the midst of

wolves. Do not take a purse or a wallet or sandals. Greet no one on the road. Into whatever house you go, say first of all, 'Peace to this house!' If it is a child of peace who lives there, your peace will remain upon it; but if not it will return to you. Remain in the same house eating and drinking whatever they give you; for the workers deserve their pay. Do not go from house to house. If you go into any town and they receive you, eat what is put before you. Heal those in it who are ill, and say to them, 'The Kingdom of God has come near you!'

24. "If you go into any town and they do not receive you, go out into its streets and say, 'The dust which clings to our feet from this town, we wipe off against you. But realize this, the Kingdom of God has come near you!' I tell you, things will be easier for Sodom in that day than for that town. Woe to you Chorazin! Woe to you Bethsaida! For if the miracles which have been done by you had been done in Tyre and Sidon, they would have repented long ago sitting in sackcloth and ashes. But at the judgment things will be easier for Tyre and Sidon than for you. And you, Capernaum, will you be exalted to Heaven? You will be cast down to Hell. Whoever listens to you, listens to Me; and whoever rejects you, rejects Me; and whoever rejects Me, rejects Almighty God, the One who sent Me."

Seventy Return

25. The Seventy returned with joy saying, "Lord, in Your name the demons are subject to us."

26. He said to them, "I saw Satan fall like lightning from Heaven. Look, I have given you authority to tread upon snakes and scorpions and over all the power of the enemy. Nothing will hurt you.

But do not rejoice in this, that the spirits are subject to you; but rejoice that your names are written in Heaven."

God's Revelations

27. At that time Jesus was filled with great joy by the Holy Spirit and said, "I thank You, Almighty God, Lord of Heaven and earth, that You have hidden these things from the wise and intelligent and that You have revealed them to babes. Yes, Almighty God for so it was Your good pleasure in Your sight. All things have been handed over to Me by Almighty God. No one knows who Emmanuel is except Almighty God; and no one knows who Almighty God is except Emmanuel, and to whomever Emmanuel wishes to reveal God."

28. He turned to His disciples when they were in private and said, "Happy are the eyes which see the things you are seeing for I tell you that many prophets and kings desired to see the things that you are seeing and did not see them, and to hear the things that you are hearing and did not hear them."

THE PARABLE OF THE GOOD SAMARITAN
LUKE 10:25-37

November, 29 - Judea

29. Look, an expert in the law stood up and asked Jesus a test question saying, "Teacher, what is it I am to do to inherit eternal life?"

He said to him, "What is written in the Law? What does it mean to you?"

30. He answered, "You must love the Lord your God with all your spirit, and with all your soul, and with all your strength, and with all your mind, and your neighbor as yourself."

"Your answer is correct," Jesus said.

31. But wishing to justify himself, he said to Jesus, "And who is my neighbor?"

Jesus answered, "There was a man who went down from Jerusalem to Jericho. He fell amongst robbers who stripped him and beat him, and went away and left him half-dead.

32. "Now, by chance, a priest came down by that road and he saw him, and he passed by on the other side. In the same way when a Levite came to the place he saw him and passed by on the other side.

33. "But a Samaritan who was on the road came to where he was. When he saw him, he felt compassion. So he came up to him and bound up his wounds, pouring in wine and oil; and he put him on his own beast and brought him to an inn and cared for him. On the next day he took two denarii and gave it to the innkeeper. 'Take care of him,' he said, 'and whatever more you spend, when I come back this way, I will repay you.'

34. "Which of these three, do you think proved to be a neighbor to the man who fell into the hands of robbers?"

He said, "He who showed mercy on him."

Jesus said to him, "Go, and do likewise."

JESUS VISITS MARTHA AND MARY
LUKE 10:38-42

November, 29 - Bethany

35. As they journeyed, Jesus entered into a village. A woman called Martha welcomed Him into her house. She had a sister called Mary, and she sat at Jesus' feet and was listening to His words.

Martha was worried with all her preparations. She came to them and said, "Lord, don't you care that my sister has left me alone to do the serving? Tell her to give me a hand."

36. But the Lord answered her, "Martha, Martha, you are worried and bothered about so many things, but only one thing is necessary. Mary has chosen the better part, and it is not to be taken away from her."

CHAPTER 19
HOW TO PRAY

LUKE 11:1-13; 13:10-17

November, 29 - Judea

1. Jesus was praying in a certain place, and when He stopped, one of His disciples said to Him, "Lord, teach us to pray, as John taught His disciples."

2. He said to them, "When your pray, say;
Expanded Literal Greek translation
"Our Father, who art in Heaven
   "Almighty God, our source and creator, who is through the universe
Hallowed be thy name.
   Blessed and worshiped be Your Name.
Your kingdom come
   Let Your Kingdom come now and always,
Your will be done *Same*
On earth as it is in Heaven
   On earth, in our lives through us as it is in Your Kingdom.
Give us this day our daily bread,
   Please give us each day what we need daily to live,
And forgive our debts
   And forgive us our debts to You,
As we forgive our debtors.
   In the same way as we forgive the debts owed to us.
And lead us not into temptation,
   Keep us clear of temptations and trials,
But deliver us from evil.
   But save and protect us from evil and the Evil One.
       Amen

Persistence

3. Jesus said to them, "Suppose one of you has a friend and goes to him at midnight and says to him, 'Friend, lend me three loaves because a friend of mine has come to me from a journey and I have nothing to set before him'; and suppose his friend answers from within, 'Don't bother me; the door has already been shut and my children are in bed with me; I can't get up and give you anything.' I tell you if he will not rise and give him because he is his friend, yet he will rise and give him as much as he needs because of his persistence.

Pray with Belief

4. "For I say to you,

> 'Ask and it will be given to you;
> seek and you will find;
> knock and it will be opened to you.
> For everyone who asks, receives;
> and whoever seeks, finds;
> and to whoever knocks,
> it will be opened.

Gift of God

5. "If a child asks any parent among you for bread, will the parent give the child a stone? Or, if the child asks for a fish, with the parent, instead of a fish, give the child a serpent? Or if the child asks for an egg, will the parent give the child a scorpion? If you then, who are evil, know how to give good gifts to your children, how much

more will your Almighty God, who is in Heaven give the Holy Spirit to those who ask God?"

Healing on Sabbath

6. Jesus was teaching in one of the synagogues on the Sabbath; and look, there was a woman there who had a spirit of weakness for eighteen years. She was bent double and could not straighten up properly. When Jesus saw her He called her to Him and said, "Woman, you are set free from your sickness;" and He laid His hands on her; and immediately she was straightened.

7. The official of the synagogue was indignant that Jesus had healed on the Sabbath. "Are there not six days," he said to the crowd, "in which work ought to be done? Come and be healed on them and not on the Sabbath day."

8. The Lord answered, "You hypocrites! Does each one of you not lose his ox or his donkey from the stall on the Sabbath, and lead them out to water? And as for this woman, a daughter of Abraham, whom Satan bound for eighteen years, should she not have been released from this bond on the Sabbath day?"

As He said this, His opponents were being humiliated, and all the crowd rejoiced over all the glorious things that were done by Him.

Dr. Patrick Pierce

THE FEAST OF DEDICATION
JOHN 10:22-42

January, 30 - Jerusalem

Jesus and Almighty God are One

9. It was the Festival of the Dedication in Jerusalem. It was wintry weather, and Jesus was walking in the Temple in Solomon's Porch. So the Jews surrounded Him. And they said to Him, "How long are You going to keep us in suspense? If You really are God's Anointed One, tell us plainly."

10. Jesus answered them, "I did tell you and you did not believe Me. The works that I do in the name of Almighty God, these are evidence about Me. But you do not believe because you are not My sheep. My sheep hear My voice, and I know them, and they follow Me. And I give them eternal life, and they will never perish, and no one will snatch them from My hand. Almighty God, Who gave them to Me, is greater than all; and no one can snatch them from the hand of Almighty God. I and Almighty God are One."

Attempt to Stone Jesus

11. The Jews again picked up stones to stone Him. Jesus said to them, "I have shown you many good works, which came from Almighty God. For which of these deeds are you trying to stone Me?"

12. The Jews answered Him, "It is not for any good work that we want to stone You; it is for insulting God, and because You, being a man, make Yourself out to be God."

Almighty God in Jesus

13. Jesus answered them, "Is it not written in your law, 'I said, you are gods?' If he called those to whom the word came gods, and the scriptures cannot be destroyed, are you going to say to Me, whom Almighty God sanctified and sent out into the world, 'You insult God,' because I said, 'I am the One of God'?; If I do not do the works of Almighty God, do not believe Me. But if I do, even if you do not believe Me, believe the works, that you may know and recognize that Almighty God is in Me, and I am in Almighty God."

They again tried to seize Him, but He evaded their grasp.

14. And He went away again to the other side of Jordan, to the place where John first used to baptize; and He stayed there. And many came to Him, and they said, "John did no sign; but everything John said about the Man is true." And then many there believed in Him.

THE NARROW DOOR
LUKE 13:22-35

January, 30 - Perea to Jerusalem

15. Jesus continued going through towns and villages, teaching and making His way to Jerusalem. Someone said to Him, "Lord, are those who are to be saved few in number?"

16. He said to them, "Strive to enter through the narrow door, because many, I tell you, will seek to enter in and will not be able to. Once the head of the house gets up and shuts the door, and when you begin to stand outside and knock, saying, 'Lord, open up to us,' The Master will answer you, 'I do not know where you are from.' Then you will begin to say, 'We have eaten and drunk in Your presence and

You taught in our streets.' He will say, 'I tell you, I do not know where you are from. Depart from Me, all you who are evil doers.' There will be weeping and gnashing of teeth there, when you will see Abraham and Isaac and Jacob in the Kingdom of God. And look, there are those who are last who will be first, and those first who will be last."

Jesus Warned

17. At that time some Pharisees came to Jesus, and said to Him, "Depart and get on Your way from this place, because Herod is out to kill You."

18. He said to them, "Go and tell that fox, look, I cast out demons and I work cures today and tomorrow, and on the third day My work is perfected. Nevertheless, I must be on My way today, and tomorrow and the next day, because it is not possible for a prophet to perish outside of Jerusalem.

Lament Over Jerusalem

19. "Jerusalem! Jerusalem! Killer of prophets! Stoner of those who were sent to you! How often I wanted to gather together your children as a hen gathers her brood under her wings, and you would not let it! Look, your house is desolate. I tell you, you will not see Me until you shall say, 'Blessed is the One Who comes in the name of the Lord.'"

DINING WITH A PHARISEE
LUKE 14:1-24

January, 30 - Perea

20. On the Sabbath day Jesus had gone into the house of one of the rulers of the Pharisees to eat bread; and they were watching Him closely. And look, there was a man in front of Him who had dropsy. Jesus said to the Scribes and Pharisees, "Is it lawful to heal on the Sabbath? Or, is it not?"

21. But they kept silent. So He took him and healed him and sent him away. He said to them, "Suppose one of you had a donkey or an ox fall into a well, will you not immediately pull it out on the Sabbath day?" And they had no answer to this.

Place of Honor

22. Jesus spoke a parable to the invited guests, for He noticed how they chose the places of honor at the table. He said to them, "When you are invited by someone to a wedding feast, do not take the place of honor, in case someone more distinguished than you has been invited, for then the person who invited you will come and say to you, 'Give this place to this person.' And then, in disgrace, you will take the lowest place. But, when you have been invited, go and sit down in the lowest place, so that, when the person who has invited you comes to say to you, 'Friend move up higher.' Then you will have honor in front of all who sit at the table with you. For everyone who exalts themselves will be humbled, and whoever humbles themselves will be exalted."

Unselfishness

23. Jesus said to the man who had invited Him, "Whenever you give a dinner or a banquet do not call your friends, or your brothers, or your kinsfolk or your rich neighbors, unless they also invite you in return and you receive a repayment. But when you give a feast, invite the poor, the maimed, the lame and the blind and then you will be blessed, because they cannot repay you. You will receive your repayment at the resurrection of the righteous."

The Great Banquet

24. When one of those who was sitting at the table with Jesus heard this, he said, "Blessed is the person who eats bread in the Kingdom of God."

25. But Jesus said to him, "There was a man who was giving a great banquet, and who invited many people to it. At the time of the banquet he sent his servants to say to those who had been invited, 'Come, because everything is now ready.' With one accord they all began to make excuses. The first said to him, 'I have bought a field, and I must go out and see it. Please have me excused.' Another said, 'I have bought five yoke of oxen, and I am on my way to try them out. Please have me excused.' Another said, 'I have married a wife, and, therefore, I cannot come.' So the servant came and told his master these things. The master of the house was angry, and said to his servant, 'Go out at once into the streets and lanes of the town and bring here the poor, and the maimed, and the blind and the lame.' The servant said, 'Sir, your orders have been carried out and there is still room.' So the master said to his servant, 'Go out to the roads and to the hedges, and compel them to come in, so that my house may be

filled. For I tell you that none of these people who were invited shall taste of my banquet."

THE COST OF DISCIPLESHIP
LUKE 14:25-33

January, 30 - Perea

26. Great crowds were on the way with Jesus. He turned and said to them, "If anyone comes to Me and does not think less of their father and mother, and spouse and children, and brothers and sisters, and even their own life too, they cannot be my disciple. Whoever does not carry their cross and come after Me cannot be My disciple.

27. "Which of you, if they want to build a tower, does not first sit down and calculate the cost, to see whether they have enough to finish it? Otherwise, when they have laid the foundation and are unable to complete the work, all who see them begin to ridicule them, saying, 'This person began to build and was unable to finish the job.' Or, what king when going to engage in battle with another king, does not first sit down and take counsel, whether they are able with ten thousand soldiers to meet the one who comes against them with twenty thousand? If the king finds they cannot, while they are still distant, the king sends an embassy and asks for terms of peace. So, therefore, every one of you who does not bid farewell to all their possessions cannot be My disciple."

CHAPTER 20
SECOND GROUP OF PARABLES

LUKE 15:1-7

January, 30 - Perea

Parable of the Lost Sheep

1. The tax-collectors and sinners were all coming near Jesus to listen to Him, and the Pharisees and Scribes were murmuring, saying, "This Man welcomes sinners and eats with them."

2. He spoke this parable to them saying, "What man of you, who has a hundred sheep, and has lost one of them, does not leave the ninety-nine in the open pasture and go after the one that is lost until he finds it? And when he finds it, rejoicing he lays it on his shoulders; and when he returns home he calls together his friends and neighbors, saying to them, 'Rejoice with me because I have found my sheep which was lost.' I tell you that in the same way there will be more joy in heaven over one sinner who repents than over ninety-nine righteous people who have no need of repentance."

PARABLE OF THE LOST COIN
LUKE 15:8-10

January, 30 - Perea

3. "Or what woman who has ten silver pieces, if she loses one piece, does not light a lamp and sweep the house and search carefully until she finds it? And when she has found it she calls together her

friends and neighbors, saying, 'Rejoice with me because I have found the silver piece which I lost.' In the same way, I tell you, there is joy in the presence of the angels of God over one sinner who repents.

PARABLE OF THE LOST SON
LUKE 15:11-32

January, 30 – Perea

4. And Jesus said, "There was a man who had two sons. The younger of them said to his father, 'Father, give me the share of the estate that comes to me.' So his father divided his wealth between them.

"Not many days later, the son gathered everything together and went away to a distant country, and there he squandered his wealth with loose living. When he had spent everything, a severe famine occurred in that country and he began to be in need. He went and hired himself out to a citizen of that country, and he sent him into his fields to feed pigs; and he had a desire to fill his stomach with the husks the pigs were eating; and no one gave anything to him.

5. "But when he came to his senses, he said, 'How many of my father's hired servants have more than enough bread, but I am dying here with hunger. I will get up and go to my father, and say to him, Father, I have sinned against Heaven and before you. I am no longer fit to be called your son. Make me as one of your hired servants.'"

6. "So he got up and went to his father. But while he was still a long way away his father saw him, and felt compassion and ran and put his arms around his neck and kissed him. The son said to him,

'Father, I have sinned against Heaven and in your sight. I am no longer worthy to be called your son.'

7. "But the father said to the servants, 'Quick! Bring out the best robe and put it one him; put a ring on his finger; put shoes on his feet; and bring the fatted calf and kill it and let us eat and rejoice, for this son was dead and has come back to life again; he was lost and has been found.' And they began to rejoice.

8. "Now his older son was in the field, and when he came near the house he heard the sound of music and dancing. He called one of the servants and asked what these things could mean. He said to him, 'Your brother has come, and your father has killed the fatted calf because he has gotten him back safe and sound.'

9. "He was angry and refused to come in. His father went out and urged him to come in. He answered his father, 'Look, I have served you so many years and I never neglected your order, and yet you never gave to me a kid that I might have a good time with my friends. But when this son of yours came, who consumed your wealth with harlots, you killed the fatted calf for him.'

10. "He said to him, 'Child, you are always with me and everything that is mine is yours. But we had to rejoice and be glad, for your brother was dead and has come back to life again; he was lost and has been found.'"

Dr. Patrick Pierce

PARABLE OF THE SHREWD STEWARD
LUKE 16:1-18

January, 30 - Perea

11. Jesus said to His disciples, "There was a rich man who had a steward, and he received information about the steward which reported that he was being wasteful of his goods. He called him, and said to him, 'What is this that I hear about you? Give an account of your stewardship, for you can no longer be steward.'

12. "The steward said to himself, 'What am I to do, since my master is taking the stewardship away from me? I have not the strength to dig, and I am ashamed to beg. I know what I will do, so that, when I am removed from my stewardship, they will receive me into their homes.'

13. "So he summoned each of the people who owed debts to his master. To the first he said, 'How much do you owe my master?'

"He said, 'A hundred measures of oil.'

"He said to him, 'Take your account and sit down and write quickly fifty.'

"Then he said to another, 'And how much do you owe?'

"He said, 'A hundred measures of wheat.'

"He said to him, 'Take your account and write eighty.'

14. "And the master praised the resourceful steward because he acted shrewdly; for the people of this world are shrewder in their own generation than the people of Light.

Honesty

15. "And I tell you, make friends for yourselves by means of your material possessions, even if they have been shrewdly acquired, so that when your wealth is gone they will receive you into a dwelling which lasts forever. Whoever is dishonest in a very little is also dishonest in much. If you have not shown yourself trustworthy in your ordinary business dealings about material things, who will trust you with great wealth? If you have not shown yourselves trustworthy in what belongs to someone else, who will give you what is your own?

Serve One Master

16. "No servant can serve two masters, for either one will be hated and the other loved, or one will be held to and the other despised. You cannot serve God and the world."

Things Detestable in God's Sight

17. When the Pharisees, who loved money, heard these things, they laughed at Jesus. So He said to them, "You are those who make yourselves look righteous before the world, but God knows your souls, because that which is exalted in the world is detestable in the sight of God."

The Law

18. "The Law and the prophets were proclaimed until John; since then the Good News of the Kingdom of God is proclaimed; and

everyone is trying to get their own way into it; but it is easier for Heaven and earth to pass away than for one stroke of the Law to become invalid."

Divorce

19. "Everyone who divorces their spouse by the world and marries another commits adultery, and whoever marries one who has been divorced from their spouse by the world commits adultery."

PARABLE OF LAZARUS AND THE RICH MAN
LUKE 16:19-31

January, 30 - Perea

20. "There was a rich man who always dressed in purple and fine linen, and who feasted in luxury every day. A poor man, called Lazarus, was laid at his gate. He was covered with sores, and he desired to be fed with the crumbs which fell from the rich man's table; besides, even the dogs would come and lick his sores.

21. "Now the poor man died, and he was carried by the angels to the bosom of Abraham and the rich man died also and was buried. And in Hell, being in torture, he lifted up his eyes, and from far away he saw Abraham, and Lazarus in his personal care. He called out, 'Father Abraham, have mercy on me, and send Lazarus to me that he may dip the tip of his finger in water and cool my tongue, because I am in agony in this fire.'

22. "But Abraham said, 'Child, remember that you received in full your good things in your life-time, just as Lazarus received bad things. Now he is comforted, and you are in agony. And,

besides this, between you and us is a great fixed gulf, so that those who wish to pass from here to you cannot do so, nor can any cross from there to us.'

23. "He said, 'Then, I beg you, father, to send him to my father's house, for I have five brothers, that he may warn them so they may not come to this place of torment also.'

"But Abraham said, 'They have Moses and the prophets. Let them listen to them.'

24. "He said, 'No, father Abraham; but if someone goes to them from the dead, they will repent.'

"But he said to them, 'If they will not listen to Moses and the prophets, neither will they be persuaded if someone rises from the dead.'"

CHAPTER 21
RAISING LAZARUS

JESUS' TEACHINGS
LUKE 17:1-10

January, 30 - Perea

Stumbling Blocks

1. Jesus said to His disciples, "It is inevitable that stumbling blocks should come; but woe to them through whom they do come! It would be better for them if a millstone were hung around their necks and they were thrown into the sea rather than they should cause one of these little ones to stumble.

Forgiveness

2. "Be on your guard. If one of God's children sins, reprove them; and if they repent, forgive them. Even if they sin against you seven times in the day, and if seven times they turn to you, saying, 'I repent,' forgive them."

Faith Like a Mustard Seed

3. The apostles said to the Lord, "Increase our faith!"

The Lord said, "If you have faith like a mustard seed, you would say to this mulberry tree, 'Be rooted up and be planted in the sea,' and it would obey you."

Duty

4. "But which of you has a servant plowing or watching the flock, and the slave comes in from the field, will he say to him, 'Come at once and take your place at the table'; or rather, will he not say to him, 'Prepare something for me to eat, and clothe yourself and serve me, until I eat and drink, and after that you shall eat and drink'? Does he thank a servant because he had done what he was ordered to do? So, you too, when you have done everything you were ordered to do, say, 'We are unworthy servants. We have done what was our duty to do.'"

RAISING LAZARUS
JOHN 11:1-46

January, 30 - Perea to Bethany

Lazarus' Illness Reported

5. There was a man, Lazarus of Bethany, the village where Mary and her sister Martha lived, who was ill. It was Mary who had anointed the Lord with perfumed ointment, and wiped His feet with her hair, and it was her brother Lazarus who was ill.

So the sisters sent a message to Jesus saying, "Lord, see the one You love is ill!"

6. But when Jesus heard the message, He said, "This illness is not going to be fatal, but it has happened for the glory of God, so that Emmanuel may be glorified by it." Jesus loved Martha and her sister and Lazarus.

Disciples Fear Return

7. Now, when Jesus heard that Lazarus was ill, He stayed where He was for two days. Then after that He said to His disciples, "Let us go to Judea again."

His disciples said to Him, "Teacher, the Jews were trying to find a way to stone You, and You are going back there?"

8. Jesus answered, "Are there not twelve hours in the day? If anyone walks in the day-time, they do not stumble because they have the light of this world. But if they walk in the night-time, they do stumble because the light is not in them."

9. Jesus said these things, and then He went on to say, "Our friend Lazarus is sleeping, but I am going to wake him up."

The disciples said to Him, "Lord, if he is sleeping he will recover."

10. Jesus had spoken about his death, but they thought He was speaking about natural sleep. So Jesus then said to them plainly, "Lazarus has died, and for your sakes, I am glad that I was not there so that you may believe, let us go to him."

Because of this Thomas, who was called Didymus, said, "Let us go also that we may die with him."

Jesus Talks with Martha

11. So, when Jesus came, He found that Lazarus had already been in the tomb for four days. Bethany was near Jerusalem, less than two miles away, and many of the Jews had gone to Martha and Mary to comfort them about their brother.

12. So when Martha heard that Jesus was coming, she went to meet Him, but Mary still sat in the house. So Martha said to Jesus, "Lord, if You had been here, my brother would not have died. And even as things are now, I know that whatever You ask of God, God will give You."

13. Jesus said to her, "Your brother will rise again."

Martha said to Him, "I know that he will rise at the resurrection on the last day."

14. Jesus said to her, "I am the Resurrection and the Life. Whoever believes in Me will live even if they have died; and everyone who lives and believes in Me shall never die. Do you believe this?"
She said to Him, "Yes Lord, I have believed that You are God's Anointed One, Emmanuel, the One Who is to come into this world."

15. When Martha had said this, she went away and called Mary her sister. Without letting the rest of the people know, she said to her, "The Teacher has arrived and is calling for you."

Jesus Talks with Mary

16. When she heard this, she rose quickly and began to go to Him. Jesus had not yet come into the village, but He was still in the place where Martha met Him. So when the Jews, who were in the house with Mary, consoling her, saw her rise quickly and go out, they followed her, for they thought that she was going back to the tomb to weep there.

17. When Mary came to where Jesus was, when she saw Him, she fell at His feet saying to Him, "Lord, if You had been here, my brother would not have died."

When Jesus saw her weeping, and the Jews who had come with her also weeping, He was deeply moved in spirit and was deeply troubled.

18. Jesus said to them, "Where have you laid him?"

They said to Him, "Lord, come and see."

Jesus wept. So the Jews said, "Look how He loved him!" Some of them said, "Could not this Man who opened the eyes of the blind have kept this man from dying also?"

Lazarus Raised

19. Again Jesus being deeply moved within went to the tomb. It was a cave; and a stone was lying against it. Jesus said, "Take away the stone."

Martha, the dead man's sister, said to Him, "Lord, by this time the stench of death is on him, for he has been in the tomb for four days."

20. Jesus said to her, "Did I not tell you that, if you believe, you will see the glory of God?" So they took the stone away.

Jesus lifted up His eyes and said, "Almighty God, I thank You that You have heard Me. I knew that You always hear Me. But I said this because of the crowd standing around, that they may believe that You sent Me." When He had said this, He cried with a loud voice, "Lazarus, come out!"

21. The man who had been dead came out, bound hand and foot in grave wrappings, and with his face wrapped with a cloth. Jesus said to them, "Unwrap him and let him go!"

Many of the Jews who had come to visit Mary and had seen what He did, believed in Him, but some of them went to tell the Pharisees what Jesus had done.

COUNCIL PLOTS AGAINST JESUS
JOHN 11:47-54

February, 30 - Jerusalem

22. Therefore, the Chief Priests and Pharisees assembled the Sanhedrin council and said, "What are we going to do, because this Man does many signs? If we leave Him alone like this, all will believe in Him, and the Romans will come and will take away our place and our nation."

23. But one of them, Caiaphas, who was High Priest that year, said to them, "You know nothing at all, nor do you take into account that it is better for you that one man should die for the people, rather than the whole nation should perish." It was not he who was responsible for what he said; but, since he was High Priest for that year, he prophesied that Jesus was going to die for the nation, and not only for the nation, but that the scattered children of God should be gathered into one.

24. From that day they planned together to kill Him. So Jesus walked no longer openly among the Jews, but He went away from them to a place near the wilderness, to a town called Ephraim, and He stayed there with His disciples.

CHAPTER 22
FINAL JOURNEY TO JERUSALEM

LUKE 17:11-37

March, 30 - Border of Samaria

Ten Lepers

1. When Jesus was on the way to Jerusalem, He was going between Samaria and Galilee; and as He entered a village, ten lepers, who stood at a distance, met Him. They raised their voices and said, "Jesus, Master, have mercy on us."

2. When He saw them, He said, "Go, and show yourselves to the priests."

And as they went they were cleansed. Now one of them when he saw that he had been healed, turned back, glorifying God with a loud voice. He fell on his face at Jesus' feet giving Him thanks. And he was a Samaritan.

3. Jesus said, "Were there not ten cleansed? But the nine, where are they? Were none found to turn back and give glory to God except this foreigner?"

And He said to him, "Rise and go! Your faith has made you well."

Coming of the Kingdom of God

4. When Jesus was asked by the Pharisees when the Kingdom of God was coming, He answered them, "The Kingdom of God does not come with signs that you can watch for; nor will they say, 'Look here!' or 'Look there!' For behold, the Kingdom of God is within you."

5. He said to His disciples, "Days will come when you will long to see one of the days of Emmanuel and you will not see it. And they will say to you, 'Look there! Look here!' Do not depart, and do not follow them. For, as the flashing lightening lights up the sky from one side to another, so shall be Emmanuel in that day. But first Emmanuel must suffer many things and be rejected by this generation.

6. "And just as it happened in the days of Noah, so it will be in the days of Emmanuel. They were eating, they were drinking, they were marrying, they were being given in marriage, until the day that Noah entered the ark and the flood came and destroyed them all.

7. "In the same way, so it was in the days of Lot. They were eating, they were drinking, they were buying, they were selling, they were planting, they were building, but on the day that Lot went out of Sodom, fire and brimstone rained from heaven and destroyed them all.

8. "It will the just the same on the day that Emmanuel is revealed. On that day, if anyone is on the housetop, with goods in the house, do not come down to take them. In the same way, if anyone is in the field, do not turn back. Remember Lot's wife! Whoever seeks to gain their life will lose it, but whoever loses it will save it. This is the truth I tell you, on that night there will be two in one bed, one will be

taken and the other will be left. There will be two working together at the same place, one will be taken and the other left."

9. The disciples interrupted Him, "Where. Lord?"

He said to them, "Where the body is, there the vultures will be gathered."

THE PERSISTENT WIDOW
LUKE 18:1-8

March, 30 - Galilee

10. Now Jesus told them a parable to show that they ought to always pray and not to lose heart. "There was a judge," He said, "in a town who neither feared God nor respected people. And there was a widow in the same town who kept coming to him saying, 'I want justice from you against my adversary.'

11. "For some time he refused, but afterwards he said to himself, 'Even though I neither fear God nor respect people, because she continually bothers me, I will see that justice is done this widow, or by her constant coming she exhausts me.'"

12. The Lord said, "Listen to what the unrighteous judge said. Now shall God not bring about justice for God's own chosen ones who cry to God day and night, and will God delay long over them? But when Emmanuel comes, will God find faith on earth?"

THE PHARISEE AND TAX COLLECTOR
LUKE 18:9-14

March, 30 - Galilee

13. Jesus spoke this parable to some who trusted in themselves that they were righteous and who despised others.

"Two went up to the Temple to pray, one was a Pharisee, and the other a tax-collector. The Pharisee stood and prayed thus with himself, 'O God, I thank You that I am not like other people, thieves, unjust, adulterers, or even as this tax-collector. I fast twice a week. I give tithes of all that I get.'

14. "The tax-collector stood some distance away, and would not lift even his eyes to heaven, and was beating his chest and said, 'O God, be merciful to me, a sinner.'

"I tell you, this one went down to his house justified rather than the other, because everyone who exalts themselves will be humbled, but whoever humbles themselves will be exalted."

TEACHING ON DIVORCE
MATTHEW 19:1-12; MARK 10:1-12

March, 30 - Through Perea

15. When Jesus had finished these words, He left Galilee, and came into a region of Judea on the other side of the Jordan. Many crowds followed Him, and He healed them there and taught them as was His custom.

16. Pharisees came to Him, to test Him. They asked, "Is it lawful for a person to divorce their spouse for any reason?"

He answered, "Have you not read that from the beginning the Creator made them male and female, and said, 'For this reason a person shall leave their father and mother, and be united to their spouse, and the two shall become one flesh?' They are no longer two, but one flesh. Therefore, what God has joined together, let no person separate. Only God can separate what God has joined together."

17. They said to Him, "Why, then, did Moses command that a man give his wife a certificate of divorce, and send her away?"

He said to them, "It was because of the hardness of your heart that Moses allowed you to divorce your spouses; but from the beginning that was not the way it was intended."

18. In the house His disciples again asked Him about this. He said to them, "I tell you that whoever divorces their spouse, except on the ground on marital unfaithfulness, and marries another, commits adultery; and whoever marries the one who has been divorced commits adultery."

19. His disciples said to Him, "If this is the only reason for divorce between a man and wife, it is better not to marry."

He replied to them, "Not everyone can accept this saying, but only those to whom it has been given. There are eunuchs who were born so from their mothers' womb; and there are eunuchs who have been made eunuchs by others; and there are others who have renounced marriage for the sake of the Kingdom of Heaven. Let whoever is able to accept this saying, accept it."

JESUS BLESSES CHILDREN
MATTHEW 19:13-15; MARK 10:13-16; LUKE 18:15-17

March, 30 - Perea

20. People were bringing little children and babies to Jesus that He might lay His hands on them and pray for them. When the disciples saw it they spoke sternly to them.

21. When Jesus saw what they were doing He was upset and said to them, "Let the little children come to Me, and don't try to stop them, for the Kingdom of God belongs to such as these. This is the truth I tell you, whoever does not receive the Kingdom of God as a little child will not enter into it."

22. And He took the children up in His arms and blessed them. After He had put His hands on them, He left there.

The Gospel of Jesus Christ

Dr. Patrick Pierce

THE RICH RULER
MATTHEW 19:16-30; 20:1-16; MARK 10:17-31; LUKE 18:18-30

March, 30 - Perea

The Rich Ruler

23. As Jesus was going along the road, a ruler came to Him and fell on his knees at His feet and asked Him, "Good Teacher, what good thing must I do to inherit eternal life?"

24. Jesus said to him, "Why do you call Me good? There is no one good, except God alone. If you wish to enter into life, keep the commandments."

He said to Him, "What commandments?"

25. Jesus said, "You know the commandments. You must not commit adultery, you must not murder, you must not bear false witness, you must not defraud anyone, you must honor your father and mother, and, you must love your neighbor as yourself."

And the young man said, "Teacher, I have kept all of these things from my youth. What am I still lacking?"

26. When Jesus looked at him He loved him, and when He heard that, He said to him, "You still lack one thing. If you wish to be complete, go, sell all your possessions, and give to the poor, and you will have treasure in heaven. Then come, follow Me!"

When the young man heard these things he was very sad, and he went away in sorrow, because he had great wealth.

Love of Possessions

27. When Jesus saw him He looked around and said to His disciples, "It is hard for the wealthy to enter into the Kingdom of God!"

His disciples were amazed at His words. Jesus repeated, "Children, how difficult it is for those who trust in wealth to enter into the Kingdom of God! Again I say to you, it is easier for a camel to pass through the Eye of a Needle Gate than for a rich person to enter into the Kingdom of God."

28. When the disciples heard this, they were more amazed and said, "What wealthy person then can be saved?"
Jesus looked at them and said, "With people it is impossible, but the things which are impossible with people are possible with God."

29. Then Peter said to Him, "Look, we have left all of our possessions and have followed You and became Your followers. What then will there be for us?"

Jesus said to them, "This is the truth I tell you, when all things are renewed, and when Emmanuel shall sit on the throne of God's glory, you, who have followed Me, will also sit on twelve thrones, judging the twelve tribes of Israel. Anyone who has left houses, or brothers or sisters or mother or father or children or lands for My sake and for the sake of the Good News, will receive a hundred times as much in this present time, homes and brothers and sisters and mothers and children and lands along with persecutions, and in the age to come, eternal life. But many who are first will be last, and many who are last will be first.

Workers in the Vineyard

30. "For the Kingdom of Heaven is like a landowner who went out early in the morning to hire workers for his vineyard. When he had come to an agreement with them that they would work for a denarius a day, he sent them into his vineyard. He went out again about nine o'clock in the morning, and saw others standing idle in the marketplace. He said to them, 'You go also into the vineyard, and I will pay you whatever is right.' And they went. He went out again about twelve o'clock midday, and about three o'clock in the afternoon, and did the same. And about five o'clock in the evening he went out and found others standing there and said to them, 'Why are you standing here the whole day idle?' They said to him, 'Because no one has hired us.' He said to them, 'you go also to the vineyard.'

31. "When evening came, the master of the vineyard said to the steward, 'Call the workers, and give them their pay, beginning from the last and to the first.' So, when those who had been hired about five o'clock in the afternoon came, they each received a denarius, and those who came first thought that they would receive more; but they also received a denarius each.

32. "When they received it, they complained to the landowner, saying, 'These last have only worked for one hour, and you have made them equal to us, who have borne the burden and the scorching heat of the day.'

33. "He answered and said to one of them, 'Friend, I am doing you no wrong. Didn't you agree with me to work for a denarius? Take what is yours and go your way! It is my will to give to this last person the same as you. Can't I do what I want with what is my own? Or, are you envious because I am generous?' Even so the last shall be first, and the first shall be last."

CHAPTER 23
FORETELLING HIS DEATH

MATTHEW 20:17-28; MARK 10:32-45; LUKE 18:31-34

March, 30 - Judea

Death Foretold

1. They were on their way on the road up to Jerusalem, with Jesus walking ahead of them. They were astonished, and as they followed Him they were afraid. Jesus once again took the twelve aside, and told them what was going to happen to Him.

2. "Listen!" He said, "We are going up to Jerusalem, and everything that was written through the prophets about Emmanuel will be fulfilled. Emmanuel will be handed over to the Chief Priests and the Scribes, the experts in the law, and they will condemn Him to death, and they will hand Him over to the Gentiles, and they will mock Him and spit on Him, and they will flog Him, and they will kill Him. And after three days He will rise again." But they did not understand any of this; the meaning was hidden from them; and they did not know what He was talking about.

James and John's Request

3. At that time the mother of Zebedee's sons, James and John, came to Jesus with her sons, kneeling before Him, asked a favor of Him. "Teacher," they said, "we want You to do for us whatever we ask of You."

4. "What do you want Me to do for you?" He said to them.

They said to Him, "Speak the word and grant to us that, in Your glory, we may sit one on Your right hand and one on Your left, in Your Kingdom."

5. Jesus answered, "You do not know what you are asking. Can you drink the cup I drink? Or can you be baptized with the baptism with which I am baptized?"
"We can," they said to Him.

6. Jesus said to them, "You will drink the cup I drink and be baptized also with the baptism I am baptized, but to sit on My right hand and My left is not Mine to give, but these places belong to those for whom they have been prepared by Almighty God."

To be Great

7. When the ten heard about this, they became angry about the action of James and John. Jesus called them to Him, and said, "You know that those who are regarded as good enough to rule over the Gentiles lord it over them, and their high officials exercise authority over them. It is not and shall not be so with you, but whoever wants to prove themselves great among you must first be your servant; and whoever wishes to have the highest place will be the servant of all. Just as Emmanuel did not come to be served but to serve, and to give His life as a ransom for many."

BARTIMAEUS AND COMPANION HEALED
MATTHEW 20:29-34; MARK 10:46-52; LUKE 18:35-43

March, 30 - Jericho

8. They went to Jericho and as Jesus was passing through Jericho, on His way out of the city, His disciples and a great crowd was with Him. Bartimaeus, the son of Timaeus, a blind beggar and his blind companion, were sitting by the roadside begging. When they heard the crowd passing through he asked what was happening. They told them, "Jesus of Nazareth is passing by."

9. They shouted out, "Jesus, Son of David, have mercy on us!" Those who were going on in front of the crowd rebuked them and told them to be quiet, but they shouted out all the more, "Son of David! Have mercy on us!"

10. Jesus stopped and said, "Call them here!"

They called the blind man. "Courage!" they said to them. "Get up! He is calling you!" They threw off their cloaks and jumped up and came to Jesus.

11. Jesus said to them, "What do you want Me to do for you?"

The blind men said to Him, "Master, Teacher! Our prayer is that we might see again."

12. Jesus felt deep compassion, and touched their eyes and said to them, "Go! Receive your sight; your faith has made you well." And

immediately they received their sight and followed Him glorifying God, and when the people saw it, they all praised God.

PARABLE OF MONEY (Minas)
LUKE 19:1-28

March, 30 - Jericho

Zachaeus

13. Jesus entered Jericho and was passing through it. And look, there was man called by the name Zachaeus, and he was commissioner of taxes, and he was rich. He was trying to see who Jesus was, and he could not for the crowd, because he was short in height. So he ran on ahead and climbed up into a sycamore tree, for He was to pass that way.

14. When Jesus came to the place He looked up and said to him, "Zachaeus! Hurry and come down! For this very day I must stay at your house."

So he hurried and came down, and welcomed Him gladly; and when they saw it, they all murmured, "He has gone to be the guest of a man who is a sinner."

15. Zachaeus stood and said to the Lord, "Listen Sir, half of my goods, Lord, I will give to the poor and, if I have taken anything from any person by fraud, I will give it back to them four times as much."

Jesus said to him, "Today salvation has come to this house, because he also is a son of Abraham; for Emmanuel came to save that which was lost."

Money Usage - Ten Minas

16. As they were listening to these things, Jesus went on to tell them a parable because He was near Jerusalem, and they were thinking that the Kingdom of God was going to appear immediately. So He said, "There was a nobleman who went into a distant country to receive a kingdom for himself and then return. He called ten of his servants and gave them $10,000 each and said to them, 'Do business with these until I come.' But his citizens hated him, and they sent an embassy after him, saying, 'We do not want this man to be king over us.'

17. "When he had received the kingdom and had returned, he ordered that the servants to whom he had given money be called to him so he might know what they had made by the business they had done. The first came and said, 'Sir, your $10,000 have made $10,000 more. So he said, 'Well done, good servant! Because you have shown yourself faithful in a little thing, you shall have authority over ten cities.' The second came and said to him also, 'Sir, your $10,000 have made $5,000. And he said also, 'You, too, are to be over five cities.' And then another came to him and said, 'Sir, here is your $10,000, which I was keeping laid away in a towel, for I was afraid of you, because I know that you are an exacting man. You take what you did not put down, and you reap what you did not sow.'

18. He said, 'By your own words I judge you, you worthless servant. You knew that I am an exacting man, taking up what I did not put down, and reaping what I did not sow. Then you ought to have given my money to the bankers, so that when I came, I would have received it plus interest.' He said to those standing by, 'Take the $10,000 away and give it to the one who has $10,000.'

They said to him, 'Sir, he has ten minas.'

"I tell you, that to everyone who has it will be given; but from the one who does not have, even what they have will be taken away. But these enemies of mine who did not wish me to reign over them, bring them here and slay them in my presence."

When Jesus had said these things, He went on ahead on the way up to Jerusalem.

Minas and Talents were amounts of money. A Talent was equal to about one-fourth of a person's annual wages and a Mina was equal to about $1/20^{th}$ of a Talent. The Parable was about money and possessions so one Mina was set to be equal to $1,000 for illustration purposes. Jesus was clearly talking about money and our valuable possessions.

JESUS ARRIVES AT BETHANY
MATTHEW 26:6-13; MARK 14:3-9; JOHN 11:55-57; 12:1-11

Friday, March 31, 30 - Bethany

Jesus Goes to Bethany

19. When the Passover Feast of the Jews was near; many from the country areas went up to Jerusalem before the Passover Feast to cleanse themselves. They were looking for Jesus; and as they stood in the Temple areas, they talked to each other saying, "What do you think? Surely it is impossible that He would come to the Feast?" Now the Chief Priests and Pharisees had given orders that if anyone knew where Jesus was, they should report it to them, so they might seize Him.

20. Now six days before the Passover Jesus went to Bethany, where Lazarus was whom He raised from the dead. So they made a meal there in the house of Simon the leper in Jesus' honor. Martha was serving while Lazarus was one of those who reclined at the table with Him.

Mary Anoints Jesus

21. Now Mary came to Him with an alabaster phial with a pound of very precious genuine spikenard ointment. She opened the phial and poured it over His head and feet as He reclined at the table, and anointed Jesus' feet, and wiped His feet with her hair. The house was filled with the fragrance of the ointment.

22. When the disciples saw this they were angry. Judas Iscariot, one to His disciples, the one who was going to betray Him said, "Why was this ointment not sold for a year's wages and the money given to the poor?" He said this, not that he cared about the poor, but because he was a thief and had charge of the money-box, and took from what was put into it.

23. When Jesus knew what they were saying, He said to them, "Let her be! Why do you trouble her? It is a lovely thing that she has done to Me. You have always got the poor with you, and you can do something for them any time you like, but you have not always got Me. She has done what she could. She has taken My body and anointed it beforehand against My burial. This is the truth I tell you, wherever the Good News shall be proclaimed throughout the whole world, the story of what she has done will be told, so that she will always be remembered."

Plot to Kill Lazarus

24. The mob of Jews knew that Jesus was there; and they came, not only because of Jesus, but to see Lazarus, whom He had raised from the dead. The Chief Priests plotted to kill Lazarus too, because many of the Jews were leaving them because of him and were believing in Jesus.

CHAPTER 24
JESUS' TRIUMPHAL ENTRY

MATTHEW 21:1-11; 14-17; MARK 11:1-11;
LUKE 19:29-44; JOHN 12:12-19

Sunday, April 2, 30 - Jerusalem

Jesus Sends for Donkey

1. On the next day when they had come near Jerusalem, and had come to Bethphage and Bethany, which is near the mount called the Mount of Olives, Jesus sent two of His disciples ahead, and said to them, "Go into the village ahead of you, and as soon as you enter it, you will find a donkey tied up, and a colt with her which no person has ever ridden. And if anyone asks you, 'Why are you doing this?' say, 'The Lord needs it,' and immediately he will send it."

2. This was done that it might be fulfilled that which was spoken through the prophet, when he said,
> "Say to the daughter of Zion,
> 'Look, your king comes to you,
> gentle and riding on a donkey,
> a colt, the foal of a donkey.'"

3. So the disciples went, and they carried out Jesus' orders. They found the colt tied up outside a door, on the open street, exactly as He had told them. And as they were untying the colt, it's owners said to them, "What are you doing untying this colt?"

4. They said to them what Jesus had told them to say, "The Lord needs it," and they let them go. They brought the donkey and colt to Jesus, and put their coats over it, and mounted Jesus on it.

Triumphant Entry

5. A great crowd that was coming to the Feast heard that Jesus was on His way to Jerusalem. The very large crowd spread their coats on the road, others cut branches from palm trees in the field and went out to meet Him and spread them on the road. When He was drawing near, at the descent from the Mount of Olives, the whole crowd of disciples began to rejoice, and to praise God with shouts for all the miracles they had seen. And those who were going before and those who were following shouted,

"Hosanna, to the Son of David!
Blessed in the name of the Lord
   is He who comes,
He who is the King of Israel!

Hosanna in the highest!
Blessed is the coming of the kingdom
   of our father David!

Send them salvation
   from the heights of Heaven!"

6. At first the disciples did not understand the significance of these things; but when Jesus was glorified then they remembered that these things were written about Him, and that they had done these

things to Him. The crowd who was with Him testified that He had called Lazarus from the tomb and had raised him from among the dead. It was because they had heard that He had performed this miracle that the crowd went out to meet Him. So the Pharisees said to each other, "You can see that all the steps you have taken have been completely ineffective. See! The whole world has gone off after Him!"

7. Some of the Pharisees who were in the crowd said to Him, "Teacher, rebuke your disciples."

He answered, "I tell you, if these keep silent, the stones will cry out."

Destruction of Jerusalem Foretold

8. When Jesus had come near, and when He saw the city, He wept over it and said, "Would that, even today you had known the things which would give you peace! But as it is, they are hidden from your eyes; for days will come upon you when your enemies will cast a rampart around you, and will surround you, and will hem you in on every side, and they will level you and your children within you to the ground, and they will not leave one stone upon another, because you did not recognize the day when God visited you."

Jesus' Popularity

9. As He entered Jerusalem, the whole city was stirred. "Who is this?" they asked; and the crowds said, "This is the prophet, Jesus, who comes from Nazareth in Galilee."

And Jesus entered into the areas of the Temple of God and the blind and the lame came to Him in the Temple and He healed them.

10. When the Chief Priests and Scribes saw the things that He did, and the children shouting in the Temple, "Hosanna to the Son of David!" They were angry. "Do you hear what these are saying?" They said.

11. Jesus said to them, "Yes! Have you never read, 'Out of the mouths of babes and sucklings you have perfect praise'?"

After He had looked around at everything, since it was now late, He went out of the city to Bethany with the Twelve, and stayed there.

TEMPLE CLEANSED
MATTHEW 21:12,13,18,19; MARK 11:12-18; LUKE 19:45-48

Monday, April 3, 30 - Jerusalem

Barren Fig Tree

12. On the next day, as they were leaving Bethany, Jesus was returning to the city early in the morning and He was hungry. From a distance He saw a fig tree in leaf, and He went to it to see if He would find anything on it. When He came to it He found nothing except leaves, for it was not yet the season for figs. He said to it, "Let no fruit come from you anymore!" And the disciples heard Him say it, and immediately the fig tree withered away.

Temple Cleansed

13. They came into Jerusalem, and when Jesus had come into the sacred areas of the Temple of God, He began to cast out those who sold and bought there. He overturned the tables of the money-changers and the seats of those who sold doves, and He would not allow anyone to carry their merchandise through the sacred areas.

14. His teaching and speaking was, "It is written, 'My house shall be a house of prayer for all nations, but you have made it a den of robbers.'"

15. He taught daily in the Temple; the Chief Priests and the Scribes sought a way to kill Him, as did the rulers of the nation, for they were afraid of Him. They could not think of anything they could do to Him, for all the people, as they listened to Him, did not want to miss a word, for the whole crowd was amazed at His teaching.

FIG TREE WITHERED
MATTHEW 21:20-22; MARK 11:19-26; LUKE 21:37, 38

Tuesday, April 4, 30 - Road to Jerusalem

16. During the days Jesus was teaching in the Temple, but at night He went out of the city and stayed on the mount called the Mount of Olives; and all the people came early in the morning to listen to Him in the Temple.

17. When they were going along the road early in the morning, they saw the fig-tree withered from the roots. Peter remembered what Jesus had said the day before and said, "Teacher! Look! The fig tree that your cursed has withered away!"

18. Jesus answered them, "This is the truth I tell you, if you have faith, and if you do not doubt and believe what you say is happening, not only will you do what was done to the fig tree, but you will say to this mountain, 'Be lifted up and cast into the sea,' it will be done for you, and will happen. So then I tell you, believe that you have received everything for which you pray, and it will be done for you. And whenever you stand praying, if you have anything against anyone, forgive it, so that Almighty God who is in Heaven may forgive you your trespasses."

AUTHORITY QUESTIONED
MATTHEW 21:23-27; MARK 11:27-33; LUKE 20:1-8

Tuesday, April 4, 30 - Temple in Jerusalem

19. Once again they came to Jerusalem, and when Jesus had come into the Temple areas and was walking in the Temple, teaching the people and telling them the Good News, the Chief Priests and Scribes with the elders came up and said to Him, "Tell us, by what authority do You do these things? And who gave You this authority?"

20. Jesus answered them, "I will ask you one question, and if you give Me an answer to it, I too will tell you by what authority I do these things. The baptism of John, was it from Heaven, or, was it from the world? Answer Me!"

21. They discussed the matter among themselves. They said, "If we say, 'From Heaven,' He will say, 'Why did you not believe in it?' But, if we say, 'From the world,' we fear all the people will stone us," for all truly held that John was a prophet. So they answered Jesus, "We do not know."

So Jesus said to them, "Neither do I tell you by what authority I do these things."

THE THIRD GROUP OF PARABLES
MATTHEW 21:28-32

Tuesday - Temple

The Parable of the Two Sons

22. And He began to speak to the people in parables.

Jesus said, "What do you think? A man had two children. He went to the first and said, 'Child, go and work in my vineyard today.' He answered, 'I will not.' But afterwards the child changed its mind and went. He went to the second and spoke to that child the same way. The child answered, 'Certainly, sir.' But the child did not go. Which of these two did the will of the father?"

"The first," they answered.

23. Jesus said to them, "This is the truth I tell you, the tax-collectors and harlots go into the Kingdom of Heaven before you. For John came to you to show you the way of righteousness, and you did not believe him; but the tax-gatherers and harlots believed him. And when you saw this, you did not even repent then, and believe in Him."

Dr. Patrick Pierce

PARABLE OF THE VINEYARD
MATTHEW 21:33-41; MARK 12:1-9; LUKE 20:9-16

Tuesday - Temple

24. Jesus began to speak this parable to the people. "Listen to another parable. There was a landowner who planted a vineyard, and surrounded it with a hedge, and dug a wine press in it, and built a tower, and rented it out to cultivators and went away for a long time.

25. "When the time of the harvest had come, he sent a servant to the cultivators that he might receive from the cultivators his share of the fruits of the vineyard. They seized him and beat him and sent him away empty handed. Again he sent another servant to them. They wounded him in the head and treated him shamefully. He sent yet another and they killed him. So they treated many others, beating some of them, and killed others, and stoned another of them.

26. "The owner of the vineyard said, 'What am I to do? I will send my beloved son. They will respect him.' But when the cultivators saw the son, they said to themselves, 'This is the heir. Come, let us kill him, and let us take the inheritance.' So they took him and killed him and threw him out of the vineyard. When the owner of the vineyard comes, what will he do to these cultivators? He will come and he will destroy the cultivators and he will give the vineyard to others who will pay him the fruits at the correct time."

And when they heard it, they said, "May it never be!"

THE REJECTED STONE
MATTHEW 21:42-46; MARK 12:10-12; LUKE 20:17-19; JOHN 20:17-19

Tuesday - Temple

27. Jesus said to them, "Have you not read the passage in the scripture,

> 'The stone which the builders rejected,
>   this has become the capstone.
> This came from God,
>   and it is marvelous in our eyes'?

28. That is why I tell you that the Kingdom of God will be taken from you and will be given to the nation that produces its fruits. Everyone who falls against the stone will be broken; but if it falls on anyone, it crushes them as the wind blows the chaff away."

29. When the Chief Priests and the Pharisees heard His parables, they knew He was speaking about them. They tried to find a way to seize Him, but they were afraid of the crowds, for they regarded Him as a prophet. So they left Him alone and went away.

THE PARABLE OF THE WEDDING
MATTHEW 22:1-14

Tuesday - Temple

30. Jesus again answered them in parables, "The Kingdom of Heaven may be compared to a king who arranged a wedding for his son. He sent servants to summon those who had been invited to the

wedding, and they refused to come. He again sent other servants. 'Tell those who have been invited,' he said, 'look, I have my meal all prepared; my oxen and my specially fatted animals have been killed; and everything is ready. Come to the wedding.' But they disregarded the invitation and went away, one to his estate and another to his business. The rest seized the servants and treated them shamefully and killed them. The king was angry, and sent his armies, and destroyed those murderers and set fire to their city.

31. "Then he said to his servants, 'The wedding is ready. Those who have been invited are not worthy to come. Go, then, to the highways and invite all you may find to the wedding.' So the servants went out to the roads, and collected all whom they found, both bad and good; and the wedding was filled with guests.

32. "The king came in to see those who were sitting at the table, and he saw there a person who was not wearing a wedding garment. He said, 'Friend, how did you come here with no wedding garment?' The person was speechless. Then the king said to the attendants, 'Bind the person's hands and feet, and throw that one out into the outer darkness, there shall be weeping and gnashing of teeth there. For many are called, but few are chosen."

CHAPTER 25
JESUS QUESTIONED

JEWISH RULERS ASK ABOUT TAXES
MATTHEW 22:15-22; MARK 12:13-17; LUKE 20:20-26

Tuesday - Temple

1. Then the Pharisees came, and tried to form a plan to trap Him. They watched for an opportunity, and they sent spies of the Pharisees and Herodians, who pretended that they were genuinely concerned about the right thing to do, so that they might catch Jesus in something and be able to hand Him over to the power and authority of the governor. They came to Him and asked, "Teacher, we know that You are genuine, and that You do not allow Yourself to be influenced by anyone, for You do not pay regard to the outward appearance of people, and You teach the way of God in truth. Is it right to pay tax to Caesar or not? Are we to pay, or are we not to pay?"

2. Jesus knew well they were acting and was aware of their malice. "Hypocrites," He said, "why do you try to test Me? Bring me a denarius and let Me see it." So they brought Him one. He said to them, "Whose image and inscription is on it?"

"Caesar's." they replied.

3. Jesus said to them, "Give to Caesar what is Caesar's, and to God what is God's."

When they heard the answer, they were amazed at Him. There was nothing in His statement that they could catch Him with in the presence of the people. They had nothing to say and left Him.

SADDUCEES ASK ABOUT THE RESURRECTION
MATTHEW 22:23-33; MARK 12:18-27; LUKE 20:27-39

Tuesday - Temple

4. On the day some of the Sadducees, who say there is no resurrection, came to Him. They asked the following question of Him, "Teacher, Moses wrote the law for us that, 'If a man's brother dies and leaves behind him a wife, and does not have children the law is that the brother should take his wife, and should have children for his brother.' Now amongst us there were seven brothers. The first took a wife, and died, and had no children. The second took her, and he died, and left no children. The third did the same right on down to the seventh. Last of all, the woman died. At the resurrection whose wife will she be, for the seven had her as a wife?"

5. Jesus answered, "You are in error, because you do not know the Scriptures or the power of Almighty God. The sons of this age marry and are married. But those who are deemed worthy to obtain that future age and the resurrection from the dead, they neither marry nor are given in marriage. They cannot die any more, for they are like angels and they are children of God, and the resurrection.

6. "With regard to the resurrection of the dead, and the fact that they do rise, have you not read in the Book of Moses, in the passage about the bush, how God said to him, 'I am the God of Abraham, and the God of Isaac, and God of Jacob.' Now Almighty

God is God, not of the dead, but of the living; for to God all people are alive. You are very wrong."

When the crowds heard this answer, they were amazed at His teaching. Some of the Scribes said, "Teacher, you have spoken well."

THE GREATEST COMMANDMENT
MATTHEW 22:34-40; MARK 12:28-34; LUKE 20:40

Tuesday - Temple

7. When the Pharisees heard that He had silenced the Sadducees they gathered together. One of the experts in the Law, who had listened to the discussion, and who realized that Jesus had answered well, approached Him and asked Him a question as a test, "What commandment in the Law is the greatest?"

8. Jesus answered, "'The Lord your God is one Lord, and you must love the Lord your God with all your spirit, and all your soul, and all your mind, and all your strength.' And the second is like it, 'You must love your neighbor as yourself.' On these two commandments the whole Law and the prophets depend. There is no other commandment which is greater than these."

9. The expert in the Law said to Him, "Teacher, you have spoken wisely, because God is one, and there is no other except God, and to love God with all your spirit, and all your understanding, and all your strength, and to love your neighbor as yourself is better than all burnt-offerings and sacrifices."

10. When Jesus saw that he had answered wisely, He said to him, "You are not far from the Kingdom of God."

Dr. Patrick Pierce

JESUS' QUESTION NO ONE COULD ANSWER
MATTHEW 22:41-46; MARK 12:35-37; LUKE 20:41-44

Tuesday - Temple

11. When the Pharisees had come together while Jesus was teaching in the sacred areas, Jesus asked them a question, "What is your opinion about the Anointed One? Whose son is He?"

"David's son," they said.

12. Jesus said to them, "How can the experts in the Law say that God's Anointed One is the Son of David? David himself, moved by the Holy Spirit said, 'The Lord said to my Lord, sit at My right hand until I put your enemies under your feet.' David calls the Anointed One Lord, how is He his son?" And no one was able to give Him an answer. And from that day no one any longer dared to ask Him a question.

CHAPTER 26
JESUS' LAST PUBLIC TEACHINGS

MATTHEW 23:1-39; MARK 12:38-40; LUKE 20:45-47

Tuesday - Temple

Self-Righteousness

1. Then Jesus said to the crowd of people listening with pleasure to Him, and to His disciples, "Beware of the experts in the Law. The Scribes and Pharisees sit in Moses' seat. Therefore, do everything they tell you; but do not act as they act; for they speak, but they do not do. They bind burdens that are heavy and hard to bear, and place them on people's shoulders; but they themselves refuse to lift a finger to remove them.

2. "They perform all their actions to be seen by people. They broaden the prayer boxes worn on their arms; they wear oversized tassels; they like to walk around in flowing, long robes. They love the places of honor at meals, and the front seats in the synagogues, and like to be greeted in the market place, and to be called Rabbi by all. They devour widows' houses and pretend to offer long prayers.

Leaders

3. "You must not be called Rabbi; for you have only one teacher, and you are all brothers and sisters. Call no one upon earth god; you have one God, Almighty God in Heaven. Nor must you be called leaders; you have one leader, Christ. Whoever is greatest among

you will be your servant. Whoever will exalt themselves will be humbled; and whoever will humble themselves will be exalted.

Denunciation of Scribes and Pharisees

4. "But woe to you, Scribes and Pharisees, hypocrites, because you shut the door to the Kingdom of Heaven in people's faces! You yourselves are not going into it; nor do you allow those who are trying to get into it to enter in.

"Woe to you, Scribes and Pharisees, hypocrites, because you devour widow's houses, even while for a pretense you make long prayers; therefore, you shall receive greater condemnation.

"Woe to you, Scribes and Pharisees you travel over the sea and land to make one proselyte, and when that happens, you make them twice as much the child of Hell as yourselves!

5. "Woe to you, Scribes and Pharisees! Blind guides! You say, 'If any one swears by the Temple, it is nothing; but whoever swears by the gold of the Temple is bound by their oath.' Foolish ones and blind! Which is greater? The gold? Or the Temple which hallows the gold? You say, 'If anyone swears by the alter, it is nothing; but if anyone swears by the gift that is on it, they are bound by their oath.' Blind ones! Which is greater? The gift? Or the alter which hallows the gift? Therefore, whoever swears both by the alter and everything on it, and whoever swears by the Temple, swears by it, and by the God who inhabits it. And whoever swears by Heaven, swears by the throne of God, and by Almighty God who sits upon it.

6. "Woe to you, Scribes and Pharisees, hypocrites! For you tithe mint and dill and cumin, and neglect the weightier matters of the Law; justice and mercy and faithfulness. But these you should have done without neglecting the others. Blind guides who strain out a gnat and swallow a camel!

Outward Appearances

7. "Woe to you, Scribes and Pharisees, hypocrites! For you cleanse the outside of the cup and the plate, but inside they are full of robbery and self-indulgence. Blind Pharisees! Clean the inside of the cup and the plate first, so that the outside of it also may be clean.

8. "Woe to you, Scribes and Pharisees! For you are like whitewashed tombs, which look beautiful on the outside, but inside are full of the bones of dead people, and of all corruption. Even so you too outwardly look righteous to people, but inwardly you are full of hypocrisy and lawlessness.

Persecution Condemned

9. "Woe to you Scribes and Pharisees, hypocrites! For you build the tombs of the prophets, and adorn the memorials of the righteous, and say, 'If we had lived in the days of our ancestors, we would not have been partners with them in the murder of the prophets.' Consequently you witness against yourselves that you are the offspring of those who murdered the prophets. Fill up the measure of your ancestors. Serpents, brood of vipers, how are you to escape being condemned to Hell fire! For this reason, behold, I send you the prophets and the wise men and the Scribes. Some of them you will kill and crucify; and some of them you will scourge in your synagogues,

and pursue them with persecution from city to city, that on you there may fall the responsibility for all the righteous blood shed upon the earth, from the blood of righteous Abel, to the blood of Zacharias, the son of Barachios, whom you murdered between the Temple and the altar. This is the truth I tell you, the responsibility for all these crimes shall fall on this generation.

Jerusalem Lamented

10. "Jerusalem, Jerusalem, killer of prophets, stoner of those sent to you, how often have I wished to gather your children together, as a bird gathers her nestlings under her wings, and you refused. Behold, your house is left to you desolate, for I tell you, from now on you will not see Me until you say, 'Blessed is the One who comes in the name of the Lord.'"

THE WIDOW'S MITES
MARK 12:41-44; LUKE 21:1-4

Tuesday - Temple

11. When Jesus had sat down opposite the treasury, He was watching how the crowd put their money into the Temple treasury, and many rich people put in large amounts. But a poor widow came and put in two small copper coins which are worth about a penny. He called His disciples and said to them, "This is the truth I tell you, this poor widow has put in more than all the people who put money into the treasury, for all of them gave their contributions out of their abundance, but she, out of her poverty has put in everything she had to live on."

GREEKS SEE JESUS
JOHN 12:20-50

Tuesday - Temple

Purpose of Jesus' Death

12. There were some Greeks among those who were going up to worship at the feast. Now these came to Philip, who came from Bethsaida in Galilee, and made a request to him saying, "Sir, we wish to see Jesus." Philip went and told Andrew, and Andrew and Philip went and told Jesus.

13. Jesus answered them, "The hour has come that Emmanuel should be glorified. This is the truth I tell you, unless a grain of wheat falls into the ground and dies, it remains by itself alone; but if it dies, it bears much fruit. Whoever loves their life loses it; and whoever hates their life in this world will keep it to life eternal. If anyone serves Me, let them follow Me; and where I am, there will My servants also be. If anyone serves Me, Almighty God will honor them.

14. "Now, My soul is troubled. And what shall I say? 'Almighty God, rescue Me from this hour.' But it was for this purpose that I came to this hour. Almighty God, glorify Your name."

A voice came from Heaven, "I have both glorified It and I will glorify It again."

Jesus Foretells that He Will Draw All People to Him

15. So the crowd who were standing by, and who heard it, said that there had been thunder. Others said, "An angel spoke to Him."

Jesus answered, "It was not for My sake that this voice came, but for yours. Now is the judgment on this world. Now the ruler of this world will be cast out. And I, if I be lifted up from the earth, will draw all people to Myself." He said this to indicate by what kind of death He was going to die.

Walk in the Light

16. The crowd answered Him, "We have heard from the Law that God's Anointed One remains forever. And how can you say, 'Emmanuel must be lifted up'? Who is this Emmanuel?"

17. Jesus said to them, "For a little while longer the Light is among you. Walk while you have the Light, that the darkness may not overtake you. Whoever walks in the darkness does not know where they are going. While you have the Light, believe in the Light, that you may become the children of the Light."

Disbelief Fulfills Prophecy

18. When Jesus had said these things, He went away and hid Himself from them. Although He had done such great signs in their presence they did not believe Him. It happened this way that the word which Isaiah the prophet spoke might be fulfilled, "Lord, who has believed our report? And to whom has the arm of the Lord been revealed?" It was for this reason that they could not believe, because Isaiah said again;

> 'God has blinded their eyes,
> and God has hardened their heart,
> so that they may not see with their eyes

and understand with their heart
and be converted,
and I will heal them.'

Isaiah said these things because he saw God's glory and spoke about God. Nevertheless many of the rulers believed in Him, but because of the Pharisees they did not publicly confess their faith for they did not wish to be put out of the synagogue for they loved the approval of people rather than the glory of God.

Final Public Appeal

19. Jesus cried out and said, "Whoever believes in Me does not believe in Me only, but in Almighty God who sent Me. And whoever looks upon Me, looks upon the One who sent Me. I came as a Light into the world, that everyone who believes in Me may not remain in darkness.

20. "If anyone hears My words and does not keep them, it is not I who judge them. I did not come to judge the world, but to save the world. There is a judge for whoever rejects Me, and does not receive My words. The words I spoke is what will condemn them at the last day. For it was not out of My own initiative that I spoke. But Almighty God who sent Me has given Me commandments about what to say and what to speak. And I know that God's commandment is eternal life; therefore, the things that I speak, I speak just as Almighty God had told."

CHAPTER 27
FUTURE SIGNS FORETOLD

MATTHEW 24:1-28; MARK 13:1-23; LUKE 21:5-24

Tuesday - Temple and Mount of Olives

Temple to be Destroyed

1. When Jesus had left the area of the Temple, He was leaving and His disciples came to Him to point out to Him the buildings in the Temple saying "Teacher, what wonderful stones, what wonderful buildings."

Jesus said to them, "Do you see all these great buildings? As for these things at which you are looking, this is the truth I tell you, days will come in which not one stone here will be left upon another, which will not be pulled down."

Jesus Tells of Future Signs

2. As He was sitting on the Mount of Olives, opposite the sacred areas of the Temple, Peter, James, John and Andrew, His disciples, came to Him privately and asked, "Teacher, when will these things happen? And what will be the sign when these things are going to happen? And tell us what will be the sign of Your coming, and the start of the end of the age?"

3. Jesus said to them, "Watch out that no one misleads you. For many will come in My name, claiming, 'I am God's Anointed One!'

and, 'The time is at hand!' Do not go after them for they will lead many astray. When you hear of wars and reports of wars, do not be alarmed. These things must happen first, but the end is still to come."

4. Then He said to them, "Nation will rise against nation, and kingdom against kingdom. There will be great earthquakes in certain places; in some places there will be famines and pestilences; there will be terrifying things, and great signs from Heaven. All these things are the beginning of the birth-pangs of the new age.

5. "Before all these things, they will lay hands upon you, and they will hand you over to the synagogues and prisons and whip you, and you will be brought before kings and governors. Then they will deliver you to affliction, kill you, and you will be hated by all nations because of My name. It will all be an opportunity for you to bear witness to them of Me. And when they hand you over and bring you before authorities, do not worry beforehand about what you will say in your defense, but speak whatever is given you in that hour, for it is not you who speaks but the Holy Spirit, I will give you a mouth and wisdom against which all your opponents will be unable to stand or argue.

6. "And then many will stumble, and will betray each other, and will hate each other. And many false prophets will arise, and they will lead many astray. And the love of many will grow cold, because lawlessness will be multiplied.

7. "You will be handed over even by parents, brothers, kinsfolk and friends. Brother shall hand over brother to death, and parents their children. Children will rise up against parents, and will kill them. Some of you will be put to death; and you will be hated by all for the

sake of My name. Not one hair on your head will perish. But it is the one who endures to the end who will be saved. By your endurance you will win souls. And the gospel will be proclaimed to the whole world, for a testimony to all nations, and then the end will come.

8. "When you shall see Jerusalem encircled by armies, then know that the time of the desolation is at hand. When you see the abomination of desolation, which was spoken of by the prophet Daniel, standing in the Holy Place (let whoever reads understand), then let whoever is in Judea flee to the mountains. At that time let those in Jerusalem flee to the mountains, and let not those in the country enter into Jerusalem. Let whoever is on the house-top not come down, nor let them go in to remove their goods from their house. Let whoever is working in the field not come back to pick up their coat, because these are days of vengeance, to fulfill all that is written. Woe to women who are with child and to those whose babes are at their breasts in these days! For great distress will be upon the earth and wrath upon all the people. They shall fall by the edge of the sword, and they will be taken away captive to all nations. Jerusalem will be trodden underfoot by the Gentiles, until the time of the Gentiles are completed.

9. "Pray that your flight may not happen in the stormy weather of winter, nor on the Sabbath. For at the time there will be great affliction, such as has never happened from the beginning of the creation which God has created until now, and such as never will happen. And if the day had not been shortened by the Lord, no human being or living creature would have survived. But for the sake of the chosen ones who God chose, God shortened the days.

10. "And if someone then says to you, 'See! Here is the Messiah!' or, 'See! There is Emmanuel!' do not believe them. For false Messiahs and false prophets will arise, and they will produce great signs and wonders, the consequences of which will be, if possible, to lead the elect astray. But do you look to yourselves! See! I have told you about these things before they happen.

11. "If anyone says to you, 'Look, He is in the wilderness.' do not go out. 'Look, He is in the inner chambers,' do not believe them. For as the bright light comes from the east and shines as far as the west, so shall the coming of Emmanuel be. Where the body is, there the vultures will be gathered."

SECOND COMING OF CHRIST FORETOLD
MATTHEW 24:29-51; MARK 13:24-37; LUKE 21:25-36

Tuesday Evening - Mount of Olives

12. "And in those days, after the tribulations, the sun will be darkened, and the moon will not give its light, and the stars will fall from the sky, and the powers of Heaven will be shaken. The nations will be in distress and will not know what to do in the roaring of the sea and of the wave, while people's hearts will faint from fear and from expectations of the things that are coming on the world.

13. "Then there will appear the sign of Emmanuel in Heaven. And then all the tribes of the earth will mourn. Then they will see Emmanuel coming in the clouds with great power and glory. And then Emmanuel will send God's angels with a great trumpet call, and they will gather the chosen ones from the four winds, from one boundary of Heaven to the other. When these things begin to happen, look up and be elated for your deliverance is near."

14. And He spoke this parable to them, "Learn the lesson from the fig tree. Look at the fig tree and all the trees; as soon as the branch has become tender, and puts out its leaves you see it for yourselves and you know that the harvest and summer is near. Even so, when you see all these things, you know that the Kingdom of God is near.

15. "This is the truth I tell you, this generation shall not pass away until these things have happened. Heaven and earth will pass away but My words will never pass away.

Exact Time Unknown

16. "No one knows about that day or hour, not even the angels in Heaven, but only Almighty God. As it was in the days of Noah, so will be the coming of Emmanuel. For, as in those days before the flood they spent their time eating and drinking, marrying and giving in marriage, until the day that Noah entered into the ark, and they were quite unaware of what would happen until the flood came and swept them all away, so will the coming of Emmanuel be. At that time there will be two men in the field; one is taken and the other is left. There will be two women grinding with the mill; one is taken, and the other left.

Stay Ready

17. "Keep watch, therefore, for you do not know on what day your Lord will come. But understand this, if the household had known what time of the night the thief was coming, they would have been awake, and would not have let the thief break into the house. That is why you too, must be ready; for Emmanuel is coming at an hour you do not expect.

18. "Be careful or your hearts will be weighed down with dissipations, drunkenness and the worries of this life, and that day will come suddenly upon you like a trap closing, for it will come upon all who dwell upon the face of the earth.

The Faithful Servant

19. "Who, then, is the dependable and wise servant who the master put in charge of the household staff, to give them their food at the right time? Happy are the servants whose master finds them acting so when the master returns. This is the truth I tell you, the master put them in charge of all the belongings. But if the bad servant says, 'My master will not be back for a long time yet,' and if then begins to beat the fellow-servants, and then eats and drinks with drunkards, then the master of the servant will come on a day when the servant is not expecting, and at an hour which the servant does not know, and will cut the servant in pieces, and assign the servant a place with the hypocrites where there will be weeping and gnashing of teeth.

Be Watchful

20. "Be watchful at all times, and keep praying that you may have strength to escape all the things that are going to happen, and to be able to stand before Emmanuel.

"So be watchful! For you do not know when the Master comes, late in the evening, at midnight, at cockcrow, or in the early day. Watch! In case Emmanuel comes suddenly and finds you sleeping. What I say to you, I say to all, be on the watch!"

THE JUDGMENTS
MATTHEW 25:1-46

Tuesday Evening - Mount of Olives

Ten Virgins Parable

21. "Then the Kingdom of Heaven is comparable to ten virgins who took their lamps and went out to meet the bridegroom. Five of them were foolish and five were wise. The foolish took their lamps, but did not take oil with them, but the wise took oil in flasks along with their lamps.

"When the bridegroom was delayed, all of them settled down to rest and slept. In the middle of the night the cry went up, 'Look, the bridegroom! Come out and meet him!' Then all these virgins awoke, and they prepared their lamps. The foolish ones said to the wise ones, 'Give us some of your oil, for our lamps are going out.' But the wise answered, 'No; there will not be enough for us and for you. Go instead to the dealers, and buy it for yourselves.'

"While they went away to buy oil, the bridegroom came; and those who were ready entered with him into the marriage celebrations, and the door was shut. Later the rest of the virgins came too, saying, 'Lord, Lord, open the door to us.' But he answered, 'This is the truth I tell you, I do not know you.' Be on the alert then, for you do not know the day nor the hour."

Money and Possessions (Talents) Parable

22. "For it is just like the man going on a journey, who called his servants, and handed over his belongings to them. To one he gave

$50,000; to another $20,000; and to another $10,000; to each according to their own ability. So he went away. Straightway the one who had received the $50,000 went and traded with them, and made another $50,000. In the same way the one who had received $20,000 made $20,000 more. But the one who had received $10,000 went away and dug up the ground, and hid the master's money.

23. "After a long time the master of those servants came, and settled accounts with them. The one who had received the $50,000 came and brought another $50,000 and said, 'Master, you gave me $50,000. See, I have made another $50,000.' His master said, 'Well done, good and faithful servant! You have been faithful in a few things; I will put you in charge over many things; enter into the joy of your master.' The one who had received the $20,000 came and said, 'Master, you entrusted to me $20,000. See, I have made another $20,000.' His master said, 'Well done, good and faithful servant! You have been faithful in a few things. I will put you in charge over many things; enter into the joy of your master.' The one who had received the $10,000 came also and said, 'Master, I knew that you are a hard man, reaping where you did not sow, and gathering where you scattered no seed. So I was afraid, and I went away and hid your $10,000 in the ground. See, you have what is yours.'

24. The master answered, 'Wicked and lazy servant! You knew that I reap where I have not sowed, and that I gather where I scattered no seed. Then you ought to have put the money in the bank, and when I came I would have received back what is my own with interest. Therefore, take the $10,000 and give it to the one who has the $100,000. For to everyone who has, will be given, and they will have abundance; but from whoever has not, even what they have will it be taken away

from them. And cast the worthless servant into the outer darkness, into the place where there shall be weeping and gnashing of teeth."

Minas and Talents were amounts of money. A Talent was equal to about one-fourth of a person's annual wages and a Mina was equal to about $1/20^{th}$ of a Talent. The Parable was about money and possessions so one Mina was set to be equal to $1,000 for illustration purposes. Jesus was clearly talking about money and our valuable possessions.

The Judgment of Righteous Workers

25. "When Emmanuel comes in God's glory, and all the angels with Emmanuel, then Emmanuel will take God's seat upon the throne of God's glory, and all nations will be gathered before God, and Emmanuel will separate them from each other, as the shepherd separates the sheep from the goats, and Emmanuel will place the sheep on the right side and the goats on the left. Then the King will say to those on the right side, 'Come, you who are blessed by Almighty God enter into possession of the Kingdom which has been prepared for you since the creation of the world. For I was hungry, and you gave Me something to eat; I was thirsty, and you gave Me something to drink; I was a stranger, and you invited Me in; naked, and you clothed Me; I was sick, and you came to visit Me; in prison, and you came to Me.

26. "The righteous will answer, 'Lord, when did we see You hungry, and fed You? Or thirsty, and gave You drink? When did we see You a stranger, and invite You in? Or naked, and clothed You? When did we see You sick, or in prison, and come to You?' And the King will answer them, 'This is the truth I tell you, inasmuch as you did it to one of the least of these children of Mine, you did it to Me.'

27. "Then He will say to those on the left, 'Go from Me, you cursed ones, into the eternal fire prepared for the devil and the wicked angels. For I was hungry, and you did not give Me anything to eat; I was thirsty, and you did not give Me anything to drink; I was a stranger, and you did not invite Me in; naked, and you did not clothe Me; sick and in prison, and you did not come to visit Me.'

28. "Then these too will answer, 'Lord, when did we see You hungry, or thirsty, or a stranger, or naked, or sick, or in prison, and did not take care of You?'

29. "Then Emmanuel will answer them, 'This is the truth I tell you, in so far as you did not do it to one of the least of these, you did not do it to Me.' And these will go away to eternal punishment, but the righteous will go into eternal life."

JUDAS MAKES HIS BARGAIN
MATTHEW 26:1-5; 14-16; MARK 14:1,2,10,11; LUKE 22:1-6

Wednesday, April 5, 30 - Mount of Olives

Jesus Foretells of Crucifixion

30. The Feast of Unleavened Bread, which is called the Passover, was in two days. When Jesus had finished these sayings, He said to His disciples, "You know that in two days it is the Passover Feast, and Emmanuel is going to be delivered to be crucified."

31. At that time the Chief Priests, the Scribes, and the elders of the people gathered in the courtyard of the High Priest, whose name was Caiaphas, and they plotted together to seize Jesus by craftiness and to kill Him. They said, "Not at the time of the Feast, or there will

be a riot among the people." They searched to find a way to destroy Jesus, for they were afraid of the people.

Judas' Bargain

32. Then Satan entered into Judas, called Iscariot, one of the Twelve. So he went away to the Chief Priests and captains to betray Jesus to them. He said, "What are you willing to give me, if I hand Him over to you?" When they had listened to his offer, they were delighted, and they settled with him and promised to give him a sum of thirty silver coins. He agreed and began to watch for an opportunity to betray Him, when the crowd was not present.

CHAPTER 28
JUDAS' BETRAYAL

PASSOVER PREPARATION
MATTHEW 26:17-19; MARK 14:12-17; LUKE 22:7-13,24-30

Thursday Evening, April 6, 30 - Bethany

Preparations

1. Then came the first day of the Feast of Unleavened Bread, on which the Passover lamb had to be sacrificed. Jesus' disciples came to Him and said, "Where do You wish us to go and make the necessary preparations for You to eat the Passover?"

2. Jesus sent two of His disciples, Peter and John, and said to them, "Go and make the Passover ready for us that we may eat it."

They said to Him, "Where do You want us to prepare for it."

3. He said to them, "Listen carefully. As you enter into the city a man carrying a jar of water will meet you. Follow him to the house that he enters; and say to the master of the house, 'The Teacher says to you, My time is near. I will keep the Passover with My disciples at your house. Where is the guest room that I may eat the Passover with My disciples?' And he will show you a large upper room, furnished and prepared."

4. So the disciples went away, and they came into the city, and found everything just as He had told them. And they got everything

ready for the Passover Feast as Jesus instructed them. When it was evening, Jesus came with the Twelve.

A Servants Reward

5. There arose a dispute among them about which was to be considered the greatest. Jesus said to them, "The kings of the gentiles lord it over them and those who have authority over them are called 'Benefactors.' It must not be so with you; but let whoever is greatest among you be like the youngest; and let whoever is the leader be as the servant. For who is greater, the one who sits at the table, or the one who serves? Is it not the one who sits at the table? But I am among you as One who serves. You are those who have stayed with Me in My tribulations; and I grant to you a kingdom, just as Almighty God has granted one to Me, that you may eat and drink at My table in My kingdom; and you will sit upon thrones judging the twelve tribes of Israel."

JESUS WASHES THE DISCIPLES' FEET
JOHN 13:1-20

Thursday Evening - Upper Room

6. Before the Festival of the Passover, Jesus knowing that His hour had come to leave this world and to go to Almighty God, having loved His own people who were in the world, He loved them to the end.

7. And during the meal the devil had already put into the heart of Judas Iscariot, the son of Simon, to betray Him. Knowing that Almighty God had given all things into His hands, and that He had come forth from Almighty God, and was going back to God, He rose

The Gospel of Jesus Christ

from the meal and laid aside His outer robe, and took a towel and put it round Himself. Then He poured water into a basin and began to wash the feet of His disciples and to wipe them with the towel which He had put round Himself.

8. He came to Simon Peter. Peter said to Him, "Lord, are You going to wash my feet?"

Jesus answered him, "You do not know what I am doing, but you will understand afterwards."

Peter said to Him, "You will never wash my feet."

Jesus answered him, "If I do not wash you, you have no part of Me."
Simon Peter said to Him, "Lord, if that is so, do not wash my feet only, but my hands and my head too."

9. Jesus said to him, "Whoever has been bathed has need only to have their feet washed. After that is done, they are completely clean. And you are clean, but not all of you."

Jesus Explains Washing

10. So when He had washed their feet, taken His robe again, and taken His place at the table, He said to them, "Do you understand what I have done to You? You call Me 'Teacher,' and 'Lord.' And you are right to do so, for so I am. If then I, the Teacher and Lord, have washed your feet, you also ought to wash each other's feet, for I have given you an example, that as I have done to you, you too should do to each other. This is the truth I tell you, the servant is not greater than

the master, nor the messenger greater than the one who sent the messenger. If you know these things, you are blessed if you do them.

Jesus Predicts His Betrayal

11. "It is not about all of you that I am speaking. I know the ones whom I have chosen. It is all happening that the Scripture may be fulfilled, 'He who eats My bread has lifted up his heel against Me.' I am telling you this now, before it happens, so that when it does happen, you may believe that I am the One. This is the truth I tell you, whoever receives whomsoever I send, receives Me; and whoever receives Me, receives Almighty God who sent Me."

JUDAS' BETRAYAL
MATTHEW 26:20-25, 31-35; MARK 14:18-21, 27-31
LUKE 22:21-23, 31-38; JOHN 13:21-38

Thursday Evening - Upper Room

Betrayer Identified

12. When Jesus said these things, as they were reclining at the table eating, He was troubled in spirit. Solemnly Jesus declared, "This is the truth I tell you, one of you will betray Me, one who is eating with Me. And look, the hand of him who betrays Me is on the table with Me."

13. The disciples began to look at each other, because they were at a loss to know about whom He was speaking. They were very sad, and began to question one another as to which of them could be the one who was going to do this, and said to Him one by one, "Surely it cannot be me, Lord?"

14. Jesus answered, "He who has dipped his hand with Me in the bowl, it is he who will betray Me. Emmanuel will go as it has been determined and is written about Emmanuel, but woe to that man through whom Emmanuel is betrayed. It would be better for him, if he had not been born."

15. One of the them, the disciple whom Jesus loved, was reclining next to Jesus. So Simon Peter motioned to him and said, "Ask who it is whom He is speaking about." The disciple leaned back against Jesus and asked Him, "Lord, who is it?"

16. Jesus said, "It is he for whom I will dip this piece of bread in the dish and give it to him." So He took the piece of bread and dipped it in the dish and gave it to Judas Iscariot, the son of Simon.
Judas, who betrayed Him, said, "Master, can it be I?"
He said to him, "It is you who have said it." And after that man had taken the piece of bread. Satan entered into him. So Jesus said to him, "Hurry on what you are going to do."

17. But none of those who were reclining at the table understood why He said this to him. Some of them thought that, since Judas had the money box, Jesus was saying to him, "Buy the things we need for the feast"; or that He was telling him to give something to the poor. As soon as Judas took the piece he went out. And it was night.

Love One Another Commandment

18. When Judas had gone, Jesus said, "Now Emmanuel has been glorified, and God is glorified in Emmanuel; and now God will be glorified in Emmanuel; and God will glorify Emmanuel at once.

19. "My children, I am still going to be with you for a little while. You will search for Me; and as I said to the Jews, so now I say to you too, 'You cannot go where I am going.'

20. "I give you a new commandment,

> Love one another,
> as I have loved you.

It is by this that all will know that you are My disciples, if you love one another."

Peter will Stumble

21. Then Jesus said to them, "Every one of you will be made to stumble because of Me during this night; for it is written, 'I will smite the shepherd, and the sheep of the flock shall be scattered abroad.' But after I have been raised to life again, I will go before you into Galilee."

22. Simon Peter said to Him, "Lord, where are you going?"

"Where I am going," Jesus answered, "you cannot follow now; but you will follow later."

23. Peter said to Him, "Lord, why can I not follow You now? I will lay down my life for You."

Jesus answered, "Will you lay down your life for Me? Simon, Simon, listen to Me, Satan has been allowed to have you that you may be sifted like wheat. But I have prayed for you that your faith may not completely fail. And when you have turned back again, strengthen your brothers and sisters."

24. He said to Him, "Lord, I am ready to go with You to prison and to death. All the others may fall away from you, but I will not."

Jesus said to him, "This is the truth I tell you, today, this night, before the cock crows twice you will deny Me three times."

Peter insisted, "If I must die with You I will not deny You." So also spoke all the disciples.

Be Wary of the World

25. And He said to them, "When I sent you out without purse or wallet or shoes, did you lack for anything?"

They said, "For nothing."

26. But He said to them, "But now, let him who has a purse take it, and so with a wallet; and let whoever has no sword sell their coat and buy one. For I tell you that this which is written must be fulfilled in Me, 'And he was reckoned with the law-breakers'; for that which was written of Me finds its fulfillment."

They said, "Lord, here are two swords."

He said to them, "It is enough."

CHAPTER 29
THE LORD'S SUPPER

MATTHEW 26:26-29; MARK 14:22-25; LUKE 22:14-20; I CORINTHIANS 11:23-26

Thursday Evening - Upper Room

1. When the time came He took His place at the table as did His disciples. "I have intently desired to eat this Passover with you before I suffer," He said to them. While they were eating the night on which He was delivered up, the Lord Jesus took bread, and after He had given thanks, He broke it and said, "This is My body which is given for you. Do this so you will remember Me."

2. Then, after the meal, He took a cup, and when He had given thanks, He gave it to them. "Drink all of you from it," He said, "for this is My blood of the new covenant, which is shed for many, that their sins may be forgiven. Do this, as often as you drink it, so you will remember Me.

3. "For as often as you eat this bread and drink this cup you proclaim the death of the Lord until Emmanuel will come. Truly I tell you, I will no longer drink of the fruit of the vine, until that day when I drink it again in the Kingdom of God."

FAREWELL TEACHING TO DISCIPLES
JOHN 14-16

Thursday Late Evening - Upper Room

Jesus Will Prepare a Place

4. "Do not let you heart be troubled. Believe in God and believe also in Me. There are many dwelling places in Almighty God's house. If it were not so, I would have told you, for I go to prepare a place for you. And if I go and prepare a place for you, I am coming again, and I will receive you to Myself, that where I am, there you may be also.

5. "And you know the way to where I am going."

Thomas said to Him, "Lord, we do not know where You are going. How do we know the way?"

Jesus is Almighty God

6. Jesus said to him, "I am the Way, the Truth and the Life. No one comes to Almighty God except through Me.

"If you had known Me, you would have known Almighty God also. From now on you know Almighty God, and you have seen Almighty God."

7. Philip said to Him, "Lord, show us Almighty God, and that is enough for us."

Jesus said to him, "Have I been with you for so long, and you did not know Me, Philip? Whoever has seen Me has seen Almighty God. How can you say, 'Show us Almighty God?' Do you not believe that I am in Almighty God and Almighty God is in Me? I am not the source of the Words that I speak to you. It is Almighty God who dwells in Me who is doing God's work. Believe Me that I am in Almighty God and that Almighty God is in Me. If you cannot believe it because I say it, believe it because of the works I do.

8. "This is the truth I tell you, whoever believes in Me will do the works I do, and they will do greater works than these, because I go to Almighty God. And I will do whatever you ask in My name, that Almighty God may be glorified in Emmanuel. If you ask Me anything in My name I will do it. If you love Me, keep My commandments.

Holy Spirit Promised

9. "I will ask Almighty God and God will give you another Helper to be with you forever. That is the Spirit of Truth. The world cannot receive the Spirit, because it does not see the Spirit or know the Spirit. But you know the Spirit because the Spirit abides with you and will be in you.

Jesus Foretells Return

10. "I will not leave you as orphans. I am coming to you. In a little while the world will no longer see Me; but you will see Me because I will be alive and you will be alive also. In that day you will know that I am in Almighty God, and that you are in Me, even as I am in you. It is whoever has My commandments and keeps them who

loves Me. Whoever loves Me will be loved by Almighty God, and I will love them and reveal Myself to them."

11. Judas, not Iscariot, said to Him, "Lord, what has happened that You are going to reveal Yourself to us, and not to the world?"

Jesus answered, "If any one loves Me, they will keep My Words; and Almighty God will love them, and We will come to them, and We will make our abode with them. Whoever does not love Me does not keep My Words. The Words which you hear are not Mine, but belong to Almighty God Who sent Me.

12. "I have spoken these things to you while I am still with you. The Helper, the Holy Spirit, whom Almighty God will send in My name, will teach you all things, and will remind you of all that I have said. I am leaving you peace; I give you My peace. I do not give it to you as the world gives peace. Let not your soul be troubled nor let it be fearful. You heard that I said to you, 'I am going away and I will come to you.' If you loved Me, you would rejoice because I go to Almighty God, for Almighty God is greater than I. And now I have told you before it happens, so when it does happen, you may believe. I shall not say much more to you, because the Ruler of this world is coming and has no hold over Me. Satan's coming will only make the world know that I love Almighty God, and that I do as Almighty God has commanded Me. Rise, let us go from here.

Vine and Branches

13. "I am the true vine and Almighty God is the vine-dresser. God destroys every branch in Me which does not bear fruit; and God takes away every branch which does not bear fruit, and prunes it, so it

will bear more fruit. You are already clean because the word which I have spoken to you. Abide in Me and I in you. As the branch cannot bear fruit of its own strength, unless it abides in the vine, so neither can you, unless you abide in Me. I am the vine; you are the branches, whoever abides in Me, and I in them, bears much fruit, because apart from Me you can do nothing. If anyone does not abide in Me, they will be cast out like a withered branch. And they gather these branches and throw them into the fire and they are burned.

14. "If you abide in Me, and My Words abide in you, ask whatever you wish and it will be done for you. It is that you bear much fruit, and prove yourselves to be My disciples, that Almighty God is glorified. Just as Almighty God has loved Me, so I have also loved you. Abide in My love. If you keep My commandments, you will abide in My love, just as I have kept Almighty God's commandments. And abide in God's love.

"I have spoken these things to you that My joy might be in you, and that your joy might be complete.

Disciples Relationship to Each Other

15. "This is My commandment, that you love one another, just as I have loved you. No one has greater love than this, that a person should lay down their life for a friend. You are My friends, if you do what I command you. I no longer call you slaves, because the slave does not know what their master is doing. I have called you friends because I have made known to you everything that I heard from Almighty God.

16. "You did not choose Me, but I chose you, and appointed you that you should go and bear fruit, and that your fruit should remain, so that Almighty God will give you whatever you ask in My name. This I command you, that you love one another.

Disciple's Relationship to the World

17. "If the world hates you, you know that it hated Me before it hated you. If you were of the world, the world would love its own; but the world hates you, because you are not of the world, but I chose you out of the world. Remember the Word which I spoke to you, 'The servant is not greater than the master.' If they persecuted Me, they will also persecute you. If they kept My Word, they will keep yours also. But they will do all these things to you because of My name, because they do not know the One who sent Me.

18. "If I had not come and spoken to them, they would not be guilty of sin. But now, they have no excuse for their sins. Whoever hates Me hates Almighty God also. If I had not done the works among them, which no one else has ever done, they would not be guilty of sin. But now, they have seen and they have heard both Me and Almighty God. But they have done all this that the Word that is written in their Law might be fulfilled, 'They have hated Me without a cause.'

The Holy Spirit

19. "When the Helper comes, whom I will send to you from Almighty God, that is the Spirit of Truth who comes forth from Almighty God, the Spirit will be a witness of Me. And you will bear witness about Me also because you have been with Me from the beginning.

Jesus' Warning

20. "I have spoken these things to you that you may be kept from stumbling. They will make you outcasts from the synagogue. But a time is coming when anyone who kills you will think that they are rendering a service to God; and they will do these things because they have not known Almighty God or Me. But I have spoken these things to you, so when their time comes, you will remember that I told you of them. I did not tell you these things at the beginning, because I was with you.

The Holy Spirit Promised

21. "But now I am going away to Almighty God who sent Me, and none of you asks Me, 'Where are You going?' But sorrow has filled your hearts because I have said these things to you. But it is the truth I am telling you, it is to your advantage that I go away, for if I do not go away, the Helper will not come to you, but if I go, I will send the Spirit to you. And when the Spirit has come, the Spirit will convict the world of sin, righteousness and judgment; concerning sin, because they do not believe in Me; and concerning righteousness, because I go to Almighty God, and you no longer see Me; and concerning judgment, because the ruler of this world has been judged.

22. "I have many things to say to you, but you cannot bear them now. But when the Spirit of Truth has come, the Spirit will guide you into all truth. For the Spirit will not speak on the Spirit's own initiative, but the Spirit will speak all that the Spirit will hear, and will disclose to you what is to come. The Spirit will glorify Me, for the Spirit will talk of the things which are Mine. That is why I said that the Spirit will take of the things which belong to Me, and tell them to you.

Jesus' Death and Resurrection Foretold

23. "In a little while you will not see Me anymore; and again in a little while you will see Me."

Some of His disciples said to each other, "What is the meaning of this that He is saying to us, 'In a little while you will not see Me, and again in a little while you will see Me?' And what does He mean when He says, 'I am going to Almighty God'? What does He mean when He talks about 'A little'? We do not know what He means."

24. Jesus knew that they wished to ask Him their questions, and He said to them, "You are discussing among yourselves what I meant when I said, 'In a little while you will not see Me, and again in a little while you will see Me.' This is the truth I tell you, you will weep and lament, but the world will rejoice. You will be sorrowful, but your sorrow will be turned into joy. Whenever a woman bears a child she has sorrow, because her hour has come. But when the child is born, she does not remember her pain because of her joy that a child is born into the world. So you too for the present have sorrow. But I will see you again, and your heart will rejoice, and no one will take your joy away from you.

Prayer

25. "In that day you will not have any questions to ask Me. This is the truth I tell you, if you ask Almighty God for anything, God will give it to you in My name. Until now you have asked for nothing in My name. Ask, and you will receive, that your joy may be made full.

Sayings Will Be Made Clear

26. "I have spoken these things to you in sayings that are hard to understand; but the hour is coming when I will no longer speak to you in sayings that are hard to understand, but I will tell you plainly about Almighty God. In that day you will ask in My name. I do not say to you that I will ask Almighty God for you, because Almighty God loves you, because you have loved Me and have believed that I came forth from Almighty God. I came forth from Almighty God, and have come into the world; I am leaving the world again, and I am going to Almighty God."

27. His disciples said, "See, now You are speaking clearly, and are not speaking in hard to understand sayings. Now we know that You know all things, and have no need for anyone to question you. Because of this we believe that You came from God."

28. Jesus answered them, "Do you believe at this time? Behold, the hour is coming and has already come, when each of you will be scattered to your own homes, and to leave Me alone. And yet I am not alone, because Almighty God is with Me. I have spoken these things to you that you may have peace in Me. In the world you will have tribulation, take courage; I have overcome the world."

Dr. Patrick Pierce

EMMANUEL'S PRAYER
JOHN 17

Thursday Night - Upper Room

Emmanuel's Glory and Authority

29. When Jesus had said these things, He lifted up His eyes to Heaven, and said, "Almighty God, the hour has come. Glorify Emmanuel that Emmanuel may glorify You, just as You gave Emmanuel authority over all people that Emmanuel may give life to everyone whom You have given to Emmanuel. This is eternal life, to know You, the only true God, and to know Jesus Christ whom You sent. I have glorified You on the earth, because I have finished the work which You gave Me to do; and now Almighty God glorify Me in Your presence, with the glory which I had with You before the world was.

30. "I have manifested Your name to the people whom You gave Me out of the world. They were Yours and You gave them to Me, and they have kept Your Word. Now they have come to know that everything You gave Me comes from You, because I gave to them the Words You gave Me, and they received them, and they truly know that I came forth from You, and they believe that You sent Me.

31. "It is for them that I ask, it is not for the world that I ask, but for those whom you have given Me because they are Yours. All that I have is Yours, and all that You have is Mine. And through them I have been glorified. I am no longer in the world, and yet they are in the world, and I come to You. Almighty God, keep them in Your name, which You gave to Me, that they may be one, even as We are One. While I was with them I kept them in Your name, which You

gave to Me. I guarded them and none of them were lost, except the one who was destined to be lost, that the scriptures might be fulfilled.

Disciples in the World

32. "But now I come to You. I am saying these things while still in the world that they may have My joy made full in themselves. I gave them Your Word, and the world hated them, because they are not of the world even as I am not of the world. I do not ask You to take them out of the world, but that You keep them from the evil one. They are not of the world, just as I am not of the world. Sanctify them in the truth; Your Word is truth. As You sent Me into the world, I also send them into the world. And for their sakes I sanctify Myself, that they also may be sanctified in the truth.

33. "It is not only for these that I ask, but also for those who are going to believe in Me through their word; that they may all be one, even as You, Almighty God, are in Me, and I in You, so that they may be in Us, so that the world may believe that You sent Me.

The Future Glory

34. "And I have given them the glory which You gave Me, that they may be one just as We are One. I am in them, and You are in Me, that they may be perfected in unity. I ask that the world may know that You sent Me, and that You loved them even as You loved Me. Almighty God, it is My will that those whom You have given Me should be with Me where I am, that they may see My glory which You have given Me; for You loved Me before the foundation of the world. Righteous Almighty God, the world did not know You, but I knew You, and these know that

Dr. Patrick Pierce

You did send Me. I have told them what You are like, and I will go on making it known, that the love with which You loved Me may be in them, and I in them."

CHAPTER 30
GOING TO GETHSEMANE

MATTHEW 26:30, 36-46; MARK 14:26, 32-42; LUKE 22:39-46; JOHN 18:1

Thursday Night, very late - Mount of Olives

Mount of Olives

1. When Jesus had said these things and after they had sung a hymn, Jesus left with His disciples and, as was His custom, went across the Kidron Valley to the Mount of Olives to a place where there was a garden called Gethsemane, into which He and His disciples entered. When He had come to the place Jesus said to His disciples, "Sit here, while I go and pray in this place. Pray that you may not enter into temptation." He took Peter and James and John with Him, and withdrew about a stone's throw, and began to be in great distress and troubled. He said to them, "My soul is overcome with sorrow to the point of death. Stay here, and keep watch."

Final Prayers

2. He went a little further, knelt down and prayed that if it be possible, this hour might pass from Him. He prayed, "Almighty God, everything is possible to You. If You are willing take this cup from Me, but not My will, but Your will be done." An angel from heaven appeared and strengthened Him. He was in agony, and He prayed still more intensely, and His sweat was like drops of blood falling to the ground.

3. So He rose from prayer and came to His disciples, and found them sleeping exhausted from sorrow. He said to Peter, "Simon, are you sleeping? Could you not stay awake for one hour? Watch and pray so you will not fall into temptation. The spirit is willing, but the flesh is weak."

4. He went away a second time and prayed in the same words, "Almighty God, if it is not possible for this cup to be taken from Me unless I drink it, may Your will be done." He came again and found them sleeping, for their eyes were heavy with sleep. And they did not know how to answer Him. So He left them and went away again, and prayed the third time, saying the same words again. Then He returned to His disciples and said to them, "Sleep on now. Take your rest, this is enough for the hour has come. Rise and pray that you may not enter into temptation. Look, Emmanuel is being betrayed into the hands of sinners. Rise, let us go! He who betrays Me has come!"

JESUS IS BETRAYED
MATTHEW 26:47-56; MARK 14:43-52; LUKE 22:47-53; JOHN 18:2-11

Friday morning before dawn - Gethsemane

5. Now Judas, who betrayed Him, knew the place for Jesus often met with His disciples there. And while He was still speaking, Judas came bringing a company of soldiers, together with the officers from the Chief Priests, elders and Pharisees, and went there with lanterns, torches and carrying weapons of swords and clubs.

6. Jesus knew the things which were going to happen to Him, so He went out and asked, "Who are you looking for?"
They answered, "Jesus of Nazareth."

7. Jesus said to them, "I am He." And Judas, His betrayer stood there with them. When He said to them, "I am He," they stepped back and fell to the ground. So Jesus asked them again, "Who are you looking for?"

They said, "Jesus of Nazareth."

8. Jesus said, "I told you that I am He. If you are looking for Me, let these go on their way." So that the Word might be fulfilled which He said, "I have lost none of those whom You have given Me."

9. The traitor had given them a sign saying, "Whoever I shall kiss, that is the Man. Seize Him and lead Him away under guard!" Immediately he went up to Jesus and said, "Greetings, Master!" And kissed Him lovingly.

10. Jesus said to him, "Judas is it with a kiss that you will betray Emmanuel? Friend, do what you have come to do!"

11. Then they came and seized Jesus and arrested Him. When those who were around Him saw what was going to happen. They said, "Lord, shall we strike with the sword!" Simon Peter had a sword, drew it and struck the high priest's slave, and cut off his right ear; and the slave's name was Malchus.

12. But Jesus said, "Stop! No more of this." And He touched his ear and healed him. And He said to Peter, "Put your sword away in the sheath; shall I not drink the cup which Almighty God has given Me? All those who take up the sword shall perish by the sword. Or do you think I cannot request to Almighty God, and God will immediately put at My disposal more than twelve legions of angels? How then will

the scriptures be fulfilled, that it must happen this way?" So the Roman detachment and the commander, and the officers of the Jews, arrested Jesus and bound Him.

13. At that time Jesus said to the crowd, "Have you come out with swords and clubs to arrest Me like a robber? Every day I used to sit with you in the temple teaching and you did not seize Me, but this hour and the power of darkness are yours. But all this has happened that the Scriptures of the prophet may be fulfilled."

14. Then they left Him and fled, and a certain young man was following Him, wearing a linen sheet over his naked body; and they seized him. But he left the linen sheet behind, and escaped naked.

CHAPTER 31
THE FIRST STAGE OF JESUS' TRIAL

EXAMINATION BY ANNAS
MATTHEW 26:69-70; MARK 14:66-68A; JOHN 18:12-24

Friday Morning before dawn – Annas' house

1. They led Him to Annas' first; for he was father-in-law to Caiaphas, who was the high priest that year. Now Caiaphas was the one who had advised the Jews that it would be good for one man to die on behalf of the people.

Peter's First Denial

2. Simon Peter and another disciple were following Jesus. Now that disciple was known to the high priest and entered with Jesus into the court of the high priest, but Peter was standing outside at the door. So the other disciple, who was known to the high priest, went out and spoke to the doorkeeper, and brought Peter in.

3. The slave girl who kept the door said to Peter, "Aren't you also one of Jesus the Galilean's, this Man's disciples?"

And He denied it before all of them saying, "I am not. I do not know what you are talking about." Now the slaves and officers were standing there, having made a charcoal fire, for it was cold and they were warming themselves; and Peter was with them also standing and warming himself.

Jesus before Annas

4. The high priest therefore questioned Jesus about His disciples, and about His teaching. Jesus answered Him, "I have spoken openly in the temple, where all the Jews come together; and I spoke nothing in secret. Why do you question Me? Question those who have heard what I spoke to them, for they know what I said."

5. And when He had said this, one of the officers standing by struck Jesus in the face, saying, "Is this the way You answer the high priest?"

Jesus answered him, "If I have spoken something wrong, bear witness of what is wrong; but if rightly, why do you strike Me?"

6. Annas therefore sent Him bound to Caiaphas the high priest.

JESUS CONDEMNED BY CAIAPHUS AND SANHEDRIN
MATTHEW 26:57-68; 71-75; MARK 14:53-65; 68b-72; LUKE 22:54-71; JOHN 18:25-27

Friday early morning, April 7, 30 - Caiaphas' Palace

7. And those who had seized Jesus led Him away to Caiaphas, the high priest, where the Scribes and the elders were gathered together. But Peter was following Him at a distance, also, as far as the courtyard of the high priest, and entered in, and sat down with the officers and warmed himself at the fire, to see the outcome.

8. Now the Chief Priests and the whole council kept trying to obtain false testimony against Jesus, in order that they might put Him to death; but they did not find any, even though many false witnesses came forward giving false testimony against Him; and yet their testimony was not consistent. But later on two came forward and said, "This man stated, 'I am able to destroy the temple of God and to rebuild it in three days without hands.'"

9. And the High Priest stood up and said to Him, "Do You make no answer? What is it that these people are testifying against You?" But Jesus kept silent and gave no answer. And the High Priest said to Him, "I direct You by the Living God that You tell us whether you are the Christ, the Emmanuel."

10. Jesus said to him, "I am. You have said it yourself. Nevertheless I tell you, hereafter you shall see Emmanuel sitting at the right hand of power and coming on the clouds of Heaven."

11. Then the High Priest tore his robes, saying, "He has blasphemed! What witnesses do we have need further? Behold, you have now heard the blasphemy; what do you think?"

12. They answered and said, "He is deserving of death!" Then they spat in His face, and blindfolded Him, and beat Him with their fists; and others slapped Him, and said, "Prophesy to us, You Christ; who is the one who hit You?" And they were saying other things against Him, blaspheming.

Peter's Denials

13. And when Peter had gone out to the gateway onto the porch, another maid saw Him and said to those who were there, "This man was with the Jesus of Nazareth." And again he denied it with an oath, "I do not know this Man." And a little later the bystanders came up and said to Peter, "Surely you are one of them also, for the way you talk as a Galilean gives you away." And one of the slaves of the High Priest who was a relative of the one whose ear Peter cut off, said, "Didn't I see you in the garden with Him?"

14. Then Peter began to curse and swear, "I do not know this Man you are talking about!" Immediately a cock crowed twice. And the Lord turned and looked at Peter. Then Peter remembered the word of the Lord, when He had told him, "Before the cock crows twice today, you will deny Me three times." He threw his coat around his head, went outside and wept bitterly.

Jesus in the Council Chambers Before the Sanhedrin

15. And when it was day, the Council of Elders of the people assembled, both Chief Priests and Scribes, and they led Him away to their council chamber, saying, "If You are the Christ, tell us."

But He said to them, "If I tell you, you will not believe; and if I ask a question, you will not answer. But from now on Emmanuel will be seated at the right hand of the power of God."

16. And they all said, "Are You Emmanuel, then?"

And He said to them, "Yes, I am."

17. And they said, "What further need do we have of testimony? For we have heard it from His own mouth ourselves." And all the Chief Priests and the elders of the people took council against Jesus to put Him to death.

JUDAS COMMITS SUICIDE
MATTHEW 27:3-10

Early Friday Morning, April 7, 30

18. Then when Judas, who had betrayed Him, saw that He had been condemned, he felt remorse and returned the thirty silver coins to the Chief Priests and elders, saying, "I have sinned by betraying innocent blood."

But they said, "What is that to us. That is your problem."

19. And he threw the silver coins into the sanctuary and left; and he went away and hanged himself.

20. And the Chief Priests took the silver coins and said, "It is against the law to put them into the temple treasury, since it is the price of blood."

And they decided together that the money would buy the Potter's Field as a burial place for strangers. For this reason that field has been called the Field of Blood to this day.

21. Then that which was spoken through Jeremiah the prophet was fulfilled. "And they took the thirty silver coins, the price of the One whose price had been set by the people of Israel; and they used them for the Potter's Field, as the Lord directed me."

CHAPTER 32
JESUS BEFORE PILATE

MATTHEW 27:2,11-14; MARK 15:1-5; LUKE 23:1-7; JOHN 18:28-38

Early Friday Morning - The Governor's Palace

1. And early in the morning the Chief Priests with the elders and Scribes and the whole council, immediately held a meeting; and binding Jesus, they led Him away into the Praetorium of Pilate, the Governor. They themselves did not enter into the Praetorium in order that they might not be defiled, but might eat the Passover. So Pilate went out to them, and said, "What charges do you bring against this Man?"

2. And they began to accuse Him, saying, "We found the Man misleading our nation and forbidding paying taxes to Caesar, and saying that He Himself is Christ, a King. If the Man were not a criminal, we would not have delivered Him up to you."

3. Pilate therefore said to them, "Take Him yourselves, and judge Him according to your own law."

The Jews said to him, "We are not permitted to put anyone to death." This happened that the Word of Jesus might be fulfilled, which He said, signifying by what kind of death He was about to die.

4. So Pilate then entered again into the Praetorium and summoned Jesus, and said to Him, "Are You the King of the Jews?"

Jesus answered, "Are you asking this on your own, or did others tell you about Me?"

5. Pilate answered, "I am not a Jew, am I? Your own people and the Chief Priests delivered You up to me; what have You done?"

Jesus answered, "My kingdom is not of this world. If My kingdom were of this world, then My servants would be fighting, that I might not be delivered up to the Jews; but as it is, My kingdom is not of this realm."

6. Pilate therefore asked Him, "So You are a King?"

Jesus answered, "You say correctly that I am a King. For this I have come into the world, to testify to the truth. Everyone who is of the truth listens to My voice."

7. Pilate said to Him, "What is the truth?" When he had said this he went out again to the Jews, and said to the Chief Priests and the crowds, "I find no guilt in the Man."

8. But they kept on insisting and saying, "He stirs up the people, teaching all over Judea, starting in Galilee, even as far as this place. And the Chief Priests began to accuse Him harshly.

9. And Pilate questioned Him again saying, "Do You make no answer? See how many charges they bring against You!" But Jesus did not answer a single charge, so that Pilate was quite amazed.

10. When Pilate heard it, he asked whether the Man was a Galilean. And when he learned that He was under Herod's jurisdiction, he sent Him to Herod, who was also in Jerusalem at the time.

JESUS BEFORE HEROD
LUKE 23:8-12

Friday Morning - Herod's Palace

11. Now Herod was very glad when he saw Jesus; for he had wanted to see Him for a long time, because he had heard about Him and hoped to see some miracle performed by Him.

12. He questioned Him intently; but Jesus never answered him. The Chief Priests and Scribes were standing there accusing Him vehemently. Herod with his soldiers, after treating Him with contempt and mocking Him, dressed Him in an elegant robe and sent Him back to Pilate. Now Herod and Pilate became friends with each other that day; for before this they had been enemies of each other.

JESUS BEFORE PILATE A SECOND TIME
MATTHEW 27:15-31; MARK 15:6-20; LUKE 23:13-25; JOHN 18:39-19:16

Friday Morning - Pilate's Palace

13. Pilate summoned the Chief Priests and the rulers, and the people said to them, "You brought this Man to me as one who incites the people to rebellions, and yet, having examined Him before you, I have found no guilt in this Man regarding the charges which you make against Him. Neither Herod, for he sent Him back to us; and look, nothing deserving death has been done by Him. I will therefore punish Him and release Him."

Jesus Scourged

14. Then Pilate took Jesus into the Praetorium and gathered the entire Roman garrison around Him and scourged Him. The soldiers wove a crown of thorns and put it on His head and a reed in His right hand and stripped Him and put on Him a purple robe; and they kneeled down before Him and came up to Him and mocked Him saying, "Hail, King of the Jews." And gave Him blows in the face, spat on Him and took the reed and began to beat Him on the head.

15. And Pilate came out again, and said to them, "Behold, I bring Him out to you, that you may know that I find no guilt in Him." Jesus therefore came out, wearing the crown of thorns and the purple robe. And Pilate said to them, "Behold, the Man!"

16. Then when the Chief Priests and the officers saw Him, they yelled out saying, "Crucify, Crucify!"

Pilate said to them, "Take Him yourselves and crucify Him, for I find no guilt in Him."

17. The Jews answered him, "We have a law, and by that law He ought to die because He made Himself out to be Emmanuel."

Pilate Questions Jesus Again

18. When Pilate heard this statement, he was more afraid, and he entered into the Praetorium again, and said to Jesus, "Where are You from?" But Jesus did not answer him. Pilate then said to him, "Why do You not speak to me? Don't You know that I have authority to release You, and I have authority to crucify You."

19. Jesus answered, "You would have no authority over Me, unless it had been given you from above; because of this he who has delivered Me up to you has the greater sin."

20. As a result of this Pilate made efforts to release Him, but the Jews cried out saying, "If you release this Man, you are no friend of Caesar; everyone who makes themselves out to be a king opposes Caesar. When Pilate heard these words, he therefore brought Jesus out, and sat down on the judgment seat at the place called The Pavement, but in Hebrew, Gabbatha. Now it was the day of preparation for the Passover; it was about 6:00 A.M. He said to the Jews, "Behold, your King!"

21. They then yelled out, "Away with Him, Away with Him, Crucify Him!"

Pilate said to them, "Shall I crucify your king?"

The Chief Priests answered, "We have no king but Caesar."

22. And while he was sitting on the judgment seat, his wife sent a message to him saying, "Have nothing to do with this righteous Man; for last night I suffered greatly in a dream because of Him."

Barabbas Released

23. Now Pilate was obligated to release to them at the Feast any one prisoner whom they wanted. And at that time they were holding a notorious prisoner called Barabbas. When they were gathered together, Pilate said to them, "Whom do you want me to release for you? Barabbas, or Jesus who is called Christ?" For he knew that because of envy they had delivered Him up.

24. But the Chief Priests and the elders persuaded the crowds to ask for Barabbas and to put Jesus to death.

25. But the Governor answered and said to them, "Which of the two do you want me to release for you?"

And they said, "Barabbas."

26. Pilate said to them, "Then what shall I do with Jesus, who is called Christ?"

They said, "Let Him be crucified!"

27. And he said, "Why, what evil has He done?"

But they kept shouting all the more, saying, "Let Him be crucified!"

28. And when Pilate saw that he was accomplishing nothing, but instead that a riot was starting, he took water and washed his hands in front of the crowd, saying, "I am innocent of this Man's blood; it is your responsibility."
And the people answered, "His blood be on us and on our children!"

29. And Pilate pronounced the sentence that their demand should be granted. And he released Barabbas for them, who had been thrown into prison for insurrection and murder, but he delivered Jesus to their will to be crucified.

CHAPTER 33
JESUS IS CRUCIFIED

JESUS IS CRUCIFIED
MATTHEW 27:32-56; MARK 15:21-41;
LUKE 23:26-49; JOHN 19:17-30

Friday, April 7, 30, 9 AM to 3 PM - Golgotha

The Road to Golgotha

1. They took His purple robe off and put His garments on Him, and led Him away to crucify Him, bearing His own cross. And as they were coming out, they found a man and laid hold of the passer-by coming from the country, Simon of Cyrene (the father of Alexander and Rufus) and placed the cross on him to carry behind Jesus.

2. And there were following Him a great multitude of people, and the women were mourning and lamenting Him. But Jesus turned to them and said, "Daughters of Jerusalem, stop weeping for Me, but weep for yourselves and for your children. For behold, the days are coming when they will say;

3. "Blessed are the barren
    and the wombs that never bore,
    and the breasts that never nursed.
They will begin to say
    to the mountains, 'Fall on us,'
    and to the hills, 'Cover us up.'

Dr. Patrick Pierce

> For if they do these things
> > when the tree is green,
> What will happen when it is dry?"

4. And two others also, who were criminals, were being led away to be put to death with Him. And they came to the place called the Place of the Skull, which in Hebrew is called Golgotha. There at nine in the morning they crucified Him, and with Him two other men, one on either side, and Jesus in between. And the scripture was fulfilled which says, "And He was numbered with transgressors."

Pilate's Inscription

5. Pilate wrote an inscription also, and put it on the cross. And it was written, "This is Jesus the Nazarene, The King of the Jews." This inscription was then read by many of the Jews, for the place where Jesus was crucified was near the city; and it was written in Hebrew, Latin and in Greek. And so the Chief Priests of the Jews said to Pilate, "Do not write, 'The King of the Jews'; but that He said, 'I am King of the Jews.'"

Pilate answered, "What I have written, I have written."

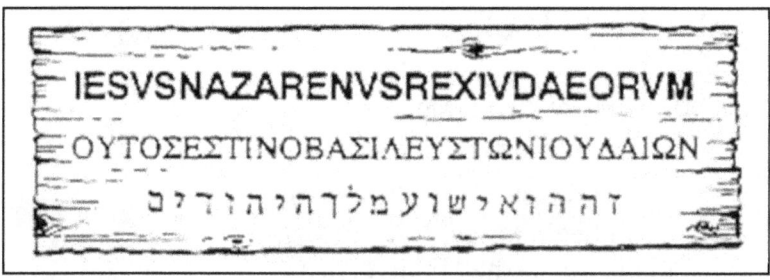

Jesus is Crucified

6. And they tried to give Him wine mixed with myrrh, but He did not take it. But Jesus said, "Almighty God, forgive them; for they do not know what they are doing."

7. When they had crucified Jesus, the soldiers took His outer garments and made four parts, a part for each soldier, and also the tunic; now the tunic was seamless, woven in one piece. They said, therefore, to one another, "Let us not tear it, but cast lots for it, to decide whose it shall be." This happened that the Scriptures might be fulfilled, "They divided My outer garments among them, and for My clothing they cast lots." So this is what the soldiers did.

Jesus Mocked

8. Those passing by were hurling insults at Him, shaking their heads and saying, "Ha! You who are going to destroy the Temple and rebuild it in three days, save Yourself! If You are the Emmanuel, come down from the cross."

9. In the same way the Chief Priests also, along with the Scribes and elders, were mocking Him, and saying, "He saved others, He cannot save Himself! He is King of Israel; let Him come down from the cross, and we shall see and believe in Him. He trusts in God; let God deliver Him now, if God takes pleasure in Him, for He said, 'I am Emmanuel.'"

10. And one of the criminals who was crucified was hurling insults at Him, saying, "Aren't You the Christ? Save Yourself and us!"

11. But the other answered and rebuking him said, "Don't You even fear God, since you are under the same sentence of condemnation? And we indeed justly, for we are receiving what we deserve for our deeds; but this Man has done nothing wrong." And he said, "Jesus, remember me when You come into Your Kingdom!"

12. And He said to him, "I tell you the truth, today you shall be with Me in Paradise."

Mary's Care Arranged

13. But there were standing near the cross of Jesus His mother, and His mother's sister, Mary the wife of Clopas, and Mary Magdalene. Then when Jesus saw His mother, and the disciple whom He loved standing nearby, He said to His mother, "Woman, behold your son!" And He said to the disciple, "Behold your mother!" And from that time the disciple took her into his own household.

Jesus Dies

14. After this, Jesus, knowing that all things had already been accomplished, in order that the Scripture might be fulfilled, said, "I am thirsty." A jar full of sour wine was standing there; so they put a sponge full of the sour wine on a hyssop branch, and brought it up to His mouth. Jesus then received the sour wine.

15. Now from noon darkness fell upon all the land until three in the afternoon. And about three o'clock Jesus cried out with a loud voice saying, "Eli, Eli, lama sabachthani?" That is, "My God, My God, why have You forsaken Me?"

16. And some of those who were standing there, when they heard it, said, "This Man is calling for Elijah." But the rest of them said, "Let's see whether Elijah will come to save Him."

17. And Jesus, cried out with a loud voice, saying, "Almighty God, into Your hands I commit My spirit. It is Finished!" And He bowed His head and gave up His spirit.

The Earth is Shaken

18. And behold, the veil of the temple was torn in two from top to bottom, and the earth shook; and the rocks were broken, and the tombs were opened; and bodies of many righteous people who had died were raised to life; and coming out of their tombs; and after His resurrection they entered the Holy City and appeared to many people.

19. Now the centurion, and those who were with him keeping guard over Jesus, saw the earthquake and the things that were happening, became very frightened and said, "Truly this was Emmanuel!"

20. All the multitudes who came together for this spectacle, when they observed what had happened, began to return, beating their chests. And all His acquaintances and many women who accompanied Him from Galilee, ministering to Him, were looking on from a distance, among whom was Mary Magdalene, Mary the mother of James and Joseph, and the mother of the sons of Zebedee, and Salome.

JESUS IS BURIED
MATTHEW 27:57-66; MARK 15:42-47;
LUKE 23:50-56; JOHN 19:31-42

Friday afternoon, from 4 to 6 PM - Joseph's Tomb

Jesus' Side is Pierced

21. The Jews, because it was the day of preparation, required that the bodies should not remain on the cross on the Sabbath (for the Sabbath was a High Day), they asked Pilate that their legs might be broken, and that they might be taken away. The soldiers therefore came, and broke the legs of the first man, and of the other man who was crucified with him; but coming to Jesus, when they saw that He was already dead, they did not break His legs. But one of the soldiers pierced His side with a spear, and immediately there came out blood and water.

22. And he who has seen it has borne witness, and his witness is true; and he knows that he is telling the truth, so that you may also believe. For these things came to pass, that the Scripture might be fulfilled, "Not a bone of Him shall be broken." And again another Scripture says, "They shall look on Him whom they pierced."

Joseph Gets Jesus' Body

23. And after these things, because it was the preparation day, that is the day before the Sabbath, a rich man came, Joseph of Arimathea, a prominent member of the Council, a good and righteous man who was waiting for the Kingdom of God (he had not consented to their plan and action) had also become a disciple of Jesus in secret for fear of the Jews. He gathered up courage and went in before Pilate,

and asked for the body of Jesus. Pilate wondered if He was dead by this time, and summoning the centurion, he questioned him as to whether He was already dead. And learning this to be so from the centurion, he granted the body to Joseph.

24. And Joseph bought a linen cloth and took Him down. Nicodemus came also, who had first come to Him by night; bringing a mixture of myrrh and aloes, about seventy-five pounds. And so they took the body of Jesus, and bound it in the linen wrapping with the spices, as is the burial custom of the Jews.

25. Now in the place where He was crucified there was a garden; and in the garden Joseph's own new tomb, which he had hewn out in the rock, in which no one had yet been laid. They laid Him in the tomb; and he rolled a large stone against the entrance of the tomb and went away. And it was the preparation day and the Sabbath was about to begin. Now the women who had come with Him out of Galilee, Mary Magdalene and Mary the mother of Jesus, followed after them and saw the tomb and how His body was laid. And they returned and prepared spices and perfumes.

And on the Sabbath they rested according to the commandment.

Guarding the Tomb - Saturday, April 8, 30

26. Now on the next day, which is after the preparation day, the Chief Priests and the Pharisees gathered together with Pilate, and said, "Sir, we remember that while He was still alive that deceiver said, 'After three days I will rise again.' So give orders to make the grave secure until the third day, otherwise the disciples may come and steal

His body away and say to the people, 'He has risen from the dead.' The last deception will be worse than the first."

27. Pilate said to them, "You have a guard. Go, make it as secure as you know how." And they went and made the grave secure, and along with the guard they set a seal on the stone.

CHAPTER 34
THE RESURRECTION

MATTHEW 28:1-15; MARK 16:1-13; LUKE 24:1-12; JOHN 20:1-17

Sunday, April 9, 30 -

Jesus Rises

1. Now after the Sabbath, as it began to dawn toward the first day of the week, behold, a severe earthquake occurred, for an angel of the Lord descended from Heaven and came and rolled away the stone and sat on it. And the angel's appearance was like lightening, and the angel's garments as white as snow; and the guards shook with fear of the angel, and became like dead men.

Women Come to the Tomb

2. When the Sabbath was over very early on the first day of the week, Mary Magdalene and Mary the mother of James and Salome, came to the tomb when the sun had risen and brought spices that they might come and anoint Him. They were saying to one another, "Who will roll away the stone for us from the entrance of the tomb?" And looking up, they saw that the stone, although it was extremely large, had been rolled away.

3. And the angel said to the women, "Do not be afraid; for I know that you are looking for Jesus who has been crucified. He is not here, for He has risen, just as He said. Come, see the place where He was lying.

4. And entering the tomb they did not find the body of the Lord Jesus. And it happened that while they were wondering about this, suddenly two angels stood near them, one at the head, and one at the feet, where the body of Jesus had been lying, in clothes that shown like light; and the women were terrified and bowed down with their faces to the ground. The angels said to them, "Woman, why are you weeping?"

She said to them, "Because they have taken away my Lord, and I do not know where they have put Him."

5. "Why do you seek the Living One among the dead? He is not here, but He has risen. Remember how He told you while He was still in Galilee, saying, 'Emmanuel must be delivered into the hands of sinful people, be crucified, and the third day rise again.' Go quickly and tell His disciples and Peter that He has risen from the dead; and He is going ahead of you into Galilee, there you will see Him; just as I have told you.

Jesus Appears to the Women

6. And they departed quickly from the tomb with fear and great joy and ran to report it to His disciples. And when they turned around, behold, Jesus met them and greeted them and said, "Woman, why are you weeping? Whom are you seeking?"

7. Supposing Him to be the gardener, she said to Him, "Sir, if you have carried Him away, tell me where you have put Him, and I will take Him away."

8. Jesus said to her, "Mary!"

She turned and said to Him in Hebrew, "Rabboni!" (Which means Teacher) And they came up and took hold of His feet and worshipped Him.

9. Then Jesus said to them, "Stop clinging to Me, for I have not yet ascended to Almighty God, My God and your God. Do not be afraid, go and tell My people to leave for Galilee, and there they will see Me.

10. And they returned from the tomb for trembling and astonishment had taken control of them; and they said nothing to anyone. For they were afraid. And they returned running from the tomb and came to Simon Peter, and to the other disciple whom Jesus loved and reported all these things to the eleven and to all the rest. Now they were Mary Magdalene and Joanna and Mary the mother of James; also the other women with them were telling these things to the Apostles. Mary Magdalene announced to the disciples, "I have seen the Lord." And that He had said these things to her. And these words appeared to them as nonsense, and they would not believe them.

11. Peter arose, and the other disciple and the two were running together; and the other disciple ran ahead faster than Peter, and came to the tomb first; and stooping and looking in, he saw the linen wrapping lying there; but he did not go in. Simon Peter then also came, following him, and entered the tomb; and he saw the linen wrappings lying there, and the face cloth, which had been on His head, not lying with the linen wrappings, but rolled up in a place by itself. So the other disciple who had first come to the tomb entered also, and he saw and believed. For as yet they did not understand the Scripture, that He must rise again from the dead. So the disciples went away again to their own homes.

Dr. Patrick Pierce

The Guards are Silenced

12. Now while they were on their way, some of the guards came into the city and reported to the Chief Priests all that had happened. When they had assembled with the elders and counseled together, they gave a large sum of money to the soldiers, and said, "You are to say, 'His disciples came by night and stole Him away while we were asleep.' And if this should be heard by the Governor, we will satisfy him and keep you out of trouble." So they took the money and did as they had been instructed; and this story was widely spread among the Jews and is to this day.

JESUS ON THE ROAD TO EMMAUS
LUKE 24:13-35

Sunday, April 9, 30 - Road to Emmaus

13. Now on the same day two of them were going to a village called Emmaus, which was about seven miles from Jerusalem. They were talking with each other about all these things which had taken place. And it came about that while they were talking and discussing, Jesus Himself approached, and began traveling with them. But their eyes were prevented from recognizing Him.

14. He said to them, "What are these words that you are exchanging with one another as you are walking."

They stood still looking sad. And one of them named Cleopas, answered and said to Him. "Are You the only one visiting Jerusalem who is unaware of the things which have happened here in these days?"

15. And He said to them, "What things?"

And they said to Him, "The things about Jesus the Nazarene, who was a prophet mighty in deed and word in the sight of God and all the people. How the Chief Priests and our rulers delivered Him up to the sentence of death and crucified Him.

16. "But we were hoping that it was He who was going to redeem Israel. Besides all this, now it is the third day since these things happened. But also some women among us amazed us, when they were at the tomb early in the morning and did not find His body, they came, saying that they had also seen a vision of angels, who said that He was alive. And some of those who were with us went to the tomb and found it just exactly as the women also had said; but they did not see Him.

17. And He said to them, "You are foolish and slow of spirit to believe in all that the prophets have spoken! Was it not necessary for the Christ to suffer these things to enter into His glory!" And beginning with Moses and with all the prophets, He explained to them the things concerning Himself in all the Scriptures. And they approached the village where they were going, and He acted as though He would go farther.

18. They urged Him, saying, "Stay with us, for it is getting near evening, and the day is now almost over." And He went to stay with them.

19. When it came about that He had reclined at the table with them, He took the bread and blessed it, and breaking it, He began giving it to them. And their eyes were opened and they recognized

Him; and He disappeared from their sight. They said to one another, "Were not our spirits burning within us while He was explaining the Scriptures to us?"

20. They arose that very hour and returned to Jerusalem and found gathered together the eleven, and those who were with them, saying, "The Lord has really risen, and has appeared to Simon." And they began to relate their experiences on the road, and how He was recognized by them in the breaking of the bread.

JESUS APPEARS TO DISCIPLES
LUKE 24:36-49; JOHN 20:20-29

Sunday, April 9, 30 & April 16, 30 - Jerusalem

Jesus Appears

21. Then when it was evening, on that day, the first day of the week, the doors were shut where the disciples were, for fear of the Jews.

22. While they were telling these things, Jesus Himself stood in their midst. But they were startled and frightened and thought that they were seeing a spirit.

23. And He said to them, "Peace be with you. Why are you troubled, and why do doubts arise in your minds? See My hands and My feet, that it is I Myself; touch Me and see, for a spirit does not have flesh and bones as you see that I have. And when He had said this, He showed them His hands and His feet and His side. And while they were marveling, He said to them, "Have you anything to eat?" And they gave Him a piece of broiled fish; and He took it and ate it before them.

24. Now He said to them, "These are My Words which I spoke to you while I was still with you, that all things which are written about Me in the Law of Moses and the Prophets and the Psalms must be fulfilled." Then He opened their minds to understand the Scriptures, and He said to them, "Thus it is written, that the Christ will suffer and rise again from the dead on the third day; and that repentance for forgiveness of sins will be proclaimed in His name to all the nations, beginning at Jerusalem. You are witnesses of these things. And behold, I am sending forth the promise of Almighty God upon you; but you are to stay in the city until you are clothed with power from on high."

25. Jesus then said to them again, "Peace be with you; as Almighty God has sent Me, I also send you." And when He had said this He breathed on them, and said to them, "Receive the Holy Spirit. If you forgive the sins of anyone, their sins have been forgiven them; if you retain the sins of anyone, they have been retained."

Thomas Doubts

26. But Thomas, one of the twelve, called Didymus, was not with them when Jesus came. The other disciples therefore were saying to him, "We have seen the Lord!"

27. But he said to them, "Unless I shall see in His hands the imprint of the nails, and put my finger into the place of the nails, and put my hand into His side, I will not believe."

28. And again after eight days His disciples were inside, and Thomas with them, Jesus came, the doors having been shut, and stood in their midst, and said, "Peace be with you." And He said to Thomas, "Reach here your finger, and see My hands; and reach here your hand, and put it into My side; and be not unbelieving, but believing."

29. Thomas answered and said to Him, "My Lord and my God!"

30. Jesus said to him, "Because you have seen Me you have believed? Blessed are they who did not see, and yet believed."

JESUS APPEARS AT THE SEA OF GALILEE
JOHN 21:1-17

April 23 to May 18, 30 - Sea of Galilee

Jesus Gives the Miracle of Fish

31. After these things Jesus Himself appeared again to the disciples at the Sea of Tiberias, and He appeared in this way. Together there were Simon Peter, and Thomas called Didymus, and Nathanael of Cana in Galilee, and the sons of Zebedee, and two others of His disciples. Simon Peter said to them, "I am going fishing."

32. They said to him, "We will come with you also. They went out and got into the boat; but that night they caught nothing. When the day was breaking, Jesus stood on the beach; but the disciples did not know that it was Jesus.

33. Jesus said to them, "Children, you do not have any fish, do you?"
They answered Him, "No."

34. And He said to them, "Cast the net on the right side of the boat, and you will find some." So they cast, and then they were not able to haul it in because of the great number of fish.

35. That disciple therefore whom Jesus loved said to Peter, "It is the Lord." And so when Simon Peter heard that it was the Lord, he put his outer garment on (for he was stripped for work), and threw himself into the sea. But the other disciples came in the little boat, for they were not far from the land, but about one hundred meters away, dragging the net full of fish. And so when they got out upon the land, they saw a charcoal fire already laid, and fish placed on it, and bread.

36. Jesus said to them, "Bring some of the fish which you have just caught." Simon Peter went up, and drew the net to land, full of large fish, a hundred and fifty-three; and although there were so many, the net was not torn.

Jesus Cooks Breakfast

37. Jesus said to them, "Come and have breakfast." None of the disciples ventured to question Him, "Who are You?" knowing that is was the Lord.

38. Jesus came and took the bread and gave them, and the fish likewise. Now this is the third time that Jesus had appeared to the disciples, after He was raised from the dead.

Peter Forgiven

39. So when they had finished breakfast Jesus said to Simon Peter, "Simon, son of John, do you love Me more than these?"

He said to Him, "Yes, Lord; You know that I love You."

40. He said to him, "Feed My lambs." He said to him again a second time, "Simon, son of Jonah, do you love Me?"

He said to Him, "Yes, Lord; You know that I love You."

41. He said to him, "Shepherd My sheep." He said to him the third time, "Simon, son of Jonah, do you love Me?" Peter felt hurt because He said to him the third time, "Do you love Me?" And he said to Him, "Lord, You know all things; You know that I love You."

42. Jesus said to him, "Keep My sheep."

CHAPTER 35
THE ASCENSION

JESUS TEACHES
JOHN 21:18-24

April 23, 30 - Sea of Galilee

1. "I tell you the truth, when you were younger, you used to dress yourself and walk wherever you wished; but when you grow old, you will stretch out your hands, and someone else will dress you, and bring you where you do not wish to go."

2. Now He said this, signifying by what kind of death Peter would glorify God. And when He had spoken this, He said to him, "Follow Me!"

3. Peter turned around and saw the disciple whom Jesus loved following them; the one who also had leaned back on His chest at the supper, and said, "Lord, who is the one who betrays You?" When Peter saw him he said to Jesus, "Lord, what about this man?"

4. Jesus said to him, "If I want him to remain until I come, what is that to you? You follow Me!"

This rumor then spread among the disciples that this disciple would not die. But Jesus did not say to him that he would not die; but only, "If I want him to remain until I come, what is that to you?"

5. This is the disciple who bears witness of these things, and wrote these things; and we know that his testimony is true.

ADDITIONAL APPEARANCES BY JESUS
JOHN 21:25; ACTS 1:2b-5; CORINTHIANS 15:16

April 23 to May 18, 30 - Sea of Galilee and Jerusalem

6. There are also many other things which Jesus did, which if they were written in detail, I suppose that even the world itself would not contain the books which would be written.

7. He had by the Holy Spirit given orders to the Apostles whom He had chosen. To these He also presented Himself alive, after His suffering, by many convincing proofs, appearing to them over a period of forty days, and speaking of the things concerning the Kingdom of God. And gathering them together, He commanded them not to leave Jerusalem, but to wait for what Almighty God had promised, "Which," He said, "you heard of but you shall be baptized by the Holy Spirit not many days from now."

8. He appeared to Cephas, then to the twelve. After that He appeared to more than five hundred disciples at one time. Then He appeared to James, then to all the Apostles; and last of all, as it were to one untimely born, He appeared to Paul also.

THE GREAT COMMISSION
MATTHEW 28:16-20

April 23 to May 18, 30 - A Mountain in Galilee

9. The eleven disciples proceeded to a mountain in Galilee, which Jesus had designated. And when they saw Him, they worshipped Him; but some were doubtful.

10. And Jesus came up and spoke to them, saying, "All authority has been given to Me in Heaven and on earth. Go therefore and make disciples of all nations, baptizing them in the name of Almighty God, Emmanuel, and the Holy Spirit, teaching them to observe all that I commanded you; and surely I am with you always, even to the end of the age."

THE ASCENSION
LUKE 24:50-53; ACTS 1:6-11

May 18, 30 - Mount Near Jerusalem

11. And He led them out as far as Bethany, and He lifted up His hands and blessed them. They asked Him saying, "Lord, is it at this time You are restoring the kingdom of Israel?"

12. He said to them, "It is not for you to know times or dates which Almighty God has fixed by God's own authority; but you shall receive power when the Holy Spirit has come upon you; and you shall be My witnesses both in Jerusalem, and in all Judea and Samaria, and even to the remotest parts of the world."

13. And after He had said these things, He was lifted up while they were looking on, and a cloud received Him out of their sight. And as they were gazing intently into the sky while He was departing, behold, two angels in white clothing stood beside them; and they also said, "People of Galilee, why do you stand looking into the sky? This Jesus, who has been taken up from you into Heaven, will come in just the same way as you have watched Him go into Heaven."

THE HOLY SPIRIT
JOHN 20:30,31; ACTS 1:12-20; 2:1-6

14. And they returned to Jerusalem from the mount called Olivet, which is near Jerusalem, a Sabbath's day's journey away, with great joy, and were continually in the Temple, praising God.

15. They went up to the upper room, where they were staying; that is, Peter and John and James and Andrew, Philip and Thomas, Bartholomew and Matthew, James the son of Alphaeus, and Simon the Zealot, and Judas the son of James. These all with one mind were continually devoting themselves to prayer, along with the women, and Mary the mother of Jesus, and with His disciples.

16. And at this time Peter stood up in the midst of the disciples (a gathering of about one hundred and twenty persons were there together), and said, "Disciples, the Scripture had to be fulfilled, which the Holy Spirit foretold by the mouth of David concerning Judas, who became a guide to those who arrested Jesus."

17. And when the day of Pentecost had come, they were all together in one place. And suddenly there came from Heaven a noise like a violent, rushing wind, and it filled the whole house where they were sitting. And there appeared to them flames as of fire distributing

themselves, and they rested on each one of them. And they were all filled with the Holy Spirit and began to speak in other tongues, as the Spirit was giving them utterance.

18. Now there were Jews living in Jerusalem, devout people, from every nation under heaven. And when this sound occurred, the multitude came together, and were bewildered, because they were each one hearing them speak in their own language.

Gospel's Purpose

19. Many other signs Jesus also performed in the presence of the disciples which are not written in this book; but these have been written that you may believe that Jesus is the Christ, Emmanuel; and that believing you may have life in His name.

The End

Dr. Patrick Pierce

"The Gospel of Jesus Christ"

The Gospel of Jesus Christ

God Bless You!

Matthew Verses

Matthew 1:1-17	51
Matthew 1:18-25	62
Matthew 2:1-12	68
Matthew 2:13-18	69
Matthew 2:19-23	70
Matthew 3:1-12	73
Matthew 3:13-17	75
Matthew 4:1-11	76
Matthew 4:12	89
Matthew 4:13-16	94
Matthew 4:17	93
Matthew 4:18-22	95
Matthew 4:23-25	99
Matthew 5:1-2	111
Matthew 5:3-12	111
Matthew 5:13-16	113
Matthew 5:17-48	114
Matthew 6:1-4	117
Matthew 6:5-8	118
Matthew 6:9-15	118
Matthew 6:16-18	119
Matthew 6:19-34	119
Matthew 7:1-6	120
Matthew 7:7-11	121
Matthew 7:12	123
Matthew 7:13-23	123
Matthew 7:24-29	124
Matthew 8:1,5-13	125
Matthew 8:2-4	100

Matthew 8:14-17 97
Matthew 8:18-22 153
Matthew 8:23-27 154
Matthew 8:28-34 155
Matthew 9:1-8 100
Matthew 9:9 102
Matthew 9:10-17 157
Matthew 9:18-26 158
Matthew 9:27-34 162
Matthew 9:35-38 165
Matthew 10:1-4 109
Matthew 10:5-42 165
Matthew 11:1 165
Matthew 11:2-30 127
Matthew 12:1-8 106
Matthew 12:9-14 107
Matthew 12:15-21 108
Matthew 12:22-37 132
Matthew 12:38-45 134
Matthew 12:46-50 136
Matthew 13:1-2 145
Matthew 13:3-23 145
Matthew 13:24-30 149
Matthew 13:31-35 150
Matthew 13:36-43 149
Matthew 13:44-53 151
Matthew 13:54-58 163
Matthew 14:1-12 170
Matthew 14:13 171
Matthew 14:14-21 172
Matthew 14:22-36 175

Matthew 15:1-20	182
Matthew 15:21-28	184
Matthew 15:29-38	187
Matthew 15:39-16:12	189
Matthew 16:13-20	193
Matthew 16:21-28	194
Matthew 17:1-13	195
Matthew 17:14-21	197
Matthew 17:22-23	199
Matthew 17:24-27	199
Matthew 18:1-14	201
Matthew 18:15-35	203
Matthew 19:1-12	258
Matthew 19:13-15	260
Matthew 19:16-30	262
Matthew 20:1-16	262
Matthew 20:17-28	267
Matthew 20:29-34	269
Matthew 21:1-11; 14-17	275
Matthew 21:12,13,18,19	278
Matthew 21:20-22	279
Matthew 21:23-27	280
Matthew 21:28-32	281
Matthew 21:33-41	282
Matthew 21:42-46	283
Matthew 22:1-14	283
Matthew 22:15-22	285
Matthew 22:23-33	286
Matthew 22:34-40	287
Matthew 22:41-46	288
Matthew 23:1-39	289

Matthew 24:1-28 297
Matthew 24:29-51 300
Matthew 25:1-46 303
Matthew 26:1-5:14-16 306
Matthew 26:6-13 272
Matthew 26:17-19 309
Matthew 26:20-25:31-35 312
Matthew 26:26-29 317
Matthew 26:30;36-46 329
Matthew 26:47-56 330
Matthew 26:57-68; 71-75 334
Matthew 26:69-70 333
Matthew 27:3-10 337
Matthew 27:2; 11-14 339
Matthew 27:15-31 341
Matthew 27:32-56 347
Matthew27:57-66 352
Matthew 28:1-15 355
Matthew 28:16-20 367

Mark Verses

Mark 1:1	55
Mark 1:1-8	73
Mark 1:9-11	75
Mark 1:12-13	76
Mark 1:14a	89
Mark 1:14b-15	93
Mark 1:16-20	95
Mark 1:21-28	96
Mark 1:29-34	97
Mark 1:35-39	99
Mark 1:40-45	100
Mark 2:1-12	100
Mark 2:13-14	102
Mark 2:15-22	157
Mark 2:23-28	106
Mark 3:1-6	107
Mark 3:7-12	108
Mark 3:13-19	109
Mark 3:20-30	132
Mark 3:31-35	136
Mark 4:1-2	145
Mark 4:3-25	145
Mark 4:26-29	148
Mark 4:30-34	150
Mark 4:35-41	154
Mark 5:1-21	155
Mark 5:22-43	158
Mark 6:1-6	163
Mark 6:7-13	165

Mark 6:14-29	170
Mark 6:30-32	171
Mark 6:33-44	172
Mark 6:45-56	175
Mark 7:1-23	182
Mark 7:24-30	184
Mark 7:31-37;8:1-9	187
Mark 8:10-26	189
Mark 8:27-30	193
Mark 8:31-38; 9:1	194
Mark 9:2-13	195
Mark 9:14-29	197
Mark 9:30-32	199
Mark 9:33-50	201
Mark 10:1-12	258
Mark 10:13-16	260
Mark 10:17-31	262
Mark 10:32-45	267
Mark 10:46-52	269
Mark 11:1-11	275
Mark 11:12-18	278
Mark 11:19-26	279
Mark 11:27-33	280
Mark 12:1-9	282
Mark 12:10-12	283
Mark 12:13-17	285
Mark 12:18-27	286
Mark 12:28-34	287
Mark 12:35-37	288
Mark 12:38-40	289
Mark 12:41-44	292

The Gospel of Jesus Christ

Mark 13:1-23 297
Mark 13:24-37 300
Mark 14:1,2,10,11 306
Mark 14:3-9 272
Mark 14:12-17 309
Mark 14:18-21; 27-31 312
Mark 14:22-25 317
Mark 14:26; 32-42 329
Mark 14:43-52 330
Mark 14:53-65; 68b-72 334
Mark 14:66-68a 333
Mark 15:1-5 339
Mark 15:6-20 341
Mark 15:21-41 347
Mark 15:42-47 352
Mark 16:1-13 355

Luke Verses

Luke 1:1-4 49
Luke 1:5-25 55
Luke 1:26-38 57
Luke 1:39-45 58
Luke 1:46-56 59
Luke 1:57-66 60
Luke 1:67-80 61
Luke 2:1-7 64
Luke 2:8-20 64
Luke 2:21-39 66
Luke 2:40-52 71
Luke 3:1-18 73
Luke 3:19-20 89
Luke 3:21-22 75
Luke 3:23 78
Luke 3:24-38 51
Luke 4:1-13 76
Luke 4:14 93
Luke 4:15 93
Luke 4:16-31 163
Luke 4:31-37 96
Luke 4:38-41 97
Luke 4:42-44 99
Luke 5:1-11 95
Luke 5:12-16 97
Luke 5:17-26 100
Luke 5:27-28 100
Luke 6:1-5 106
Luke 6:6-11 107

Luke 6:12-16 109
Luke 6:17-20a 111
Luke 6:20b-26 111
Luke 6:27-30; 32-36 114
Luke 6:31 123
Luke 6:37-42 120
Luke 6:43-45 123
Luke 6:46-49 124
Luke 7:1-10 125
Luke 7:11-17 126
Luke 7:18-35 127
Luke 7:36-50 130
Luke 8:1-3 131
Luke 8:4 145
Luke 8:5-18 145
Luke 8:19-21 136
Luke 8:22-25 154
Luke 8:26-40 155
Luke 8:41-56 158
Luke 9:1-6 165
Luke 9:7-9 170
Luke 9:10 171
Luke 9:11-17 172
Luke 9:18-21 193
Luke 9:22-27 194
Luke 9:28-36 195
Luke 9:37-43 197
Luke 9:44-45 199
Luke 9:46-50 201
Luke 9:51-56 206
Luke 9:57-62 153

Luke 10:1-24	223
Luke 10:25-37	225
Luke 10:38-42	227
Luke 11:1-13	229
Luke 11:14-23	132
Luke 11:24-36	134
Luke 11:37-54	137
Luke 12:1-3; 11-50; 54-59	139
Luke 12:4-10; 51-53	165
Luke 13:1-9	144
Luke 13:10-17	227
Luke 13:18-21	150
Luke 13:22-35	233
Luke 14:1-24	234
Luke 14:25-33	236
Luke 14:34-35	113
Luke 15:1-7	239
Luke 15:8-10	239
Luke 15:11-32	240
Luke 16:1-18	242
Luke 16:19-31	244
Luke 17:1-10	247
Luke 17:11-37	255
Luke 18:1-8	257
Luke 18:9-14	258
Luke 18:15-17	260
Luke 18:18-30	262
Luke 18:31-34	267
Luke 18:35-43	269
Luke 19:1-28	270
Luke 19:29-44	275

Luke 19:45-48	278
Luke 20:1-8	280
Luke 20:9-16	282
Luke 20:17-19	283
Luke 20:20-26	285
Luke 20:27-39	286
Luke 20:40	287
Luke 20:41-44	288
Luke 20:45-47	289
Luke 21:1-4	292
Luke 21:5-24	297
Luke 21:25-36	300
Luke 21:37,38	279
Luke 22:1-6	306
Luke 22:7-13; 24-30	309
Luke 22:14-20	317
Luke 22:21-23; 31-38	312
Luke 22:39-46	329
Luke 22:47-53	330
Luke 22:54-71	334
Luke 23:1-7	339
Luke 23:8-12	341
Luke 23:13-25	341
Luke 23:26-49	347
Luke 23:50-56	352
Luke 24:1-12	355
Luke 24:13-35	358
Luke 24:36-49	360
Luke 24:50-53	367

John Verses

John 1:1-18	49
John 1:19:34	78
John 1:35-42	81
John 1:43-51	82
John 2:1-12	83
John 2:13-25	84
John 3:1-21	85
John 3:22-36	87
John 4:1-4	89
John 4:5-42	89
John 4:43-45	93
John 4:46-54	93
John 5:1-18	102
John 5:19-29	104
John 5:30-47	105
John 6:1	171
John 6:2-13	172
John 6:14-21	175
John 6:22-71	177
John 7:1	182
John 7:2-10	205
John 7:11-52	207
John 7:53- 8:11	211
John 8:12-59	212
John 9:1-41	217
John 10:1-21	221
John 10:22-42	231
John 11:1-46	248
John 11:47-54	252

John 11:55-57; 12:1-11 272
John 12:12-19 275
John 12:20-50 293
John 13:1-20 310
John 13:21-38 312
John 14 – 16 318
John 17 326
John 18:1 329
John 18:2-11 330
John 18:12-24 333
John 18:25-27 334
John 18:28-38 339
John 18:39- 19:16 341
John 19:17-30 347
John 19:31-42 352
John 20:1-16 355
John 20:17-19 283
John 20:20-29 360
John 20:30,31 368
John 21:1-17 362
John 21:18-24 365
John 21:25 366

Other Bible Verses

Acts 1:2b-5	366
Acts 1:6-11	367
Acts 1:12-20; 2:1-6	368
I Corinthians 11:23-26	317
I Corinthians 15:16	366

EXPLANATORY NOTES

1. Combined Gospels:

There are two main approaches to combining the four Gospel accounts for study, reading and discussion purposes. Each of these approaches has its strengths and weaknesses. There are several editions from which the student, reader or discussion group can choose. The two approaches are "Harmony" and "Combination."

There have been several "Harmonies" and "Combinations" of the Gospels developed. A Harmony is a presentation of the Gospel accounts in parallel without any attempt to combine the different Gospels into one account. A Combination is a blending of the Gospels into one account.

In actuality Luke was the first person to write a Combination of the Gospel accounts. Several of the Gospel accounts that Luke used as his sources for his research have been lost. However, Luke did use Mark's Gospel as one of his main sources.

The first known Combination Gospel after Luke is Tatian's Diatessaron in about 160 A.D. in the Syriac language. This work was lost long ago, but an Arabic translation of it and an English version by Hamlyn Hill in 1894 were found. Tatian blended the Gospels into one narrative. There have been several other modern Combination Gospels, each of which has its strengths. The Combination can either provide as close as possible an accurate translation or an expanded or paraphrased rendition. Each style can be used for study or discussion and provide the student and reader with additional knowledge and help.

Academians have taken the position that a Combination presentation is not the preferred presentation. The "gain" that is achieved through the Combination does lose the difference in the style of each Gospel account. In an academic exercise it would be a better source to have the different Gospels presented in a parallel manner so each Gospel retains its individual material and style attributes.

However, if the purpose being served is for individual study, reading or group discussions, the Combination presentation would be more helpful. The readers must determine if they want to have an accurate translation or an expanded, paraphrased rendition. It is this author's position that it is important to use as accurate a translation as possible in study and discussion. An expanded, paraphrased presentation can be used for casual reading. There is a place for each type of Gospel presentation.

In the third century the Gospels were arranged in four parallel columns by Ammonius. This was one of the first Harmonies of the Gospels that we still have. In the fourth century Eusebius enabled the reader to see the parallel passages of the Gospel side by side in his Canons and Sections.

Edward Robinson's edition in 1845 has had the most influence over the more recent Gospel Harmonies. This Harmony was revised by Riddle in 1889.

There have been several others who have used the Authorized Version and divided Christ's life by feasts. The first to break away from the feasts were Broadus in 1893 and Waddy in 1887. These attempted to show the life of Jesus in historical chronology. Gospel Harmonies continued to appear with most of these works produced for academic purposes and used in scholarly research and study. Several of the Harmonies struggled with the Gospel of John since it is focused not on the "what" Jesus did or said, but on the "why." The Gospel of John doesn't present the same problem for a Combined Gospel in that it provides the answer to the important question "Why did Jesus do what He did," and "What did Jesus mean by His teachings and parables."

2. *Gospel Sources*

The validity of the Gospels are, beyond question, legitimate first and second-hand accounts of the life and teachings of Jesus. This has been tested and debated over the centuries and has held up under the most rigorous examination. Persons who would question this fact now have not taken advantage of the research that has gone on before and, therefore, closed their eyes and minds to the facts.

The number of Combination and Harmony Gospels provide evidence as to the agreement of the Gospels in the story and teachings of Jesus. The pages of <u>The Gospel of Jesus Christ</u> provide proof of the cohesiveness of the Gospels.

Mark was the first of the Gospels written and was used by Matthew and Luke in writing their Gospel versions. Almost all of Mark's verses are contained in Matthew and Luke. Both Matthew and Luke also had another source document called "Q" for "Source" document. The Q document has not been preserved over time and has been lost. Luke tells us that he had several sources that were used and that he was going to provide us with a complete account of the life of Jesus.

The continuing archeological research is providing us with more information about the first century writings than ever before. The Gospels were eventually written or translated into Greek. Matthew originally wrote his Gospel in Aramaic and then may have been involved in the translation into Greek. There are several authoritative books on the source of and contents of the original Gospel accounts.

3. Translations

Completing a meaningful translation from Greek to English and from the first century culture to the modern times is in many ways the most difficult step. This difficulty has resulted in hundreds of different translations, transliterations, paraphrases and expanded versions of the Bible and various parts of the Bible. None of these versions are perfect or fulfills everyone's purposes for reading, studying or as the sole basis for discussion groups.

One of the first widely accepted versions of the Bible is the King James Version which is still a wonderful and authoritative Bible translation. The English words used were common to the day of the translation and are still held by many as the preferred Bible version. The use of "ye" and "thou" and other older English words and phrases does not make the version better or more authoritative or accurate. However, many people feel like these words and phrases add to the "Holiness" of the text. This is good for those people and should be used for that purpose. Remember, there is "No" perfect Biblical version and each version of the Bible can be used by people for different purposes that are meaningful and important to them.

In <u>The Gospel of Jesus Christ</u> one of the most difficult and basic questions was what version or versions of the Bible should be used in the Gospel Combination. The goal was to provide the reader with a Biblical version that can provide the following:

1. An accurate translation from the Greek to Modern American English

2. A fair presentation from the first century culture to the modern American culture

3. An emphasis on the Holy nature of God, the Holy Spirit and Jesus as one God

4. An easy to read and understand Gospel account to be used in mainly non-academic discussions and reading

1. The accurate translation from Greek to Modern American English is made difficult because of the very nature of the two languages. Greek is a language of ideas and concepts that deals with the abstracts of thought. English, on the other hand, is a language that has as its basis things and the tangible matter of the world and life. There are many instances where the Greek word is made up of a combination of Greek words to express a concept. The Greek word will require several English words or perhaps a full sentence to express the same thought or concept.

Greek is an inflected language so the meaning can be made quite complex by adding or changing the ending of a word. Also, Greek has more tenses than English. English is a word order language so the meaning in English is established by the word order. Greek is completely different in this respect with the inflections and additional tenses.

Most people think of a translation as converting one word from one language to one word in the new language. If this is a constraint, it is impossible to complete a translation that will convey the meaning of the original language to the reader of the new language translation. The "Gospel of Jesus" is a Combination Gospel and is an accurate translation of the thoughts and meanings of the life and teachings of Jesus. It is not a paraphrase, but a delivery of the concept of the original Greek into modern American English. To complete this several Biblical versions were used as source materials as well as the original Greek.

2. The cultural setting in which the original Gospels were written was substantially different than the modern American cultural setting. There isn't any judgment as to whether either culture is better or preferred. There are only factual, cultural differences that impacted the accounts.

One of the basic cultural differences in the two cultures is the position of men and women. In the first century women were property like livestock that were owned and controlled by men. Because of this all references to teachings or instructions were to men and not to women or people in general. Also, all of the references to Jesus and God were masculine.

Today men and women in modern American culture have equal status, and the Bible's teachings apply equally to both. All of the Biblical teachings and references were directed to men, but today they are directed to all people. <u>The Gospel of Jesus Christ</u> makes this change in the translation. This is probably the most controversial change in this translation. There are many Christians and Christian denominations that still hold to a basic difference in status between males and females. The thing to remember is that whether or not you continue to hold on to this belief about males and females has nothing to do with the message of the Gospel. God's grace and mercy are equally available to males and females as they believe in Jesus as their Lord and Savior.

3. The Triune God is one of the more difficult concepts of God and God's nature. The Bible clearly says that there is one God, and then breaks God apart into three roles. The first is as God the Father, or Almighty God. Almighty God is at the top of the God Head and is the ultimate source of power, creation and everything else.

There is Jesus, God physically to this world. Jesus is the sacrifice for our sins, our Savior, our creator and ultimately our judge. Jesus tells us in several different ways that He and Almighty God are One. How God can be in Heaven and on earth, be Almighty God and Jesus at the same time is one of the mysteries of God. If people could understand all about God, then God wouldn't be greater than people.

Even though we can act like we know everything, we are still limited in our knowledge and understanding.

The third "person" of the God Head is the Holy Spirit. Again, the Bible tells us that the Holy Spirit is Jesus' Spirit and God's Spirit given to people after Jesus left this world. The Holy Spirit is not a person, but is the same as Almighty God and Jesus. It seems like Almighty God chose to explain Himself to this world in His three main roles to the universe, this world and to people using three different names for those roles. Since God is all knowing, all present, all powerful and not constrained by time, it is impossible for people to ever comprehend God or what God has done, is doing or is going to do.

4. In completing the translation of <u>The Gospel of Jesus Christ</u> the ease of reading and understanding was one of the primary concerns. However, it was important that accuracy of the translation not be sacrificed. There are several places in the Gospels where this balance between accuracy and ease of reading was difficult to achieve. When this was the case, accuracy was the overriding concern.

4. The Gospel of John

The first three Gospels of Matthew, Mark and Luke are called the Synoptic Gospels because they are telling the same story of Jesus' life and teachings and, much of the three Gospels are the same. However, John does not try to tell the same story and assumes that the reader is familiar with the Synoptic Gospel accounts. There is much scholarly debate over who wrote which parts of the Gospel of John. This debate will have no end or reach any real consensus of a conclusion.

It is the belief that the Gospel of John was written by the Apostle John and therefore has great importance to the teachings and explanations given to us in John. These teachings and explanations are missing in the Synoptic Gospels, but are very important to have along with the factual accounts of Jesus' life.

The Gospel of Jesus Christ combines John's teachings with the other Gospels to give us not only what Jesus did and said, but what Jesus meant by His actions and words. John was Jesus' personal confidant and spent many hours with Jesus asking questions and listening. We have the privilege of listening in on their conversations through the passages given to us in the Gospel of John.

5. List Difficulties

There are two lists given in the Gospels that scholars have been struggling over for centuries. There are just about as many conclusions as there are scholars who have made them. These lists are some of the focal points of disbelievers trying to point out that the Bible is full of errors and is not to be believed. These lists are not in error and the Bible is the Word of God given to us through specific men of history.

The Genealogies of Jesus

There are two genealogies of Jesus given in the Gospels. One of these is given by Matthew and the second by Luke. The most plausible explanation is that Matthew has given us the genealogy of Joseph and Luke has given us the genealogy of Mary. Why Luke decided to include Mary's genealogy instead of Joseph's is just as curious as why Matthew included women in Joseph's genealogy.

The List of Apostles

There are four lists of the Apostles given to us in Matthew, Mark, Luke and Acts. There are three groupings of Apostles in each list, but the Apostles within each of the groupings are given in a different order by the authors. We don't really know if there is any significance to the order of the Apostles within the groupings.

The first group is Peter, Andrew, James and John.

The second group is Philip, Bartholomew (Nathaniel), Matthew and Thomas.

The third group is James the son of Alpheus, Thaddeus (Judas the brother of James), Simon the Cananaean (Simon the Zealot), and Judas Iscariot (omitted from Acts).

People are known by different names to different people. The Apostles have different names as shown in the (parenthesis) but they are the same person.

There are no discrepancies in any of these lists.

6. Summary

God's coming to earth in human form, for all to see and hear, is a monumental point in history. God's own words and actions are a pivotal point in our reading and understanding. The Gospels, taken together, provide us with a unique opportunity to sit at the feet of our Lord and Master, Emmanuel, God with us.

Use The Gospel of Jesus Christ as your time to become better acquainted with the God of the Universe. God took the time and the effort to build this bridge to us so that we might have an everlasting relationship with God.

Dr. Patrick Pierce

God Bless You and Your Family

www.ingramcontent.com/pod-product-compliance
Lightning Source LLC
Chambersburg PA
CBHW022058150426
43195CB00008B/189